The
EVERYTHING.
Games Book

Dear Reader:

In this fast-paced world with its honking horns and long lines, we need to learn to slow down and have fun. Somewhere along the way, we've forgotten how to play. Children have the answer; their games create those silly smiles and goofy giggles that we adore and even covet. Learn from them—play those classic games that used to brighten your day and learn new games that will challenge and strengthen your skills.

Whatever your age, whatever your skill level, whatever your physical abilities, there is a game for you—and quite possibly many more than just one! Whether you use the games in this book to create quality family time or to revive your competitive spirit, one thing is certain: You'll be glad you played.

Make no excuses. Find the time to play and allow yourself to have fun. Enjoy!

Lesley Bolton

The EVERYTHING® Series

Editorial

Publishing Director	Gary M. Krebs
Managing Editor	Kate McBride
Copy Chief	Laura M. Daly
Acquisitions Editor	Gina Chaimanis
Development Editor	Julie Gutin
Production Editor	Jamie Wielgus

Production

Production Director	Susan Beale
Production Manager	Michelle Roy Kelly
Series Designers	Daria Perreault
	Colleen Cunningham
	John Paulhus
Cover Design	Paul Beatrice
	Matt LeBlanc
Layout and Graphics	Colleen Cunningham
	John Paulhus
	Daria Perreault
	Monica Rhines
	Erin Ring
Series Cover Artist	Barry Littmann
Interior Illustrator	Argosy
Illustrations on pages 26 and 275	John Paulhus

Visit the entire Everything® Series at *www.everything.com*

THE

EVERYTHING®

GAMES
BOOK
Second Edition

600 classic games and activities
for the whole family

Lesley Bolton

Adams Media
Avon, Massachusetts

For all those adults out there who still
remember how to play games like children.

An Everything® Series Book.
Everything® and everything.com® are registered trademarks of F+W Publications, Inc.
First edition copyright ©1997, Adams Media.
Published by Adams Media, an F+W Publications Company
57 Littlefield Street, Avon, MA 02322 U.S.A.
www.adamsmedia.com

ISBN: 1-59337-318-X
Printed in the United States of America.

J I H G F E D C B A

Library of Congress Cataloging-in-Publication Data
Bolton, Lesley.
The everything games book / Lesley Bolton.—2nd ed.
p.   cm.—(An everything series book)
Rev. ed. of: The everything games book / Tracy Fitzsimmons and Pamela Liflander. 1st ed. c1997.
ISBN 1-59337-318-X
1. Games—Rules. I. Fitzsimmons, Tracy Everything games book. II. Title. III. Series: Everything series.

GV1201.42.F58 2005
790.1'922—dc22

2004026777

This publication is designed to provide accurate and authoritative information with regard to the subject matter covered. It is sold with the understanding that the publisher is not engaged in rendering legal, accounting, or other professional advice. If legal advice or other expert assistance is required, the services of a competent professional person should be sought.

—From a *Declaration of Principles* jointly adopted by a Committee of the American Bar Association and a Committee of Publishers and Associations

Many of the designations used by manufacturers and sellers to distinguish their products are claimed as trademarks. Where those designations appear in this book and Adams Media was aware of a trademark claim, the designations have been printed with initial capital letters.

This book is available at quantity discounts for bulk purchases.
For information, call 1-800-872-5627.

Contents

Acknowledgments

I'd like to thank Lora Bolton for all her help during this project, for keeping me sane, and for reminding me just how much fun games can be.

Top Ten Occasions
for Playing Games

1. **Rainy Day:** When the weather won't cooperate, choose from a variety of games—card games, board games, basement games, tile or dice games, or brain teasers.

2. **Birthday Party:** What's a party without games? Need we say more?

3. **Family Together Time:** Quality time spent with the family is an important part of our daily lives; games provide entertainment everyone can participate in and enjoy.

4. **Summer Vacation:** Summer vacation offers the perfect opportunity to get fresh air and exercise with outdoor games.

5. **School Recess:** The right games can make recess the best part of the school day.

6. **Road Trip:** Dispel the boredom of road trips with games especially created for such an event.

7. **Pool Party:** Games will make a splash at any pool party.

8. **Wedding/Baby Shower:** A joyous occasion is always a great reason to bring people together. Add a little spice with games!

9. **Family Reunion:** Outdoor games help enhance relationships with those you may not see very often.

10. **Ten-Minute Break:** During stressful times, take a break to play a quick game of solitaire and allow yourself to relax before diving back into your must-do list.

Introduction

▶ Welcome to *The Everything® Games Book!* Here you will find a wide selection of the most popular games that your entire family can enjoy together. Not only will you find new and exciting games to play, but you'll have a complete set of easy-to-follow rules and regulations right at your fingertips.

Whether you are planning a party or just spending Sundays at home, *The Everything® Games Book* provides many activities that your family will love. Each game is rated for age appropriateness: **5+** for ages five and up; **8+** for ages eight and up; **12+** for ages twelve and up; **Adult** for adults.

The book is divided into twenty distinct chapters, which makes finding the right activity simple. For instance, the first two chapters include the most classic board games of all time. The next six chapters explain the best card games from around the world. You'll find card games for every member of the family, from simple children's games, including Go Fish and Crazy Eights, to the very complicated whist and euchre. Whether you want to play alone or with a large group, cards games are easily adaptable to suit every circumstance, and are sure to provide hours of competitive enjoyment.

You'll also find a chapter that focuses on tile and dice games, featuring Bunco, dice, dominoes, Yahtzee!, and the perennial Chinese favorite, mahjong. While these games do require specific equipment, once you understand how the games work, you'll easily see that it's worth a small investment.

Those games that have moved from the rec room to the bar, and now back again, are highlighted in a chapter of their own. More and more people are adding dartboards and pool tables to their homes, creating new excitement around these activities. This book provides the complete rules for each of these pastimes and several others, without the technical jargon that makes them even more confusing. The games presented do require some understanding of the basics of each of these sports; the information in this chapter is not intended to teach you how to throw a dart or hold the cue. However, once you've mastered those basics, you'll be able to play any of the games listed here.

The Everything® Games Book also offers a complete set of outdoor activities, ranging from sports such as croquet and volleyball to children's relay races and hopscotch. The wide assortment includes games for every level of physical coordination. But more important, these outdoor games will motivate you to take family time out into the fresh air. Some of the games require specific equipment, while others require little more than a standard rubber ball, or nothing at all.

The indoor games are the classic games that you grew up with and surely want to pass down to the younger generation. And to keep the kids busy, this book features chapters devoted to children's party games, road-trip games, and playground games. Most of these games require little preparation, and can be adapted to either outdoor or indoor settings.

One chapter presents a small collection of brain teasers for quieter moments during the day. Many of these games are perfect for long drives, or just spending time together before bedtime. Whenever you can squeeze one of these games in, you'll be glad that you did.

It is my hope that *The Everything® Games Book* will help create quality family time, fostering special moments that your loved ones will treasure forever. And if not, at least you'll know how to beat the pants off of them!

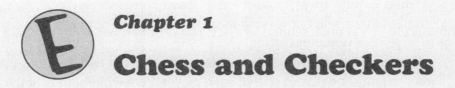

Chapter 1

Chess and Checkers

Chess and checkers are two of the best-known classic board games. While most households will already own these games, the instruction books likely are long gone. That's why this chapter includes the rules and quick lessons that will help you master each game with confidence.

Introducing Chess

Rating: 8+

Chess is played by two people, sitting opposite each other, using a board that contains sixty-four squares. The squares are colored alternately black and white, or any other two colors. Each player has sixteen pieces (or men), all of the same color, but varying in size and shape. The object of the game is to seize your opponent's King.

The game begins with the men placed on the first two lines of squares. The board must be placed so that each player has a white square at the lower right-hand corner of the board.

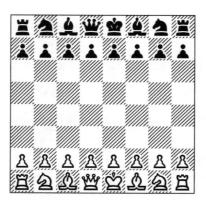

▲ The traditional chess board setup

The players flip a coin for first move and choice of color. Usually, the player who has the first move plays the white men.

The Pieces and Their Movements

The white Queen must always occupy a white square, and the black Queen a black square. The white King, on the contrary, must always occupy a black square and the black King a white one, with the Kings and Queens respectively facing each other. The Bishops on each side are posted nearest to the Kings and Queens; next come the Knights, while the Rooks occupy the corner squares.

The King

You can move the King only one square at a time in any direction—backward, forward, sideways, and diagonally. Once in the game, however, you can move the King two squares when castling. You cannot move the King onto a square next to the one occupied by the hostile King; the Kings must always be separated from each other by an intervening square.

ALERT!

After castling on the King's side, beware of uselessly pushing your King's Rook's Pawn to one square to prevent your King's Knight from being pinned by the hostile Queen's Bishop. Such a precaution is often a waste of time, and often leaves you exposed to a terrible attack.

You cannot move the King into check—that is, onto any square that is commanded by a hostile piece or Pawn. The King can, however, capture any unprotected piece or Pawn of the enemy on any square adjacent to his own in any direction. If you place the King in such a position that he cannot avoid capture, he is "checkmated," and the game is lost.

The Queen

The Queen is the most powerful of all the pieces, and you can move her any number of squares in any direction as long as the path is unobstructed. When posted on any of the four center squares, she commands twenty-seven out of the sixty-four squares of the board.

The Rook

The Rook is the next most powerful piece. You can move him in a straight line, backward, forward, and sideways, but not diagonally.

The Bishop

You move the Bishop diagonally, but only on squares of his own color. For example, you cannot move the white King's Bishop onto a black square, or the black King's Bishop onto a white one. On an unobstructed range you may move the Bishop from a corner square to the opposite corner.

The Knight

You can move the Knight two squares forward or backward, and one to the left or right. This is the only piece that can jump over another piece or Pawn, whether of his own force or the opponent's.

When you have a Knight or Bishop strongly posted either in the center of the board or in your enemy's entrenchments, try to hold that position until the end of the game or until your opponent is driven to eliminate pieces favorable to you. In general, avoid giving up similarly strong positions.

In this figure, the black Knight, standing on his King's Bishop's third square, commands eight squares. If any hostile white man were posted on any of these squares he could capture it, removing it from its square and occupying the vacated square himself.

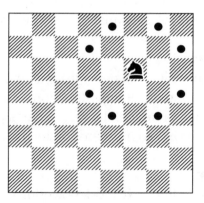

▲ The Knight has as many as eight moving options.

The Pawn

You move the Pawn move forward one square at a time, but his first move may advance either one or two squares, at your discretion. If, however, you move him two squares, and a hostile Pawn commands the square that he leaps over, the hostile Pawn has the choice of taking him and intercepting him in his leap, as if your Pawn had only moved forward one square. This is called taking *en passant*. The Pawn captures diagonally and in a forward movement only. When your Pawn reaches the eighth square of any file on which he is advancing, you may exchange him for a Queen, or any other piece that you choose; or you may refuse this promotion and allow him to remain a Pawn, as before. In such a case he is called a *dummy* Pawn.

Relative Value of the Pieces

In the middle of the game the Queen is usually better than two Rooks; but in the end two Rooks are stronger than the Queen.

Sometimes you may advantageously exchange the Queen for three minor pieces, but as a rule three minor pieces are not preferable to the Queen.

A Rook and two Pawns are usually better than two minor pieces; but a Bishop and Knight are better than a Rook and Pawn and far superior to a single Rook.

QUESTION?

Where did chess originate?
Chess traveled through several countries and underwent several changes before becoming the beloved game of today. The first version of chess was developed in India around the seventh century, though it was then called *Chaturanga*.

Two Bishops and a Knight are better than two Knights and a Bishop.

Two Bishops are stronger than two Knights; two Bishops can easily force checkmate, whereas two Knights can never do so.

Generally speaking, the Bishop is always better than the Knight, but the real relative value of these two pieces depends on their position. A Bishop and a Knight are each worth more than three Pawns.

In average positions the Queen should win against (1) a Rook, (2) a Rook and a Pawn, (3) two Knights, (4) two Bishops, (5) a Bishop and a Knight, or

(6) a Bishop or a Knight. In certain exceptional situations the weaker force can draw the game.

A Rook and Knight can win against a Rook only in very rare instances; in fact, in ninety-nine cases out of a hundred Rook and Knight versus Rook is a legitimately drawn game.

A Rook can usually win against a Bishop or Knight when there are an equal number of Pawns on each side, though in the end the Rook against Bishop is generally a draw.

Rook versus Knight also is usually a drawn game, unless you can prevent the Knight from approaching his King.

Chess Notation

The following are the English notations of chess moves, for the purpose of reading and recording games. Each square is named after the piece that occupies it. For instance, the square on which the King stands is called K sq., or K1, and all the squares are numbered vertically on the whole file from 1 to 8.

FACT

If you move a man when it is not your turn to play, you must retract the move. After your opponent moves, you must play the same man if it can be played legally.

The King and Queen are considered the center pieces on the board. All of the pieces on the right side of the King are called the King's pieces, and all of the pieces on the left of the Queen are called the Queen's pieces—in other words, Queen's Bishop=QB; Queen's Knight=QKt; Queen's Rook=QR. The same rule applies to the black pieces; thus, White King's square would be Black King's eight=K8; while Black King's square would be White King's eight=K8; and so on with all the other squares.

The horizontal divisions are called *rows,* and the vertical divisions are called *files.* Other abbreviations used in notation are: *sq.* for square, *ch.* or *(+)* for check, *x* for takes, *dis. ch.* for discovered check, *dble. ch.* for double check, *en pass.* for *en passant. P takes P,* or *P x P,* means Pawn takes Pawn.

Q.R.sq.	Q.Kt.s.	Q.B.sq.	Q.sq.	K.sq.	K.B.sq.	K.Kt.s.	K.R.sq.
Q.R.8.	Q.Kt.8	Q.B.8.	Q.8.	K.8.	K.B.8.	K.Kt.8.	K.R.8.
Q.R.2.	Q.Kt.2	Q.B.2.	Q.2.	K.2.	K.B.2.	K.Kt.2.	K.R.2.
Q.R.7.	Q.Kt.7	Q.B.7.	Q.7.	K.7.	K.B.7.	K.Kt.7.	K.R.7.
Q.R.3.	Q.Kt.3	Q.B.3.	Q.3.	K.3.	K.B.3.	K.Kt.3.	K.R.3.
Q.R.6.	Q.Kt.6	Q.B.6.	Q.6.	K.6.	K.B.6.	K.Kt.6.	K.R.6.
Q.R.4.	Q.Kt.4	Q.B.4.	Q.4.	K.4.	K.B.4.	K.Kt.4.	K.R.4.
Q.R.5.	Q.Kt.5	Q.B.5.	Q.5.	K.5.	K.B.5.	K.Kt.5.	K.R.5.
Q.R.5.	Q.Kt.5	Q.B.5.	Q.5.	K.5.	K.B.5.	K.Kt.5.	K.R.5.
Q.R.4.	Q.Kt.4	Q.B.4.	Q.4.	K.4.	K.B.4.	K.Kt.4.	K.R.4.
Q.R.6.	Q.Kt.6	Q.B.6.	Q.6.	K.6.	K.B.6.	K.Kt.6.	K.R.6.
Q.R.3.	Q.Kt.3	Q.B.3.	Q.3.	K.3.	K.B.3.	K.Kt.3.	K.R.3.
Q.R.7.	Q.Kt.7	Q.B.7.	Q.7.	K.7.	K.B.7.	K.Kt.7.	K.R.7.
Q.R.2.	Q.Kt.2	Q.B.2.	Q.2.	K.2.	K.B.2.	K.Kt.2.	K.R.2.
Q.R.8.	Q.Kt.8	Q.B.8.	Q.8.	K.8.	K.B.8.	K.Kt.8.	K.R.8.
Q.R.sq.	Q.Kt.s	Q.B.sq.	Q.sq.	K.sq.	K.B.sq.	K.Kt.s.	K.R.sq.

▲ Standard English notation for chess

Technical Terms

Chess is a game that has its own vocabulary. As you learn to play, things will go along much easier if you can make sense of all those new words and their definitions.

Check and Checkmate

The King is said to be in check when he is attacked by a hostile piece or Pawn. Warning must be given by the opponent calling "check." You then must do one of three things: you must move the King out of check, or your King must take the piece or Pawn that checks him, or you must move a piece or Pawn between the King and the attacking hostile man. If you can't do any of these things, the King is *checkmated* and the game is lost.

When check is given by a Knight, you have only one choice—the King must move. Several other kinds of check are possible. Simple check is when the King is attacked by a single piece or Pawn. Double check occurs when the King is attacked by two pieces at the same time as a result of a discovered check. The discovered check is a discovered attack that places the king in check.

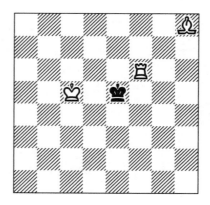

◀ **Discovered check:**
White, having to play,
can give discovered
check from the Bishop
by moving his Rook on
fourteen different squares.

Perpetual check occurs when the position is such that the attacked King cannot escape from one check without leaving himself constantly open to another. Perpetual check constitutes a drawn game, and may be resorted to, when possible, to save a losing player from defeat.

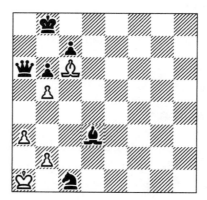

◀ **Perpetual check:**
Black draws the game
by establishing a
perpetual check; thus,
Black is threatened with
checkmate by Q to R8,
or Q to Kt7. But, it being
Black's move, he would
play Kt to Kt6: ch.; White
must play K to R2; Black
again returns to his
old position. There is
nothing to prevent his
repeatedly making these
two moves. Therefore,
the game is drawn.

Stalemate and Smothered Mate

A stalemate occurs when the King, though not in check, *cannot move without going into check,* and when no other piece or Pawn can be moved. The game is then drawn. Stalemate necessarily occurs only at the end of a game, when the King on one side stands alone or without any available pieces to move.

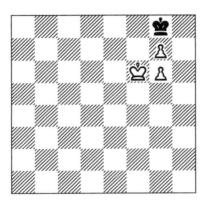

◄ **Stalemate:** Black, having to move, is stalemated, his King being unable to move on any square out of check from the Pawns, and being unable to capture the Pawn next him.

Smothered mate, also known as Philidor's Legacy, is when the King is so hemmed in that he cannot move out of check of a hostile Knight. It occasionally happens that this mate can be effected by heroically sacrificing the Queen.

Drawn Game

When neither player can checkmate his opponent, the result is a drawn game. Drawn games are brought about (1) by stalemate; (2) by perpetual check; (3) when both players persist in repeating the same moves; (4) when there is not sufficient force to give checkmate, as a King and two Knights only, or a King and Bishop; (5) when the forces on each side are equal, or nearly so, as Queen versus Queen, Rook versus Rook, etc.; (6) when a player who has sufficient force, as, for instance, a Knight and a Bishop, is unable to effect checkmate in fifty moves.

To Take En Passant

On the Pawn's *first* move, you may advance him two squares. If, in thus advancing, he passes a square occupied by one of the enemy's Pawns that has advanced to a fifth square, he is liable to be taken by that Pawn, which may intercept him in his passage or leap, as if he had only moved one square. This is called being taken *en passant.*

But, if taken *en passant,* he must be taken at once on the move. He cannot be thus captured at any subsequent stage of the game. Only Pawns—not pieces—can be taken *en passant.*

Other Vocabulary

- *En Prise*—French, meaning "exposed to capture." When a piece or Pawn is attacked by a hostile man, it is said to be *en prise*—that is, in danger of being captured.
- *J'Adoube*—French, meaning "I adjust or replace." This is used when a player touches a piece or Pawn to adjust it in the center of the square it occupies, without intending to move it.
- *Forced Move*—When a player can only make one move on the board, it is called a forced move.
- *Minor Pieces*—This is the term used for Knights and Bishops, to distinguish them from the Queens and Rooks.
- *The Exchange*—Winning or losing a Rook for a minor piece is called winning or losing the exchange.
- *Gambit*—This term is derived from an Italian word meaning "to trip up in wrestling," and is used in chess in those openings in which the first player purposely sacrifices a Pawn for the attack. The Pawn sacrificed is called the *gambit Pawn.*
- *Doubled Pawn*—When two Pawns are on the same file they are called *doubled Pawns.*
- *Isolated Pawn*—A Pawn standing alone without the support of other Pawns is called an *isolated Pawn.*
- *Passed Pawn*—A Pawn is labeled *passed* when the enemy has no Pawns either in front or on the adjacent files right or left to obstruct its march to Queen.

- *False Move*—A false move is any illegal move, such as moving a Knight like a Bishop or castling when the King is in check or has been already moved.

The Rules of the Game

Chess follows a strict set of rules that you must adopt to play the game well.

1.

The board must be placed so that each combatant has a white square in his right-hand corner. If, during the progress of a game, either player discovers that the board has been improperly placed, he may insist on its being adjusted.

2.

If, at any time in the course of the game, it is found that the men were not properly placed, or that one or more of them were omitted at the beginning, the game in question must be annulled. If at any time it is discovered that a man has been dropped off the board, and moves have been made during its absence, such moves shall be retracted and the man restored. If the players cannot agree as to the square on which it should be replaced, the game must be annulled.

3.

The right of making the first move and, if either player requires it, of choosing the color must be decided by flipping a coin. The color shall be retained for the remainder of the playing session. In any series of games between the same players at one sitting, each shall have the first move alternately in all the games, whether won or drawn. In an annulled game, the player who had the first move in that game shall move first in the next.

4.

If a player makes the first move in a game when it is not his turn to do so, the game must be annulled if the error has been noticed before both players have completed the fourth move. After four moves on each side have been made, the game must be played out as it stands.

5.

A player must never touch any of the men except when it is his turn to play, or except when he touches a man for the purpose of adjusting it; in the latter case he must inform his opponent before touching the piece. A player who touches with his hand (except accidentally) one of his own men when it is his turn to play must move it, if it can be legally moved, unless, before touching it, he says, "I adjust," as above; and a player who touches one of his adversary's men, under the same conditions, must take it if he can legally do so. If, in either case, the move cannot be legally made, the offender must move his King; but in the event of the King having no legal move, there shall be no penalty.

If a player holds a man in his hand when he can't decide which square to play it, his adversary may require him to replace it until he has decided its destination; that man, however, must be moved.

If a player, when it is his turn to play, touches with his hand (except accidentally or in castling), more than one of his own men, he must play any one of them, legally movable, that his opponent selects. If he touches two or more of the adversary's men, he must capture whichever of them his antagonist chooses, provided it can be legally taken. If it happens that none of the men so touched can be moved or captured, the offender must move his King; but if the King cannot be legally moved, there shall be no penalty.

6.

If a player makes a false move—that is, either by playing a man of his own to a square to which it cannot be legally moved, or by capturing an opponent's man by a move that cannot be legally made—he must, at the choice of his opponent, and according to the case, either move his own man legally, capture the man legally, or move any other man legally movable.

If, in the course of a game, an illegality is discovered (not involving a King being in check), and the move on which it was committed has been replied to, and not more than four moves on each side have been made subsequently, all these latter moves, including that on which the legality was committed, must be retracted. If more than four moves on each side have been made, the game must be played out as it stands.

7.

A player must audibly say "Check" when he makes a move that puts the hostile King in check. The mere announcement of check shall have no significance if check is not actually occurring. If check is occurring, but not announced, and the adversary makes a move that blocks the check, the move must stand.

If check occurs and is announced, and the adversary neglects to block it, he shall not have the option of capturing the checking piece or of covering, but must "move his King" out of check; but if the King has no legal move, there shall be no penalty.

If, in the course of the game, a King has been left in check for one or more moves on either side, all the moves subsequent to that on which the check was given must be retracted. Should these moves not be remembered, the game must be annulled.

If a player abandons the game, discontinues his moves, voluntarily resigns, upsets the board, or refuses to abide by these laws, he must be considered to have lost the game.

8.

A player is not bound to enforce a penalty. A penalty can only be enforced by a player before he has touched a man in reply. Should he touch a man in reply in consequence of a false or illegal move of his opponent, or a false cry of check, he shall not be compelled to move that man, and his right to enforce a penalty shall remain. When a King is moved as a penalty, it cannot castle on that move.

9.

Once in the game, if neither King nor Rook have been previously moved, the King has the privilege of moving two squares in conjunction with either of the Rooks. This operation is referred to as *castling*. If the space between the King and Rook is unoccupied, the King moves two squares to the right or left, and the Rook is placed on the next square that was originally occupied by the King. The King must not be in check, nor can he alight upon or pass over a square threatened by a hostile piece or Pawn.

In castling, the player shall move King and Rook simultaneously, or shall touch the King first. If he touches the Rook first, he must not let go of it before having touched the King; or his opponent may claim the move of the rook as a complete move.

10.

A player may call upon his opponent to draw the game, or to mate him within fifty moves on each side, whenever his opponent persists in repeating a particular check, or series of checks, or the same line of play, or whenever he has a King alone on the board, or one of the following occurs against an equal or superior force.

King and Queen
King and Rook
King and Bishop
King and Knight

or against King and Queen:

King and two Bishops
King and two Knights
King, Bishop, and Knight

and in all analogous cases; and whenever one player considers that his opponent can force the game, or that neither side can win it, he has the right of submitting the case to the umpire or bystanders, who shall decide whether it is one for the fifty-move counting. Should he not be mated within the fifty moves, he may claim that the game shall proceed.

For example: White has a King and Queen against Black's King and Rook. Black claims to count fifty moves. At the forty-ninth move, White, by a blunder, loses his Queen. Black can claim that the game proceed, and White in his turn may claim the fifty-move counting.

11.

Should a player be left with no other move than to take a Pawn in passing, he shall be bound to play that move.

12.

When a Pawn has reached the eighth square, the player has the option of selecting a piece, except a King (whether such piece has been previously lost or not), whose name and powers it shall then assume, or of deciding that it shall remain a Pawn. This is called either *queening a Pawn,* or a *Pawn queens.* Thus one player may have two or more Queens, Rooks, Knights, or Bishops on the board at the same time. A player can often win a game by claiming a Knight or a rook, whereas he could lose by claiming a Queen.

13.

The umpire shall have authority to decide any question that may arise in the course of a game, but must never interfere except when asked. He must always apply the laws as expressed, and not assume the power of modifying them or of deviating from them in particular cases, according to his own judgment. When a question is submitted to the umpire, or to bystanders, by both players, the umpire's decision shall be final.

A Preliminary Chess Game

The game of chess is full of intricacies, requiring both methodical play and foresight. An example of a simple game, thoroughly explained at every step, will help you to gain a better understanding. All the plays are numbered. In formal matches, the defending player always takes Black.

White	Black
1P–K4	1P–K4
2Kt–KB 3	

This is a good move, bringing out a piece and immediately attacking Black's undefended King's Pawn.

White	Black
	2 Kt–QB 3

Black defends his Pawn.

White	Black
3 B–B4	

White attacks Black's KBP, with the idea of bringing another piece to bear on it. It could not be taken at this time because it is defended by the King. Remember, a Bishop is worth at least three Pawns.

White	Black
	3 B–B4
4 P–Q3	

This move frees the Queen's Bishop.

White	Black
	4 P–Q3
5 Kt–QB 3	5 Kt–KB 3
6 Castles	6 Castles
7 B–KKt 5	

Here White pins the black Knight, which cannot be moved without losing the Queen.

White	Black
	7 P–KR 3

Black tries to drive away this troublesome Bishop.

White	Black
8 B × Kt	8 Q × B

Black retakes with Queen in order to avoid a doubled Pawn on KBP file, and the attack of Q–Q2 threatened by White.

White	Black
9 Kt–Q5	9 Q–Kt 3
10 Kt × QBP	10 B–KR 6

Black leaves the Rook open to be taken, and menacing immediate checkmate.

White	Black
11 Kt–KR 4	

White instead stops the mate and attacks the Queen.

White	Black
	11 Q–B 3
12 Kt × R	12 Q × Kt
13 P × B	13 Q × KRP
14 Kt–B7	

White is overanxious to save his piece.

White	Black
	14 Kt–Q5
15 P–KB 3	

White is vainly trying to prevent the danger.

White	Black
	15 Kt × KBP

Black discovers that he is in double check. The white King is now checked both by Bishop and Knight, and must move into the corner square.

White	Black
16 K–R sq.	16 Q × RP checkmate

Introducing Checkers
Rating: 5+

Checkers is played by two people sitting opposite each other, using a board containing sixty-four squares. The squares are colored alternately black and white, or any other two colors. The pieces (or men) are flat disks. Each player has twelve pieces of one color, usually black, red, or white. The object is to prevent an opponent from moving in his turn by capturing his twelve pieces, or blocking his remaining pieces.

To begin play, place the board so that a white corner is at the lower left in front of each player.

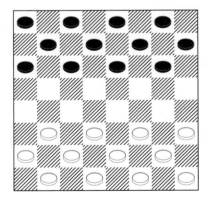

◀ Begin each checkers game by placing the pieces on the first three lines of white squares. The player who has chosen to take the black pieces leads off.

You can decide who gets the black pieces with a coin toss. The players should alternate pieces, so if you start out with white pieces, in the next game you should switch to black ones.

Moving the Pieces

To move a piece, push it forward from the square it is on to an unoccupied white square to the right or left. Stepping on the black squares isn't allowed (with one important exception that will be covered soon). You can only move the men forward, one square at a time, until they reach one of the four white squares on the opposite end of the board. When they accomplish this, they become kings and you can move them either forward or backward, but still only one square at a time.

Capturing

You can take or "capture" an opponent's man in the direction in which you are moving your man by leaping over any hostile piece that is on an adjoining square, provided that there is a vacant white square beyond it. You then place your capturing man on the vacant square, and remove the opponent's captured piece from the board. If several pieces on a forward diagonal have open squares between them, you may take all of them at one capture. You then place your capturing man on the square beyond the last piece taken.

A few judicious exchanges at the opening of the game will greatly simplify its progress; a game board full of pieces frequently causes embarrassment to the beginner. You should, however, vary your tactics according to whether you are playing against an opponent who is a more experienced or less experienced player than you are.

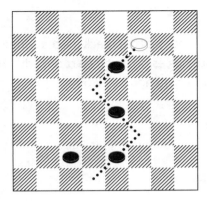

◀ A white piece placed on square 8 can capture black pieces on 11, 19, and 27 in a zigzag line.

The Huffing Option

If you do not take a piece when you are able to, your opponent has three alternatives:

1. He may allow the move to remain good.
2. He may require you to capture the man or men liable to be taken.
3. He may *huff,* which means he may remove the piece that could have made the capture but did not. In other words, he may take your man off the board.

For example: Black begins by moving one of the men placed on 9, 10, 11, or 12. Suppose he moves the man from 11 to 15. White replies by moving his piece from 22 to 18. Black can take White by leaping his man from 15 to 22, and removing the captured piece off the board. Should Black not take White but move in another direction, say from 12 to 16, he is liable to be huffed. To penalize Black for not taking a white man off the board, White may remove the man that Black should have used to make the capture.

Instead of huffing, White may, if he thinks it is more to his advantage to do so, simply leave the offending piece on the board, without any penalty. The third alternative is to require Black to replace the man played to 16, and play from 15 to 22, thereby capturing the white man on 18, thus enabling White to capture Black by playing 25 to 18.

When one player huffs the other, he does not replace the piece his opponent moved in error, but simply removes the man from the board. He then plays his own move. The technical checkers term for this strategy is to *huff and move*.

If you are entitled to huff, you must do so before you move. If you do not, you forfeit the right to do so during that turn. However, if your opponent again neglects to take the man, you can exact the penalty at his next turn.

If you are able to take a piece in more than one way, you can choose to do so in whichever way you please.

Crowning Kings

When a man belonging to either player arrives at one of the squares farthest from his own end of the board, whether by moving or capturing, he is made a King. The King is marked by having another piece of the same color placed on top of him, which is called *crowning* him. You can move a King both forward and backward along the white diagonals. A King can take any number of pieces. However, like any other man, he can be huffed for not taking the correct number of pieces off the board.

A man's turn is finished when it reaches one of the extreme squares and is made a King. You must wait until your opponent makes his move before you can move this piece again, whether to capture your opponent's piece or simply advance your own man on the board.

Never resort to a risky move unless you realize that you are losing and that you would gain a decided advantage should your move succeed. If you're in an equal position with your opponent, wait for an opportunity when you are feeling stronger; choose a draw rather than make a risky move.

And the Winner Is . . .

The game is won by whoever can first succeed in capturing or blocking all his opponent's men, so that the opponent has nothing left to move.

A draw would occur when each player has a very small and equal force remaining, and neither player can make a move to defeat his opponent.

Rules of the Game

Here's an overview of the rules for playing checkers:

1. The choice of men that each player shall take in the opening game is to be decided by tossing a coin or any other means agreed upon. Whoever gains the choice can begin with the black men, or call on his adversary to do so.
2. If a series of games is played, the choice of lead player and black men belongs to each player alternately, whether the previous game was won or drawn.
3. A player should not point over the board with his finger, or use any action that may interrupt his opponent's view of the game.
4. At any part of the game it is allowable to readjust the men on their proper squares, provided that the player warns his adversary before doing so. In the absence of such warning, if a player, whose turn it is to play, touches a piece, he must play it in one direction or another, if possible. If a piece that cannot be moved is touched, there is no penalty.
5. A move or capture of a piece is completed as soon as the hand is withdrawn from the piece played.
6. If a piece is moved so far as to be in any way visible over the angle of the square on which it is resting, that move must be completed notwithstanding that the player so moving it may incur the penalty of being huffed.
7. If a piece is illegally moved, the adversary may require the same piece to make a proper move in either direction he pleases, or may allow the false move to stand good. But if the piece cannot be legally moved in any direction, the adversary has only the option of allowing the false move to stand good.
8. If a player captures one of his own men, the opponent has the option whether the piece capturing in error shall be replaced or allowed to remain where placed in error.

9. When a player is in a position from which he can capture on either of two forward diagonals, he may do so whichever way he pleases, without regard to the one capture comprising greater force than the other. For example, if one man is one way or two are another way, a player may capture either the one man or the two at his option.

10. When a player moves a man to the end of the board, which entitles it to be made a king, the adversary is bound to crown it.

11. Each player is obliged to move within a specified time agreed upon by the players before commencing the game. A player who does not move within such time is considered to have lost the game.

12. If a player neglects to take a piece when able, his opponent has three alternatives: He may allow the move to hold good, may oblige the player in fault to capture the man or men, or may huff the pieces that could have effected the capture.

13. If a player entitled to huff has made his election to touch the piece that is liable to be huffed, he is bound to huff.

14. After a player entitled to huff has moved without exercising his right, he cannot remedy the omission unless his adversary should still neglect to take or change the position of the piece concerned, and so render himself liable again.

15. When several pieces are taken at one move, they must not be removed from the board until the capturing piece has completed its full move.

16. The act of huffing does not constitute a move, but a huff and a move go together.

17. When at the end of a game a small degree of force remains, the player who has the superiority of force may be required to win the game in a certain number of moves; and if he cannot do so, the game must be abandoned as a draw. A full move in this sense is not complete until both sides have played.

18. When three Kings remain against two, the player with the three may be required to win after not more than forty moves (twenty would be better in our opinion) have been played by each player, the moves to be computed from the point at which notice is given.

19. When two Kings remain against one, the player with the two Kings may similarly be required to win after not more than twenty moves have been played by each player.

20. In no case can these numbers be exceeded, after having been once claimed, and even if one more move would win the game, it must be declared a draw.

21. The rule is to play on the white squares; the exception is to play on the black.

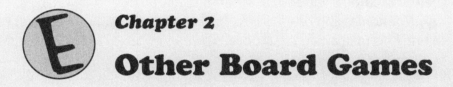

Chapter 2

Other Board Games

There are hundreds of board games on the market, but none of the newcomers compare to the classics. Whether you are looking for a board game that will simply provide an evening's worth of fun or something a little more advanced that will challenge your skill, this chapter has it all.

Backgammon

Rating: 8+

Backgammon is played by two people, sitting opposite each other. The borders of the board should be raised, and across the middle of the board, there should be a raised bar, separating the board into two tables, called *inner* (or home) and *outer* tables. The object of the game is for each player to bring his men around and into his own inner table. This is accomplished by throws of the dice.

Each player has fifteen pieces (or men), which are small, flat disks. The tables are marked with twenty-four points, colored alternately white and black, or any other two colors. The points should be long enough to hold five men, with about half of the fifth man projecting beyond the point. Between the points in White's tables and those in Black's tables is a space on which the dice are thrown.

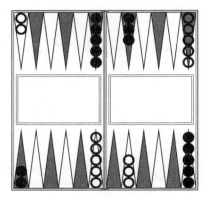

▲ Backgammon board

Each point has a name. The one to the extreme left in White's inner table is called White's Ace point; the next, White's Deuce point; the others, in order, are White's Three, Four, Five, and Six points. The Ace point in White's outer table is called his Bar point. The points on Black's table are named in the same way.

Getting Started

Each player has a box and two dice, and pieces are moved around the board depending on the number of spots that are face up when the dice are thrown.

At the start, each player takes his dice box and shakes one die in it. Place two fingers over the open end of the box to prevent the die from being shaken out.

At the beginning of the game you should try to secure your Five point, or your opponent's Five point, or both. The next best point to hold is your Bar point, and next to that your Four point.

After shaking the dice box, each player throws his die on the board. The player who throws the higher number has the first play. He may either adopt the two numbers just thrown, or he may take up the dice and throw them again.

After throwing the dice, you should call out the numbers rolled. If you throw a Four and a Two, you call "Four Two" (the higher number always being called first), and then move any of your men a number of points corresponding to the numbers thrown. The march of men is from your opponent's inner table to his outer table, then to your outer table, and last to your own home table. The White and Black men move in opposite directions.

You may move one man the entire value of the throw, or you may divide the move between two men, each one moving one of the numbers thrown. In other words, White might play Four Two by carrying one man from the Six point of Black's outer table to his own six point; or he might play one man from the Deuce point of his outer table to his Four point, and another man from his Six point to his Four point.

When you play men as in the latter example, so that two men will occupy a previously blank point, it is called *making a point*. If White plays in this way, the man who played the Four will remain on a point by himself. This is called *leaving a blot*.

If you throw two equal numbers (called doubles), you play double what you throw. For example, if you throw two Aces, you play four Aces instead of two.

The players throw and play alternately throughout the game.

Limitations in Playing

The only limitations to the play are that neither player can play beyond his own home table, or onto any point occupied by two or more of his opponent's men. If White throws Five Ace in his opening move, he cannot play a Five in Black's inner table, or an Ace from Black's outer table to his own inner table, because the points are already occupied by Black. He could play Five Ace from Black's inner table by playing the Ace first and then the Five, but not by playing the Five first. In this position the play is not affected, because the caster (person casting the dice) may choose which number to play first. Any part of a throw that cannot be played is lost, but the caster must play the whole throw if he can.

Hitting Blots

If you play a man to a point that is occupied by just one of your opponent's men, you have *hit a blot*. You take the man off the table and place him on the bar. This man has to be played into your opponent's inner table at the next throw. This is called entering. If your opponent throws an Ace, the man is entered on the Ace point, and so on for other numbers. Of course he cannot be entered on any point that is occupied by two or more of your men. If the points corresponding to both the numbers thrown are occupied, your opponent's man cannot re-enter the game. He is not permitted to play any other man while he has a man to enter; consequently, in the case above, he would lose his turn.

FACT

A leading principle of backgammon play is to make points whenever you can, especially in or close to your home table. A second general principle is to avoid leaving blots, particularly where they are likely to be hit by the adversary.

It sometimes happens that one player has a man up, and that his opponent has his home table made up; that is, each point is occupied by two or more men. In this case it is obvious that the player who is up cannot enter. Because it is useless for that player to throw, his opponent continues throwing and playing until he opens a point on his home table.

You may take up two or more blots at once, or in successive throws. You do not have to hit a blot if you can play the throw without doing so.

Bearing

The game proceeds as described until one player has carried all his men into his home table. When you reach that point you then have the privilege of taking your men off the board (this is called *bearing* them). If every point on your home table is made up and you throw Four Three, you can take off one man from your Four point and one from your Three point. Or, if you prefer, you may move a Four from your Six or Five point, and a Three from your Six, Five, or Four point; or you may move one and bear the other. If you cannot move any part of the throw, you must bear it. For example, if you have no man on your Six or Five points, you must bear the Four.

Always take up a man if the blot you leave can only be hit with double dice, except when playing for a hit only, and if you have two of your opponent's men in your home table and you seem to be winning.

If you throw a number that is higher than any point on which you have a man, you must bear the man from the highest occupied point. For example, if you have no man on your Six point and you throw a Six, you must bear from your Five point or, if that is unoccupied, from your Four point, and so on. And, of course, in the reverse case, if you throw an Ace, and your Ace point is unoccupied, you must move another man toward the Ace point. Doubles similarly entitle you to bear or play four men.

If you should be hit on a blot after you have begun bearing your men, you must enter on your opponent's inner table, and you cannot bear any more men until the one taken up has been played back again into your own home table. The player who first bears all his men wins the game.

The game counts as a single win or hit if the opponent has borne any of his men; a double game or gammon if the opponent has not removed any of his men; and as a triple or quadruple game (according to what you agreed at the beginning of the game) or backgammon if, at the time the winner bears his last man, the opponent (not having borne a man) has a man up, or one in the winner's inner table. Should a player who has borne a man be taken up, he can only lose a hit, even if he fails to enter the man before the adversary bears all his.

When you play a series of games, the winner of a hit has the first throw in the succeeding game; but if a gammon or backgammon is won, the players each throw a single die to determine the first throw of the next game.

Rules of the Game

1. The game shall be played with fifteen men on either side.
2. The players shall determine by agreement who shall command the inner and the outer table.
3. The white men are arranged as follows: Two on the Ace point of the inner table most remote from the player; five on the Six point of the outer table most remote from the player; three on the Deuce point of the outer table nearest the player; and five on the Six point of the inner table nearest the player. The Black men, in like numbers, shall occupy the points immediately opposite.
4. If a player begins to play with less than his proper number of men on the board, he cannot afterward claim to place the man or men he has omitted.
5. If, at the outset of the game, any of the men shall be placed incorrectly, either player may rectify the error before he has played; but after he has once played, he is not entitled to require such rectification. After both players have played, no rectification shall be made, except by mutual consent.
6. The dice must be thrown into one or the other of the tables.
7. If either die jumps from one table into the other, or off the board, the cast is void, and the caster shall throw both dice again.

8. If either die rests, wholly or partially, on the other die, on the bar or frame of the board, on any of the men, or in any manner other than with its underside in complete contact with the surface of the table into which it is thrown, the cast is void, and the caster shall throw both dice again.

9. The caster must call his throw before playing it.

10. If a die is touched while in the act of falling from the box, or while still in motion on the board, the player not in fault shall be entitled to name the number that shall be played for that die.

11. If a die, even at rest, is touched before the caster has called his throw, and the throw be disputed, the player not in fault shall be entitled to name the number that shall be played for that die.

12. Should the caster call his throw incorrectly, he must abide by the call, unless he shall have perceived and corrected the mistake before the dice are touched by either player.

13. If the caster, after throwing, touches one of his own men, unless for the purpose of adjusting it, he must play such man, if it is possible to do so. If he has moved a man to any point and let go of it, it shall remain on such point.

14. If a wrong number of points is played, the adversary may require the correction of the error before he has again thrown; but after he has thrown, the move shall stand, unless altered by mutual consent.

15. The total amount of a throw must be played, if it is possible to do so. If there are alternative modes of play, one only of which will enable the whole throw to be played, such alternative shall be adopted.

16. If either player bears off a man or men before he has brought the whole of his men into his home table, the man or men so borne shall be placed on the bar, and re-entered in the adversary's table.

Battleship

Rating: 8+

Battleship is played by two people. The object of the game is to sink your opponent's ships. The first person to sink all of his opponent's ships wins.

The players sit facing each other. Each player gets five ships: one patrol boat, with three holes; one submarine, with three holes; one destroyer, with three holes; one battleship, with four holes; and one carrier, with five holes. Each player places his fleet of ships on the lower of two grids that serve as each player's game board. Ships may be placed vertically or horizontally, not diagonally. A ship cannot touch another ship or the edges of the grid.

FACT

Before it became a popular commercial game, Battleship was played with paper and pencil. You can simply draw the two grids on paper and use X's to fill in the Misses and the Hits.

Players decide who will go first by flipping a coin or a similar method. The first player selects a location on the grid and calls out the location by letter (vertical axis) and number (horizontal axis)—for example, G-3. The second player finds the coordinate on his lower grid. If the first player has called out a coordinate on which the second player has a ship, the second player must declare a Hit, and which ship was hit—for example, "Hit. Battleship." The first player places a red peg in the coordinate on the upper grid. If there is no ship in the coordinate, the second player says "Miss," and the first player puts a white peg in the upper grid. Players alternate calling out shots. A ship is sunk when all its holes have been filled by red pegs. When a ship is sunk, the player must declare it sunk. The first person to sink all of his opponent's ships wins.

Chinese Checkers
Rating: 5+

Chinese Checkers can be played by two, three, or six players. If two people are playing, they sit opposite each other, choosing opposite points of the star. If three people are playing, the players sit at every other point. Each player chooses ten marbles of the same color and places them in the holes in the point of the star in front of him. The object of the game is to be the first player to get ten marbles across the board to the opposite point on the star.

Players choose among themselves who should go first, and then play moves to the left of the first player. The first player moves a marble one hole in any direction along the lines provided on the board.

You can move a marble to a hole adjacent to the marble's starting point, as long as the hole is empty, or you can jump it over a marble to the next hole along the line, if there is an empty space beyond the marble. The marble you're moving can jump either your own color or any other player's. You also can move a marble in a series of jumps over various marbles, as long as you follow the lines on the board, and there are empty spaces between marbles for yours to land. The marbles that you jump over are not removed from the board. When the first player is finished moving his marble as far as possible, his turn is over and the player on his left continues, and so on.

Connect Four

Rating: 8+

Connect Four is a sort of vertical tic-tac-toe. It is played on a vertical board with seven columns into which flat disks similar to checkers pieces are inserted. One player has red pieces; the other has black. Players take turns inserting the pieces into the board. Each player tries to get four pieces of her color in a row: diagonally, horizontally, or vertically. The first player to do so wins. If the board is filled up with neither player getting four in a row, the game is a draw, and players start again.

Cranium

Rating: 12+

Players divide themselves into teams. Each team tries to get all the way around the board and into Cranium Central. On each player's first turn and on each purple Cranium planet, she gets to choose the box from which she will pick a card. After the player successfully completes an activity, she rolls the dice and moves to the next color. Players must stop at every planet. If the player is unsuccessful, she must remain in place and try again on her next turn. The next player to the left then takes a turn.

A team may get on the fast track if its players are successful on their first Cranium activity. The team to the right of the active team selects a card detailing the activity from the box matching the color of the space the team is on and reads the card out loud. The first team to reach Cranium Central and successfully complete the final activity wins.

Monopoly

Rating: 8+

The object of the game of Monopoly is to gain as much money as possible. The game requires two or more people and can take a long time to play. Before beginning play, you must set up the board and choose tokens for each player. Players receive $1,500 from the bank in the following denominations: $500 (2), $100 (2), $50 (2), $20 (6), $10 (5), $5 (5), and $1 (5).

One player is selected as the banker. The banker doles out and collects funds from the other players, hands out the deed cards, and also auctions property. However, the banker keeps his or her personal fortune separate from the bank's money.

Playing the Game

The banker begins play by throwing the dice. Then every other player also throws the dice. The player with the highest number on the dice goes first, and so on. The first player moves her token along the board according to the number rolled on the dice, starting at "Go." The other players roll the dice and move their tokens in turn. It is possible to have more than one token on each space.

Some spaces require you to draw a card from the Chance or Community chests, pay taxes, go to jail, or pay other penalties. Each time you pass the "Go" space, you collect $200 from the bank.

Going to Jail

If you throw doubles (the dice both have the same number), you are entitled to throw again. However, if you throw doubles three times in a row you must go to the space marked "Jail." You may get out of jail by throwing doubles within your next three turns. You then move according to the number on the dice without throwing again. You also can use a Get Out of Jail Free card (either one you have drawn or one that you bought from another player). If you fail to roll doubles or use a Get Out of Jail Free card after three turns, you may pay a $50 fine and then roll and continue playing the game.

Buying Property

If the space you land on is not owned by another player, you may buy the property. You then will receive the Title Deed Card to the property. If you decline to buy the property at the printed price, the bank may auction it.

FACT

You may sell property without buildings to other players; however, you may not sell properties that already have buildings. You may sell buildings back to the bank for half the price you paid. You also may mortgage property, but only if it has no buildings. You must sell all buildings back to the bank before you can mortgage the property. You can pay off the mortgage by paying the bank the amount of the mortgage plus 10 percent.

When you own all the spaces in a color, you may double the rent that's charged when another player lands on your property, and you also may buy houses from the bank. After building four houses on a color group, you may buy hotels from the bank. You must build an equal number of houses and hotels on each property in a color group before you can build new houses on other properties; that is, building must be even. Adding houses and hotels to property makes the rent price go up.

Paying Rent

If you land on a space owned by another player, you may have to pay rent, the amount of which is printed on the deed card. If the property is mortgaged, you do not have to pay rent. If you cannot pay what is owed to either the bank or another player, you are declared bankrupt and must turn over all of your assets to the bank or the other player. If your assets go to the bank, the bank will auction off your property. A bankrupt player is out of the game. The winner is either the richest player when play stops, or the last remaining player.

Scrabble

Rating: 8+

Scrabble requires two to four players, one of whom is elected scorekeeper. To choose the order of players, shuffle the letter tiles in a bag and have each player draw a tile. Play begins in alphabetical order—that is, players with letters closer to A go first, and so on down to Z. The tiles are then returned to the bag and shuffled. Players draw seven tiles each and set them on their racks so that the tiles are not seen by other players.

Options for Play

At each turn, you have three options:

1. Exchanging tiles: You may exchange as many of your tiles as you want by drawing new tiles and returning the old ones to the bag. However, all players must always have seven tiles.
2. Passing: If you are unable to form a word, you may pass (decline your turn) and allow the next player to go. If everyone passes twice in a row, the game is over.
3. Playing: The first player uses his tiles to create a word with two or more letters. Subsequent players build on this word horizontally or vertically, but not diagonally.

After each turn, count and announce your score. To count score, add up the values on the tiles included in the word and any premium values that you get for landing on premium spaces. If you use all seven of your tiles in one play, you get fifty extra points. After you count and record your score, draw new tiles to replace the ones you played.

QUESTION?

How can I tell which words are real and which are made up?
Words must come from the Scrabble dictionary or a standard dictionary agreed upon by the players. Other players may challenge a word or its spelling. If the challenge is successful, the word is removed and the next player takes his turn.

Rules of the Game

1. Tiles placed in one play must be in the same row or column.
2. If tiles in a word touch any other tiles, they must also form a word. The player gets credit for these words.
3. New words can be formed by: adding letters to an existing word (e.g., *rain* can become *sprain*); adding words at right angles using existing tiles; or a word created at right angles may add letters to words on the board.
4. The game ends in one of two ways: Either every player passes twice— that is, no one plays for two rounds—or all of the tiles are in play from the bag, and one player uses all of his tiles.

Final scores are determined by subtracting the sum value of a player's remaining unplayed tiles. If a player has used all of his tiles, the sum of the other player's (or players') remaining tiles are added to his score. The player with the highest score wins.

Trivial Pursuit
Rating: 12+

Trivial Pursuit requires one to six players. Each player selects a game piece, which has spaces for six smaller pieces, one for each category. Categories are color-coded as follows:

- Blue—Geography
- Orange—Sports & Leisure
- Pink—Entertainment
- Brown—Art & Literature
- Green—Science & Nature
- Yellow—History

To figure out the order of play, each player rolls the dice. The player with the highest number goes first, the second-highest number goes next, and so on. Place all tokens in the center of the board.

To begin, the first player rolls the dice and moves the appropriate number of spaces down any one of the spokes. Once on the wheel of the board, you can move in either direction and up the spokes, but you are not allowed to move back and forth across spaces in one turn. Another player then draws a card from the box and reads the question that corresponds to the category of the space on which you have landed. If you correctly answer the question, you may roll again. If you answer incorrectly, the turn passes to the next player.

The object of the game is to fill your game piece with a wedge from each category. You may only collect one of each color and only on the spaces located at the intersection of the wheel and a spoke. After you collect all of the pieces, you must get the token back to the starting place at the center of the board and answer one final question from a category selected by the other players. The first player to successfully answer this final question wins.

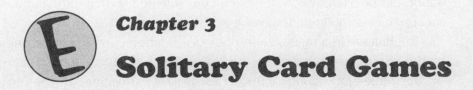

Chapter 3

Solitary Card Games

Who says games have to be social to be fun? Whether you simply cannot find anyone to play with or you just want to spend some time alone, there are plenty of games you can play by yourself, many requiring only a deck of cards. This chapter offers a variety of solitaire games to choose from.

Anno Domini
Rating: 8+

The object of this game is to build complete families upon the foundations in suit and in ascending sequence. You form the game board with four foundation cards, one of each suit, each card selected so that if the families are successfully completed, the result will show a year.

To produce this result, each of the foundation cards must be one card higher in denomination than the digits that form the date. If a zero (0) occurs in the date—2000 for instance—zero is represented by the Ten-spot, and the foundation card that corresponds is a Jack. Use one deck of cards for this game.

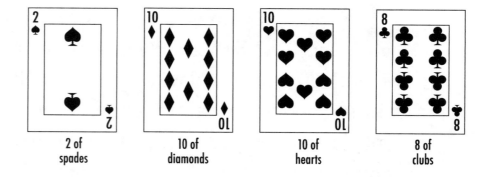

2 of spades   10 of diamonds   10 of hearts   8 of clubs

▲ For example, to play the year 1997, the foundation cards are the Deuce of Spades, Ten of Diamonds, Ten of Hearts, and Eight of Clubs .

From your stock of cards, turn over one card at a time, building upon the foundations in ascending sequence, wrapping from King to Ace when necessary. One redeal is permitted. If no play is possible, the game is blocked and ended.

Classic Solitaire

Rating: 8+

The object of this game is to build complete families upon the foundations, beginning with the King, in descending sequence, alternating colors. Use one deck of cards for this game.

Deal the cards, face down, into seven packets in a row. The first (or left-hand) packet contains seven cards; the next packet to the right, six cards; and each succeeding packet to the right, one card less than the preceding packet, so that the seventh packet will consist of one card. These cards are called the *auxiliary piles*. Turn over the top card from each auxiliary pile, exposing the face of the card.

If any Kings appear, remove them from their pile and place them in a separate row above the auxiliary piles. The Kings form the foundations on which you will build the families. You then will match up the rest of the face-up cards in descending order, alternating in color, if possible. (Note that a set that alternates red and black cards is called a *marriage*.) If any piles are left unexposed, you may turn up the next available card in that pile to see if you can use it.

ALERT!

While solitaire is traditionally played with a deck of cards, most personal computers now come with solitaire as part of their software package, making the game easily accessible both at home and at work. Be careful; this computer game can be addictive.

Once all of the preliminary marriages are complete, flip over one card from the stock that's left after you deal, and see if it can be used. If it is King, place it in the separate row above the piles. You can place a Queen of an alternating color atop the King, and so on, until you reach an Ace. You also can use cards from the stock to create marriages within the auxiliary piles.

Repeat the deal over and over again until you have exhausted the auxiliary piles. If no play has been possible during a deal, the game is blocked and ended. A winning game consists of the four families, all ending with an Ace.

Double or Quits

Rating: 8+

In this game, all the cards count for their face value from Ace (one) up to Ten. The Jack counts for eleven; the Queen, twelve; and the King, thirteen. Each succeeding card placed on the foundation must be double the value of the card preceding it. The exposed card of the stock and the auxiliary cards are available for play. Use one deck of cards for this game.

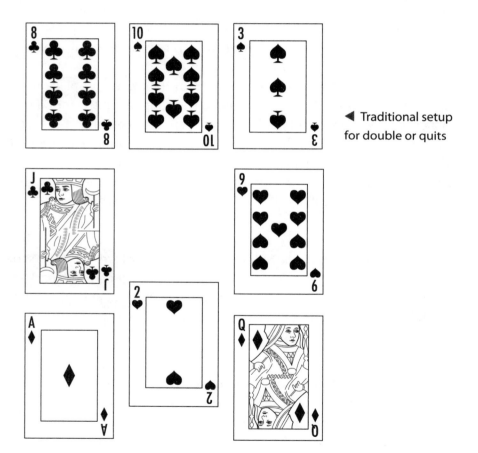

◀ Traditional setup for double or quits

Place six cards in two columns of three each, and a seventh card between the top cards of the columns. These seven cards are auxiliaries, and as vacancies occur you will fill them from the pack. Lay an eighth card between the four lower cards of the columns; this is the foundation on which you will build. In this game, cards go by value only, regardless of suit. Unsuitable cards form a stock.

If any one of the auxiliary cards first laid out is a King, place it at the bottom of the pack and substitute another card. If, in the course of play, a King becomes an auxiliary card, it must remain so.

FACT

Though winning is dependent mostly upon luck, this game of solitaire allows for pretty good chances. You have approximately a 50 percent chance of winning each time.

If the double of a card is more than thirteen, the excess of the double over thirteen denotes the card required. For example, suppose the last card played on the foundation was a Nine. The double of nine is eighteen, which is five more than thirteen, so the next required card must be a Five; the next following, the double of five, and so on.

Two redeals are allowed, if necessary. If no play has been possible after the second deal, the game is blocked and ended.

The Fan
Rating: 8+

In this game you build families upon the foundations in sequence without following suit. Sequences may be ascending or descending at your option, but the one you select at first must be adhered to for all the foundations. Several cards are always available: the right-hand exposed or released card in the fan, the four auxiliary cards, the exposed card of the reserve packet, and the top undealt card of the pack. Use two complete decks of cards for this game.

Turn the pack face up. Working from left to right, lay out twelve cards in the shape of a fan. Each successive card partly covers, but does not conceal, its left-hand neighbor. Next, place a reserve packet of twelve cards to

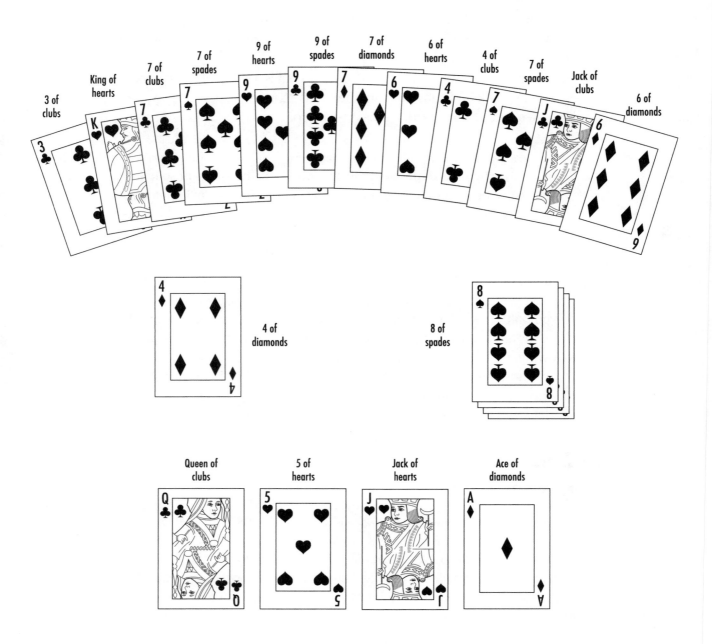

3 of
clubs

King of
hearts

7 of
clubs

7 of
spades

9 of
hearts

9 of
spades

7 of
diamonds

6 of
hearts

4 of
clubs

7 of
spades

Jack of
clubs

6 of
diamonds

4 of
diamonds

8 of
spades

Queen of
clubs

5 of
hearts

Jack of
hearts

Ace of
diamonds

▲ Traditional setup for the fan

the right of the fan; then deal four auxiliary cards in a row, a little distance below the fan, so as to leave space between them for the foundations. You will fill vacancies in the auxiliary cards from the pack.

Lay the next card dealt from the pack below the left end of the fan. This card, together with the other seven cards of the same denomination, placed in a row to the right as they appear in dealing, are the eight foundations for families. Play suitable cards upon the foundations as available. Because it is important that the fan and reserve be used up, you should play suitable cards from them in preference to playing from the pack, when you have the choice. Two redeals are allowed, if necessary.

Fascination

Rating: 8+

The object of this game is to build complete families upon the foundations in suit and ascending sequence. Make the marriages in descending sequence, alternating colors between the auxiliary cards or packets, and upon the auxiliary cards from the pack and from the reserve. Use one deck of cards for this game.

Count off thirteen cards face down from the pack, and then turn this reserve packet face up. Deal one card from the pack, and place it below the reserve packet. This is the first of the foundations. Place the other three cards of the same denomination in a row to the right of the first, as they appear in play. Deal four more cards in a row below the foundation row. These are the auxiliary cards. Fill vacancies in the auxiliaries from the reserve only until the reserve is exhausted. After that, fill vacancies with the next undealt card of the pack.

Next, deal the cards from the pack, face down, in groups of three at a time. As you deal each group, turn it face up. The exposed or released card of each successive group is available for play.

Marriages between auxiliary cards are not confined merely to exposed cards; you may lift and transfer any number of cards in a packet, provided that the bottom card of the ones you lift fits exactly in color and sequence upon the top card of another packet.

▲ Traditional set-up for fascination

Repeat the deal over and over again as long as a suitable card has appeared in the previous deal. If no play has been possible during a deal, the game is blocked and ended.

Forwards and Backwards
Rating: 8+

In this game the King counts for thirteen; the Queen, for twelve; the Jack, for eleven; and the remainder of the cards for the pips on their faces, the Ace being one. You can use a card, as dealt, only when it can make 14 points with the foundation card or packet that it's played on. Use two decks of cards for this game.

Deal twenty cards from the pack, arranging them in four rows of five cards each. These are the foundation cards. If a Seven does not appear in these twenty cards, return any one card to the pack, and fill the vacancy with a Seven selected from the pack. Deal the cards one by one. The first card dealt that is not suitable blocks and ends the game.

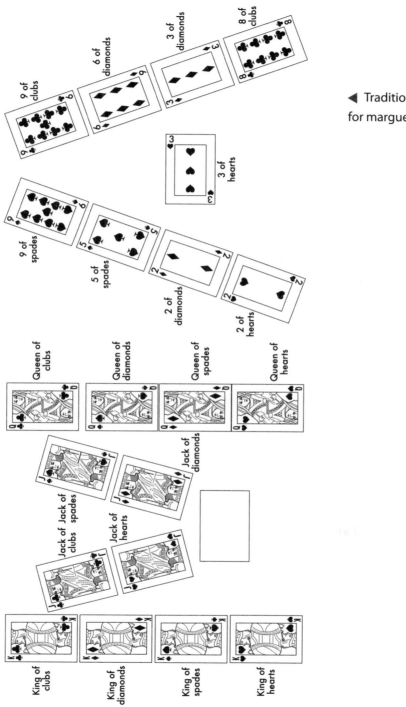

9 of clubs

6 of diamonds

3 of diamonds

8 of clubs

3 of hearts

◀ Traditional setup
for marguerite

9 of spades

5 of spades

2 of diamonds

2 of hearts

Queen of clubs

Queen of diamonds

Queen of spades

Queen of hearts

Jack of spades

Jack of diamonds

Jack of clubs

Jack of hearts

King of clubs

King of diamonds

King of spades

King of hearts

Marguerite
Rating: 8+

The object of the game is to build families upon the foundations in suit and in descending sequence. The exposed card of the stock, and any card or cards in the A group, are available. Use one deck of cards for this game.

Form the game board with the Kings, Queens, and Jacks of each suit. Take them from the pack and arrange them in the form of an M with a vacant space below the Jacks. You will complete the foundations with three cards on each in descending sequence, as follows:

On each King—the Ten, Nine, and Eight of the same suit
On each Queen—the Seven, Six, and Five of the same suit
On each Jack—the Four, Three, and Two of the same suit

Deal nine cards from the pack, arranging them in the form of the letter A. As vacancies occur in the A group, filled them from the pack. If no vacancies occur, deal the cards from the stock until suitable cards appear.

If you deal two cards of the same suit upon the stock in descending sequence—a Three on a Four, for instance—it is clear that the game is blocked. Because Aces are of no use in the game, place them, as you deal them, upon the vacant spot below the Jacks.

There is no redeal allowed. If no play has been possible during a deal, the game is blocked and ended.

The Necklace
Rating: 8+

In this game you build families upon the foundation cards, following suit in descending sequence from the Ten down to the Ace. Cards as dealt, the three auxiliary cards, and the exposed card of the stock are available. Use one deck of cards for this game.

Form the game board by degrees as you deal the necessary cards. Place the four Tens, as they appear, in the form of a cross. These are the foundation

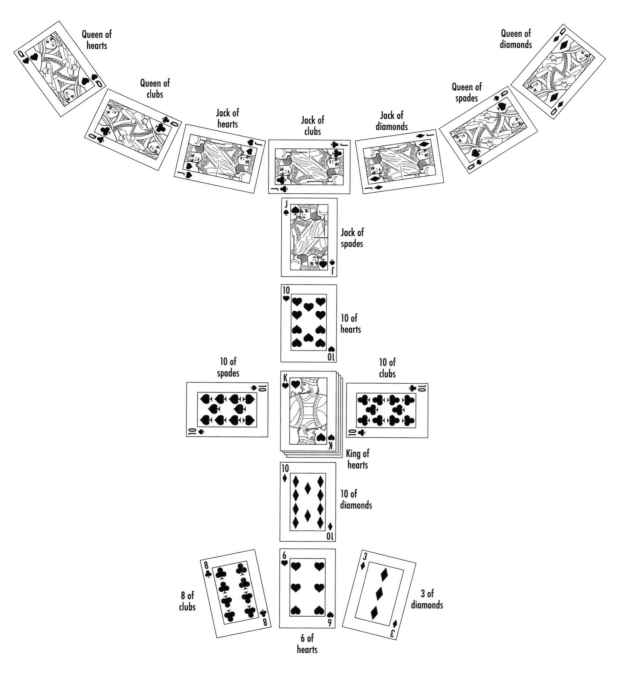

▲ Traditional setup for the necklace

cards. As you deal, lay the first three cards in a fan shape below the lower Ten. These are auxiliary cards, and you will fill their places from the stock as vacancies occur.

If a card that you deal is of the same suit and next higher in rank of any one of the auxiliary cards, you may place it upon that auxiliary card.

FACT

The court cards are merely ornamental. As they appear in dealing, place them in their respective positions in the game board—the four Kings in a packet in the space between the Tens, and the Queens and Jacks forming the necklace above the Tens.

If the game is successful, you will have used all the cards, and the packet of Kings will be surrounded by the four Aces. One redeal is allowed. If no play has been possible during a deal, the game is blocked and ended.

Odd and Even

Rating: 8+

In this game you build families in suit upon Ace foundations in ascending sequence of odd numbers—Three, Five, Seven, Nine, Jack, King; then in sequence of even numbers—Two, Four, Six, Eight, Ten, ending finally with Queen. You build the families in suit upon the Deuce foundations in ascending even numbers—Four, Six, Eight, Ten, Queen; then in odd numbers—Ace, Three, Five, and so on, finally ending with King. Cards as dealt, the auxiliary cards, and the exposed card of the stock are available. Use two decks of cards for this game.

Deal the first nine cards in rows of three each. These are the auxiliary cards. As they appear in dealing, place one Ace and Deuce of each suit side by side in a row above the auxiliary cards. These are the foundations that you will build the families upon.

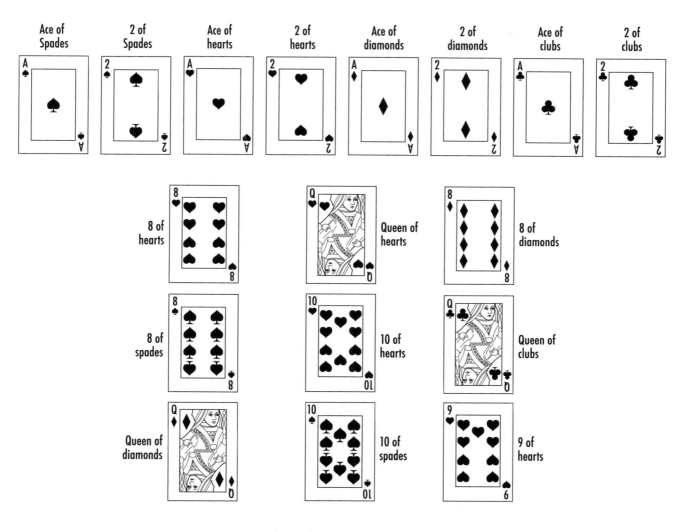

▲ Traditional setup for odd and even

In dealing, the stock is formed of cards that are not suitable for play. Fill the vacancies in the nine auxiliary cards from the stock. One redeal is allowed. The game, if successful, will result in the Kings and Queens of the four suits.

Perseverance

Rating: 8+

The object of the game is to build families upon the foundations in suit and ascending sequence from Ace up to King. You can make marriages between exposed cards of the auxiliary packets, in suit and in descending sequence. Exposed cards of the auxiliary packets are available. Use one deck of cards for this game.

Take the four Aces from the pack and place them in a row. These are the foundations. Deal the remainder of the pack into twelve packets of four cards each. These are the auxiliary packets.

When choosing to play solitaire games online, take the time to read through the instructions, even if it is a game you have played several times before. There often are slight variations in the rules, and sometimes it's up to you to change the Preferences to get the game you want to play.

Play all suitable cards upon the foundations. Marry suitable exposed cards. When the game is blocked, gather the packets and deal them again into as many packets of four cards each as the cards allow. This may be repeated as often as necessary until two such deals in succession fail to produce any suitable card for the foundations. The game is then finally blocked and ended.

The Privileged Four

Rating: 8+

In this game you build families upon the foundations in suit: upon the Aces in ascending sequence, and upon the Kings in descending sequence. The free cards are always available. During the deal, the only cards that are available in the auxiliary rows are those in a direct line below the Ace or King

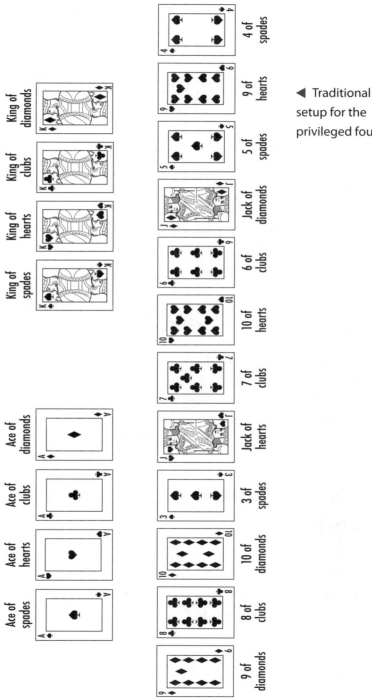

King of
diamonds

King of
clubs

King of
hearts

King of
spades

Ace of
diamonds

Ace of
clubs

Ace of
hearts

Ace of
spades

4 of
spades

9 of
hearts

5 of
spades

Jack of
diamonds

6 of
clubs

10 of
hearts

7 of
clubs

Jack of
hearts

3 of
spades

10 of
diamonds

8 of
clubs

9 of
diamonds

◀ Traditional
setup for the
privileged four

of the same suit. After all the cards have been dealt, this restriction ends. At that point, the lowest card in any column and the released cards are available. Use two decks of cards for this game.

Select the four Aces and Kings of one deck, and place them in a row, leaving a space the width of two cards between the Ace and King groups. These Aces and Kings are the foundations.

Deal twelve auxiliary cards in an unbroken row from left to right, placing the second card exactly below the left-hand Ace. In this manner, place two cards in the middle and one card at each end of the row. These four cards are the free cards.

After you have placed any suitable cards upon the foundations, fill vacancies from the pack and deal another row of twelve cards, partially covering but not concealing the cards in the row above.

Play suitable cards upon the foundations, in the same manner as in the first row. Fill vacancies as before and place new rows of twelve cards in the same manner as you did previously, until the pack is exhausted.

After the pack is exhausted, you can make marriages between available cards in suit and in ascending or descending sequence. When further play is impossible, run together the remaining cards in each column in packets from left to right and deal them again. Repeat the entire routine of play. This repetition is allowed a second time if necessary, making three deals in all.

After the last deal and as a last resource, if you have formed a column, you can transfer one card to reopen the column.

The Royal Windows
Rating: 8+

The object of this game is to form families upon the foundations in suit and ascending sequence from Ace to Queen. The Kings are not played. The exposed card in each packet and all released cards are available. Use one deck of cards for this game.

Divide the cards, face up, into eight packets in a row. The first (or left-hand) packet contains ten cards; the next packet to the right, nine cards; and each succeeding packet to the right, one card less than the preceding packet, so that the eighth packet will consist of three cards.

If the top card of any packet is an Ace, place it below the row to form a foundation, on which you will build an ascending sequence in suit. If a King appears on top of a packet, take him off and slip him under the bottom card of the same packet.

If the exposed card of a packet is of the same suit and next lower in rank to the exposed card of another packet, you can transfer it in descending sequence.

After you have made all possible changes, take the left-hand packet up, and, without disturbing their order, search for a card of the same suit and next in rank below the exposed card of any other packet. If such a card is found, transfer the discovered card and all cards above it just as they are.

Follow the same routine with each successive packet to the right, over and over again in regular rotation, transferring where possible, and employing all suitable and released cards for forming the families, until you've exhausted all the packets and the board is complete, or the game is blocked and ended.

The Sickle

Rating: 8+

The object of this game is to build upon twelve foundation cards, creating a stack of eight cards for each denomination with alternating colors. The exposed card of the stock is always available. Use two decks of cards for this game.

The Kings take no part in the game. Put them aside as they appear, and use them only to make an ornamental handle for the sickle if the game is successful, in which case there will be eight cards of the same denomination, in alternate colors, upon each of the twelve original cards.

Turn up the top card of the pack and place it at the left hand of the game board. Then turn the pack turned face up and deal onto a stock until a card of the next higher denomination, but of different color, appears. Place this card to the right of the first card that's already laid in the game board. Continue the same process until you have laid out the entire sequence of twelve cards up to the Queen, then Ace, and so on, from left to right. At all times during the dealing, cards that match or pair with the original twelve cards must be played on them in alternate colors.

Until all of the original twelve cards have been laid out, you must take care not to entirely conceal the color of each with the matched cards that you play upon them. Two redeals are permitted.

The Solid Square
Rating: 8+

In this game, you form families upon the foundations in suit, first in ascending sequence from Ace to King, and then in descending sequence from King to Ace. The cards as dealt, the auxiliary cards, and the exposed card of the stock are always available. Use two packs of cards for this game.

As you deal the first sixteen cards, arrange them in a solid four-square. These are the auxiliary cards. As the four Aces of different suits appear in the course of the deal, place them at the four corners of the square. These are the foundations.

Play suitable auxiliary cards upon the foundations without delay. Whenever vacancies occur, immediately fill them from the stock, or, if there is no stock, from the pack. You may make marriages in suit and in ascending or descending sequence among the auxiliary cards. As you deal, you may similarly marry any card that is next in rank above or below any auxiliary card and of the same suit. There is no redeal. If no play has been possible during a deal, the game is blocked and ended.

The Wedding
Rating: 8+

The game is played by building a single family upon the foundation of the Queen of Diamonds, in suit and ascending sequence, from Queen, King,

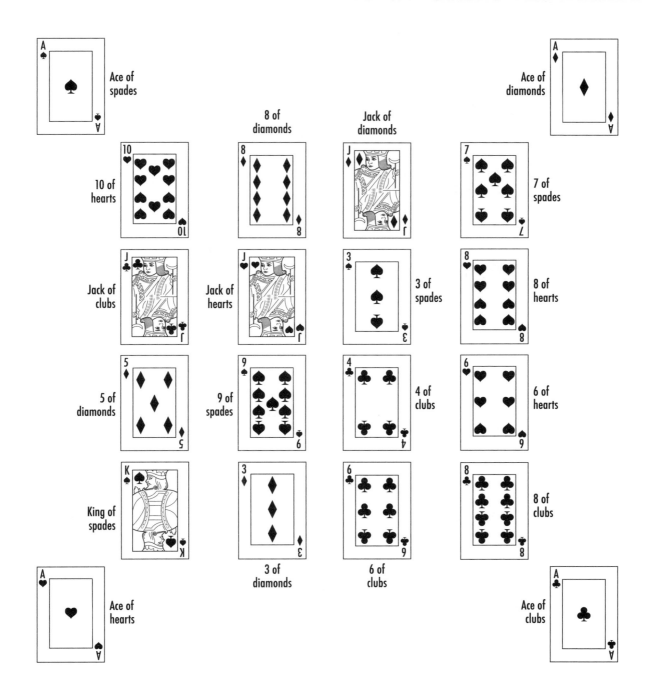

Ace of spades

Ace of diamonds

8 of diamonds

Jack of diamonds

10 of hearts

7 of spades

Jack of clubs

Jack of hearts

3 of spades

8 of hearts

5 of diamonds

9 of spades

4 of clubs

6 of hearts

King of spades

3 of diamonds

6 of clubs

8 of clubs

Ace of hearts

Ace of clubs

▲ Traditional setup for the solid square

Ace, Deuce, and so on, ending with the Jack. Build families upon each of the three Jacks in suit and in descending sequence from Jack down to Ace, then King and ending with Queen. Build the families upon each of the four Tens in suit and in similar manner, but from Ten, Nine, and so on, down to Ace, then King, Queen, ending with Jack. Cards as dealt, and exposed auxiliary cards, are available. Use two packs of cards for this game.

QUESTION?

Where did the word solitaire come from?
It's a word of French origin, and it means "solitary." The game has a long history and is said to have been a favorite of several famous persons. For example, it's believed that Napoleon spent quite a bit of his time playing solitaire when exiled to St. Helena.

Select from the pack a Queen and Jack of Diamonds, and place them side by side, the Queen on the left of the Jack. Then deal two rows of eight cards each for auxiliary cards. As soon as they appear, place the two Jacks of Hearts, one above and the other below the Queen and Jack of Diamonds.

Also, as they appear, place the two Tens of Spades and of Clubs. Place a Ten of Spades on each side of the lower Jack of Hearts, and a Ten of Clubs on each side of the upper Jack of Hearts. The Queen of Diamonds, the three Jacks, and the four Tens are the foundations for building.

After you deal the sixteen auxiliary cards and use all suitable cards for the foundations and for play, deal sixteen more cards from left to right upon the auxiliary cards and vacancies, if any, and play any suitable cards.

Repeat this sequence until you deal all of the pack. Deal the sixteenth auxiliary packet, first to fill the vacancy and then from left to right, upon the remaining fifteen packets. After this, deal the fifteenth packet in like manner, first filling vacancies, and so on. Place the first card of each new deal next to the right of the last card previously dealt. If the foundation is finally blocked, the game is over.

If, however, the game has succeeded, the wedded Jack and Queen of Diamonds will appear surrounded by a bridesmaid and two groomsmen.

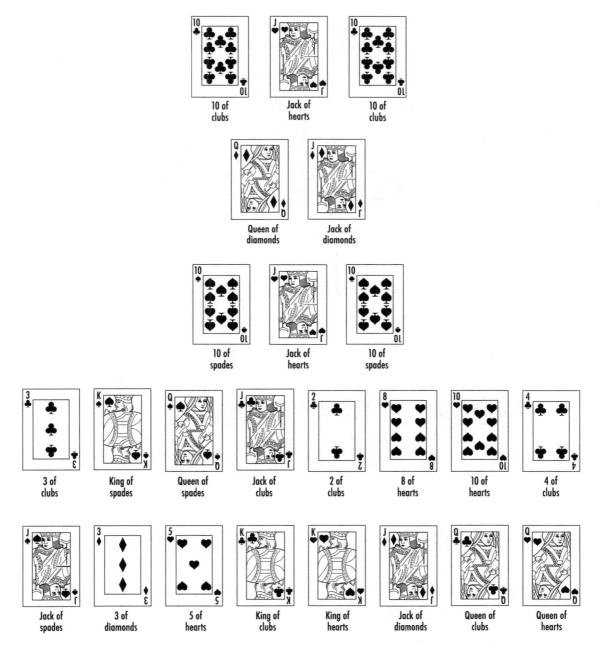

10 of
clubs

Jack of
hearts

10 of
clubs

Queen of
diamonds

Jack of
diamonds

10 of
spades

Jack of
hearts

10 of
spades

3 of
clubs

King of
spades

Queen of
spades

Jack of
clubs

2 of
clubs

8 of
hearts

10 of
hearts

4 of
clubs

Jack of
spades

3 of
diamonds

5 of
hearts

King of
clubs

King of
hearts

Jack of
diamonds

Queen of
clubs

Queen of
hearts

▲ Traditional setup for the wedding

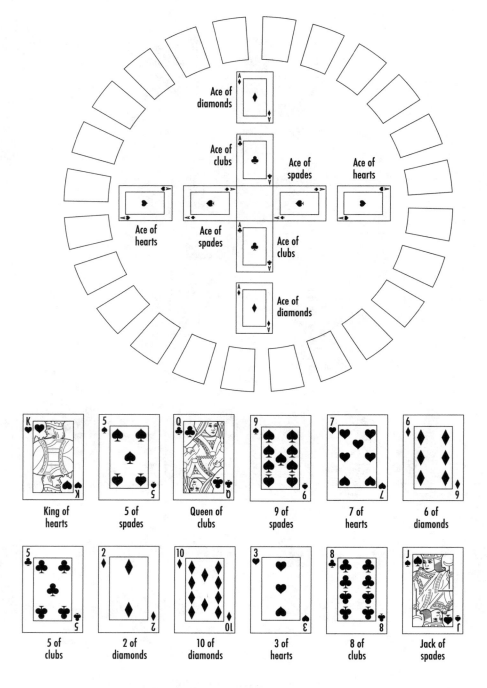

▲ Traditional setup for the wheel

The Wheel

Rating: 8+

For this game, you will select cards to form the packets; two cards of the same denomination are prohibited. There must be no interruption during each dealing of the cards, and play is not allowed until a deal is completed. Exposed auxiliary cards are available. Use two decks of cards for this game.

Take the eight Aces from the pack and arrange them in the form of a cross, with the black Aces in the center and the red Aces outside, suit opposite suit, as shown in the figure on page 60. These Aces are merely ornamental, and represent the spokes of the wheel.

Deal from the pack twelve auxiliary cards in two rows of six cards each. Select from them first a court card then any three other cards whose combined pips count exactly 18. The court card does not enter in to the count. Gather the four cards into a packet, the court card at top, and place the packet in one of the spaces that represent the circumference of the wheel in the game board. Fill up vacancies as they occur from the pack. When you have made all the packets, or no packet is possible, deal twelve more cards upon the rows. Continue the same routine until you deal all of the pack. If the game is successful, the wheel will contain twenty-four packets. There is no redeal.

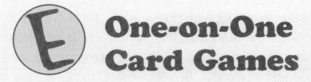

Chapter 4

One-on-One Card Games

How often have you found yourself sitting around with a friend or loved one trying to figure out what you want to do? Stop wasting quality time and grab a deck of cards. With the variety of card games for two people offered in this chapter, your only problem will be deciding which to play first.

Casino

Rating: 8+

Casino is played by two players, with a pack of fifty-two cards. The object of the game is to win by pairing and building.

To start, the players cut for deal. The dealer gives four cards to each player, and lays out four other cards face up on the table. Deal the cards two or four at a time; the opponent's hand first, the laid-out cards next, the dealer last. After the cards are all played, deal four more cards to each player the same as before, but do no lay any out. Repeat until all the cards are dealt.

Playing

After the deal is completed the dealer's opponent plays first. The object in Casino is to capture as many cards as possible, and this is done in four different ways: pairing, combining, building, and calling. One card *must* be played from the hand at each turn. If a card is played, and it cannot be used for pairing, or to take a combination, or to form a build or call, that card must remain on the table.

Pairing

This consists of capturing one or more cards from the table by matching it with a similar card played from the hand. For example, a King held in the hand will take all the Kings that are on the table. The card played and all the cards it captures become the property of the player.

Combining

You may group together two or more cards that are on the table and add their value together. For example, a Two and a Six on the table can be combined to form an eight, and thus may be taken off the table by an Eight that you hold in your hand. Two or more combinations may be made at the same time, provided that each combination produces a similar numerical result (for example, two Fours, or a Three and a Five, also add up to eight).

Building

You may lay a card from your hand upon a card or cards on the table, which can then only be captured in your next turn by a card worth the total number of points. Suppose there is a Five on the table, and you have a Seven and a Two in your hand. When it is your turn, you may lay your Two upon the Five, and say "Seven." When your next turn comes, you can capture the build with your Seven, unless your opponent has already done so, or has raised the build.

You cannot raise your own build, but your opponent can, if he holds the card needed to redeem it. Thus, in the previous instance, you have *built* a seven; you cannot raise your build by playing a Three upon it to make a ten, but your opponent can. Your opponent can play a Two upon your build, and say "Nine." If you have an Ace and a Ten, you can then play your Ace on the nine-build, and say "Ten," and then nothing but a Ten would capture it.

Casino Strategies

You may make another build, or may pair or combine other cards, or capture your opponent's build, before taking your first build.

Calling or Duplicating

This consists of grouping together similar cards, builds, or combinations, and then *calling* their denomination. Once you make a call, the cards, builds, or combinations cannot be interfered with; they can only be captured by a card of the denomination *called*.

Here's how calling works. Suppose you have two Nines in your hand, and there is a Nine (or a build or a combination of nine) on the table. Instead of pairing it or taking it, you can play one of the Nines from your hand upon it and say "Nines," and then only another Nine will capture it.

A Sweep

If you can capture all the cards on the board with one play it is called a *sweep*, which counts as 1 point for you.

When you make a sweep you turn the *sweep-card* (the card that takes the sweep) face up. This is done to keep tally of the number of sweeps made by each player. If your opponent makes a sweep, these two sweeps cancel each other, and both of you turn the canceled sweep-cards down. Score only the difference in the number of sweeps: if you make three sweeps and your opponent makes two, you deduct your opponent's two sweeps from your own three and score the difference, which is one.

Last-cards

After all the cards have been dealt, and the hands finally played out, all cards that remain upon the table belong to the player who took the last trick.

Points Value and Scoring

These are the points that may be scored:

Great casino—The Ten of Diamonds: 2 points
Little casino—The Two of Spades: 1 point
The majority of cards: 3 points
The majority of Spades: 1 point
Each Ace: 1 point
Each sweep: 1 point

FACT

The points gained by each player are counted at the end of the deal, and whoever has the greatest number of points at the end wins the game. Casino is sometimes played for a fixed number of points. If both players make the same number of points, the game is drawn.

Rules of the Game

1. The deal is determined by cutting the cards, and the player cutting the lowest card must deal. Ties are cut over. In cutting, Ace is low.

2. Each player has a right to shuffle. The dealer has the right of shuffling last.

3. If, in cutting to the dealer, or in reuniting the separated packets, a card is exposed, or if there is any confusion of the cards, there must be a fresh cut.

4. The dealer must deal the cards either two or four at a time; first to his adversary, next for the layout, and last to himself. The laid-out cards are dealt face up. After the first four cards are played, four more cards must be similarly dealt to each player, but none laid out; this is repeated until the pack is exhausted.

5. If the dealer deals without having the pack cut, or if he shuffles the pack after it has been cut with his consent, there must be a fresh deal, provided the opposing side claims it before any cards are turned up on the table. In this case the cards must be reshuffled and recut, and the dealer must deal again.

6. If a card is face up in the deck or if the dealer, while dealing, exposes any of his adversary's cards prior to turning up any of the cards in the layout, there must be a fresh deal, provided the opposing player demands it. If a card is exposed after any portion of the layout has been turned up, the opposing player may keep it or reject it; if he rejects it, the dealer must place the rejected card in the middle of the stock, and deal a fresh card. If the dealer exposes a card in the last round, he should take the exposed card, and allow his adversary to draw one card from his hand in exchange.

7. If the dealer deals too many or too few cards, it is a misdeal, and the dealer forfeits the game.

8. If a player makes a build and holds no card of the proper denomination to take it in, the opposing player may take back in his hand all the cards he has played since the error was made; and, after separating the cards composing the improper build, may use them as any other cards on the table, in every way the cards will permit, playing again and again, if he can, before his opponent is allowed to resume the play.

9. If a player makes a build, his adversary cannot raise the build by adding any card to the table. The denomination of a build cannot be changed except by a card played from the hand.

10. When a card is played for the purpose of building or calling, the player must declare the denomination of the proposed build or call so that his opponent understands. If he fails to do so, his opponent may separate the cards, and employ them in any lawful way he may deem to his advantage.

11. If a player picks up a card or cards that do not belong to the combination, the delinquent player must restore to the layout not only the card or cards thus improperly taken up, but also all the cards that rightly composed the combination.

12. Tricks that have been taken must not be examined throughout the game.

Cooncan

Rating: 8+

Cooncan is played by two people, with a pack of forty cards. Remove the the Eights, Nines, and Tens from a complete pack. The cards rank in the following order: Ace, Two, Three, Four, Five, Six, Seven, Jack, Queen, and King.

FACT

Cooncan is an early form of rummy. It began as *conquian* and was quite popular in Mexico in the nineteenth century. It moved into the United States and became known as cooncan, gradually transforming into what we know as rummy today.

Dealing

The players cut for deal; the highest card deals. After you properly shuffle and cut the cards, deal three cards to each player, then three again, and finally four cards, thus giving each player ten cards. Then place the cards that remain undealt (called the stock) face down on the table.

Playing

The object of the game is for each player to form runs of Fours, Threes, and Sequences with the assistance of cards drawn from the stock, or taken from the discard pile. By placing such combinations on the table, the players unload their original ten cards, and one card more. The winner is the player who can get rid of his cards first.

You may form the Sequences with Ace, Two, Three, and so on, or with Five, Six, Seven, and so on, of the same suit. The Ace is not in sequence with the King and Queen.

The play begins when your opponent draws one card from the top of the stock and, with the assistance of that card, tries to form any Threes or Fours, or a Sequence. If he has any of these combinations, he places them on the table and then discards one card from his hand. If he does not use the card that he drew, he places it, face up, by the side of the stock in the discard pile.

If the dealer can use the discarded card to form any combination, he takes it in hand and similarly places the combination on the table, and discards a card from his hand. If he cannot use the discard, he draws a card from the stock to try to form combinations. The play proceeds in this manner until one of the players succeeds in combining all of his ten cards and one card more, eleven in all.

If neither of the players succeeds, the game is a draw. The losing player deals, but when a draw occurs the opponent deals.

Cribbage

Rating: 8+

Cribbage is entirely different from any other card game. It is usually played by two people, with a full pack of fifty-two cards, with five cards to a player. Though more than two people can play cribbage, because the two-handed game is the most popular, only the rules for this game will be included. Sixty-one points constitute game. These points are scored on a cribbage board, which consists of two linear divisions, one division for each player's independent score. Each division contains sixty holes, and at one end, between the divisions, is another hole, called the *game-hole*. Each division is marked off in subdivisions of 5 points each.

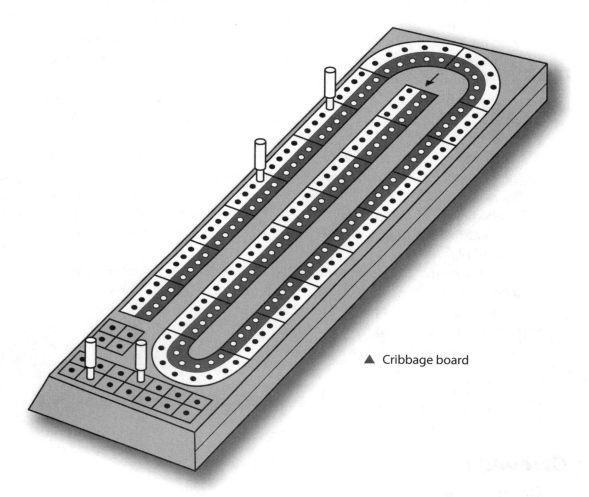

▲ Cribbage board

The players begin the game in the outside row on the side of the game hole. The pegs will travel along the outside edge, pass across the top, then down the inside row to game. Each player will use two pegs for scoring.

Dealing

Cut the deck for the deal; the low card deals. The dealer shuffles the pack, and the nondealer cuts it. The dealer reunites the deck and deals out five cards to each player, one at a time. The dealer places the undealt portion of the pack face down, between the game-hole end of the board and the edge of the table. The nondealer is entitled to mark three holes, called *three for last*, while his adversary is dealing.

Laying Out for Crib

Once the deal is completed, the players look at their hands and *lay out for crib*. Each has to put out two cards. After deciding which two cards they want to discard, the players place the cards face down in a pile on the table, by the side of the board nearest to the dealer. The cards laid out are called the *crib*.

Cutting for the Start

After the crib is laid out, the nondealer cuts the pack and the dealer turns up the top card of the bottom pile. The card turned up is called the *start*. If the start is a Jack the dealer marks two (called *two for his heels)* on his side of the board.

Playing

At this point play begins. The nondealer plays any card from his hand that he sees fit, placing it face up on the table by the side of the board nearest to himself and calling out the number at which it is valued. The King, Queen, Jack, and Ten (called *tenth cards)* are valued at ten each, the other cards at the number of pips on them. The dealer then plays any card he chooses, placing it face up by his side of the board and calling out the value of his card added to the value of the first card played.

In laying out for crib, keep in mind whether or not you are the dealer. When you are the dealer, you should lay out cards that are likely to score in crib; when you are not the dealer, you should do the reverse.

The nondealer next plays another card, and then the dealer, and so on, as long as any cards remain in hand, or until a card cannot be played without passing the number thirty-one. When it happens that a player cannot play without passing thirty-one, he says, "Go." If his opponent has a card that can be played without passing thirty-one (called *coming in)*, he is entitled to play it. When there is a *go,* or when thirty-one is reached, the game ends.

Counts and Combinations in Play

The players are entitled to score for certain combinations of cards: pairs, fifteen, sequences, the go, and thirty-one.

Pairs and Pair Royal

If, when you play a card, the next card played pairs it (for instance, if a four is played to a four), you are entitled to mark 2 points on the cribbage board.

If, after you have played a pair, the card next played is also of the same denomination, a *pair royal* is made, which entitles you to mark 6 points.

Double Pair Royal

If, after you have played a *pair royal*, the card next played is again of the same kind, it constitutes a *double pair royal* that entitles you to a score of 12 points, in addition to the pair that you already scored.

Tenth cards only pair with tenth cards of the same denomination. Thus, Kings pair with Kings, but Kings do not pair with Queens, although they are both considered tenth cards.

Fifteen

If you reach exactly fifteen by adding the pips of all the played cards, you are entitled to mark 2 points.

Sequences

The sequence of the cards is King, Queen, Jack, Ten, Nine, Eight, Seven, Six, Five, Four, Three, Two, Ace. The Ace is not in sequence with the King and Queen. If any three cards are played in sequence order, the player of the third card is entitled to mark three (called a *run* of three). If a fourth card is similarly played, that player is entitled to a run of four; if a fifth card is similarly played, a run of five accrues, and so on. If there is a break in the sequence, and in the subsequent play the break is filled up without the intervention of a card out of sequence order, the player completing the sequence is entitled to a score of 1 for each card forming the sequence.

It is not necessary for the cards forming a sequence to be played in order. For example, you play a Four; your opponent a Two; and then you play a Five. Your opponent can then come in with a Three, and mark a run of four with Two, Three, Four, Five. After the Three is played, you can come in with an Ace or a Six, making a run of five, or with a Four, making a run of four. But if any card not in sequence intervenes, the run is stopped. Thus, if Four, Two, Five, and Five are played in this order, a Three or a Six will not come in, as the second Five, which intervened, disrupted the run.

The Go

The player who gets closest to thirty-one is entitled to mark one, for the *last card, go,* or *end hole.* If you reach thirty-one exactly, you mark two instead of one.

For instance: you play two tenth cards and a Four, making twenty-four. If your opponent has no card in hand under an Eight, he cannot come in, and you mark a go. If, however, your opponent has a Seven, he may play that and score two for thirty-one; or, if he has a Four he may play it and mark two for the pair.

Compound Score

You may obtain more than one mark at the same time. In the last case given, a pair and a go are scored together. A pair and a thirty-one, or a pair and a fifteen, may occur, scoring four; or a sequence and a fifteen, and so on.

Showing

As soon as a go or thirty-one is reached, the players show their hands and try to create certain combinations within their own hands. The nondealer has the *first show.* He places his hand face up on the table, marking points for whatever he is holding, making use of the start as though it were a part of his hand, but without mixing it with his cards. The dealer does the same with his hand. He then shows the crib, and has the opportunity to use that with the remainder of his hand, and mark any points made with it and the start.

The points counted in hand or crib may be made by fifteens; by pairs or pairs royal; by sequences; by flushes; or by *his nob*.

If your opponent plays a card that you can pair or make fifteen, choose the latter. At the same time you must not forget that if a Seven or Eight is led and you make fifteen, you give your opponent a chance of coming in with a Six or a Nine.

Fifteens in hand or crib are counted by adding together all the different cards (including the start), the pips of which will make exactly fifteen, without counting the same set of cards twice. In reckoning fifteens, tenth cards are valued at ten each. Each separate fifteen that can be made with a different combination is worth two. For example: Iif you hold, either with or without the start, a tenth card and a five, you reckon two (called *fifteen-two*). If you have another five, you combine this also with the tenth card and reckon two more, or *fifteen-four*. If your other cards were a Four and an Ace, you would similarly reckon another fifteen.

Suppose you hold two tenth cards with a Five, and a Five is turned up. You reckon fifteen-eight, the combination being as follows:

Ten of Clubs	Ten of Spades	Ten of Clubs	Ten of Spades
Five of Clubs	Five of Spades	Five of Spades	Five of Clubs

Pairs are reckoned on the same principle. In the above example the total score would be twelve: eight for the fifteens, and four for the two pairs. To take a less easy example, a hand consisting of four fives would score twenty (twelve for the double pair royal and eight for the fifteens), as follows:

Five of Spades	Five of Spades	Five of Spades	Five of Hearts
Five of Hearts	Five of Hearts	Five of Clubs	Five of Clubs
Five of Clubs	Five of Diamonds	Five of Diamonds	Five of Diamonds

Sequences of three or more cards are counted as indicated in this chart, with one addition. If one card of a sequence can be substituted for another of the same kind, the sequence is counted twice. For example, a Seven, Eight, and two Nines give two sequences of seven, eight, nine, by substituting one Nine for the other, in addition to the fifteen and the pair, making the total ten.

A *flush* is counted by a player whose entire hand consists of cards of the same suit. The flush counts three; if the start is of the same suit as the hand, the flush counts four. For example, suppose you have Three, Four, Five of the same suit, and a Six is turned up. The hand counts fifteen-two: four for sequence (six), and three for the flush (nine). If the start is also of the same suit, the hand reckons ten. No flush can be counted in crib, unless the start is of the same suit as the crib, when the flush reckons five.

His nob—If a player holds a Jack in hand or crib of the suit turned up, he counts *one for his nob*.

When you finish counting all of the hands and crib, the deal is at an end. Put the cards together and shuffle them, and begin a fresh deal. The player who was the nondealer in the first hand now deals, and so on, alternately, until the game is won.

Scoring

The points made during the hand accrue in the following order: 2 for his heels; points during the play of the hand; the nondealer's show; the dealer's show; and the crib show. Each player marks the points to which he is entitled as soon as they accrue by placing a peg in the hole on the board corresponding to the number to which he is entitled. For the first score on each side, only one peg is used; for the second score, the second peg (called the *foremost peg)* is placed in front of the first. At the next score the *hindmost* peg is moved in front of the other, and becomes in turn the foremost peg.

FACT

The layout is affected by the state of the score. Toward the end of the game, if you have cards that in all probability will take you out, that is more important than laying out bad cards for your opponent's crib.

When a player arrives at the top, he proceeds to mark *down the board,* on the inner row of holes on his side of the board. The player who first scores sixty-one places his foremost peg in the game-hole and wins the game. If a player wins the game before his opponent has scored 31 points, he wins a double.

Rules of the Game

1. In cutting for the deal, the player cutting must leave sufficient cards for the player cutting last to make a legal cut. He who cuts last must not leave less than four cards in the remainder of the pack.
2. The player who cuts the lowest card deals. The Ace is lowest, the King highest.
3. If, in cutting for the deal, a player exposes more than one card, his adversary may treat whichever of the exposed cards he chooses as the one cut.
4. If, in cutting, or reuniting the separated packets, the dealer exposes a card or if there is any confusion of the cards, there must be a fresh cut.
5. There must be a fresh cut for the deal after each game.
6. Each player has a right to shuffle the cards. The dealer has the right to shuffle last. The players deal alternately throughout the game.
7. The dealer must deal the cards one at a time to each player, beginning with his adversary. If he deals two together, he may rectify the error, provided he can do so by moving one card only; otherwise, there must be a fresh deal, and the nondealer marks two holes.
8. If the dealer exposes any of his own cards, there is no penalty. If he exposes one of his adversary's, the adversary marks two holes, and has the option of a fresh deal, prior to looking at his hand. If a card is exposed through the nondealer's fault, the dealer marks two, and has the option of dealing again.
9. If there is a faced card in the pack, there must be a fresh deal.
10. If the dealer gives out too many cards, the nondealer marks two holes, and a fresh deal ensues; but, in such case, the nondealer must discover the error before he takes up his cards, or he cannot claim the two, though there must still be a new deal.
11. If the dealer gives out too few cards, the nondealer marks two holes,

and has the option, after looking at his hand, of a fresh deal, or of allowing the imperfect hand to be completed from the top of the pack.

12. If a player deals out of turn, and the error is discovered before the start is turned up, the deal in error is void, and the dealer who was supposed to have dealt deals.

13. If either player lays out with too few cards in hand, he must play out the hand with less than the right number of cards.

14. The dealer may insist on his adversary laying out first.

15. If a player takes back into his hand a card he has laid out, his adversary marks two holes, and has the option of a fresh deal.

16. The crib must not be touched during the play of the hand.

17. If the dealer turns up more than one card, the nondealer may choose which of the exposed cards shall be the start.

18. If a jack is turned up, and the dealer plays his first card without scoring his heels, he forfeits the score.

19. If a player plays with too many cards in hand, his adversary marks two holes, and has the option of a fresh deal. If he elects to stand the deal, he has the right of drawing the surplus cards from the offender's hand, and of looking at them, and the option of playing the hand again, or not.

20. If a player plays with too few cards, there is no penalty.

21. If a card that will come in is played, it cannot be taken up again. If a card that will not come in is played, no penalty attaches to the exposure.

22. If two cards are played together, the card counted is deemed to be the one played, and the other must be taken back into the player's hand.

23. If a player neglects to play when he has a card that will come in, his opponent may require it to be played, or may mark two holes.

24. There is no penalty for miscounting during the play.

25. When reckoning a hand or crib, the cards must be shown and must remain exposed until the opponent is satisfied with the claims of combinations.

26. If a player mixes his hand with the crib or with the pack before his claim is properly made, he forfeits any score the hand or crib may contain.

27. If a player scores more points than he is entitled to, the adversary may correct the score and add the same number to his own score. This rule applies even if a player places his peg in the game-hole.

28. There is no penalty for scoring too few points. A player is not bound to assist his adversary in making out his score.

29. If a player touches his opponent's pegs except to put back an overscore, or if he touches his own pegs except when he has a score to make, his adversary marks two holes.
30. If a player displaces his foremost peg, he must put it behind the other. If he displaces both his pegs, his adversary is entitled to place the hindmost peg where he believes it should go, and the other peg must then be put behind it.
31. A lurch (or double game) cannot be claimed, unless by previous agreement.
32. The three for last may be scored at any time during the game, but not after the opponent has scored sixty-one.

Pinochle
Rating: 8+

Pinochle is played with two packs of cards, retaining only the Ace, King, Queen, Jack, Ten, and Nine of each pack. Another option is to invest in a special pinochle deck. The game may be played by two, three, or four people. Here, we will focus on two-handed pinochle. The object of the game is to make points, and 1,000 points are game.

Dealing

In cutting, the highest card wins the deal, Ace being highest, the Ten next, followed by the King, Queen, Jack, and Nine. The dealer shuffles the cards and they are cut by the player on his right. The dealer then deals the cards four at a time to each player, until each has twelve cards. The dealer turns up the next card for trump, and places it face up by the side of the stock.

Playing

The first player leads any card he pleases. His opponent lays a card on top of it, constituting a trick. In playing to a card led, the second player need not follow suit, nor play a card to win the trick, unless he chooses. Trumping is optional.

The player who takes the trick leads for the next; but before he leads, he can then (and only then) announce or *meld* any one combination that he may be holding in his hand. After he makes the meld (if any) and before he leads, he must draw the top card from the stock. His opponent draws the next, thus again filling both their hands with twelve cards.

After each trick is taken, follow the same routine until the stock has been exhausted, the trump card being the last to be drawn.

One variation of the game requires that the dealer not turn up the twenty-fifth card for trump, as in the regular game. Instead, the trump suit is determined by the first marriage (King and Queen of a suit) melded. There is, therefore, no trump suit until the first marriage has been melded. With this single exception, the game proceeds in exactly the same manner as the regular two-handed game.

Each player takes up into his hand all the cards exposed. Suit must be followed, if possible; otherwise a trump must be played. If neither is possible, any card may be played. The second player to a trick must take the trick, if he can; failure to do so constitutes a revoke, and the player loses all the points he has made in that hand.

The points depend upon the face value of the cards contained in tricks won, and the value of melds declared in course of play. The last trick counts 10 points for the player who takes it. The total points, therefore, of the cards and last trick combined, amount to 250. One of the players or a third person keeps score, and the points are scored to each player as they accrue.

Rank and Value of the Cards

Ace is highest; counts for 11 points
Ten counts for 10 points
King counts for 4 points
Queen counts for 3 points
Jack counts for 2 points
Nine counts for 0 points

Value of Announcements or Melds

Eight Aces count for 1,000
Eight Kings count for 800
Eight Queens count for 400
Eight Jacks count for 400
Two Queens of Spades (double-pinochle) count for 400
Two Jacks of Diamonds count for 400
Ace, Ten, King, Queen and Jack of trumps count for 150
Four Aces of different suits count for 100
Four Kings count for 80
Four Queens count for 60
Four Jacks count for 40
Queen of Spades (pinochle) counts for 40
Jack of Diamonds counts for 40
King and Queen of trumps (royal marriage) count for 40
King and Queen of a suit not trumps (marriage) count for 20

When the dealer turns up a Nine for trump, he scores 10 points for the Nine, or *Dix* (pronounced *deece)*, at once. When a Nine is not turned up for trump, the player who holds the Nine can exchange it for the trump card and meld 10 points at any time when he has obtained the privilege of melding (that is, after he has taken a trick); he cannot meld anything else he may have in his hand.

If you and your significant other are searching for a fun way to spend quality time together and socialize at the same time, you may want to seek out another couple with whom to play four-handed pinochle.

When a player melds any combination, he must lay down the cards that make up his meld face up on the table beside him; he can make use of any of these exposed cards to play to a trick.

Melded cards cannot be used to make any new combinations of the same nature. For example, if four Kings have been melded, none of those four can be combined with other Kings for a new meld. Or, if the Queen of Spades and Jack of Diamonds have been melded for pinochle, that Queen cannot be used to combine with another Jack of Diamonds for a new pinochle.

Melded cards can be used to form different combinations, however. For example, if King and Queen of Spades have been melded, the Queen of Spades may be combined with a Jack of Diamonds to meld pinochle. It must be noted, however, that a royal marriage must have been melded first.

It requires two Queens of Spades and two Jacks of Diamonds to form a double pinochle. The cards composing a single pinochle, already melded, cannot be employed to form a double pinochle.

Points are awarded only to those players who hold better hands than does the dealer.

Sixty-Six

Rating: 8+

Sixty-six is played by two players, using twenty-four cards: the Ace, Ten, King, Queen, Jack, and Nine of each suit. The cards rank in value in the order named above; trumps are the superior suit.

Dealing

The player who cuts the highest card deals. The dealer gives each player six cards, three at a time, turning up the last card for trump, which is laid on the table. The remainder of the pack (the stock) is placed face down apart from the trump card.

The nondealer leads and may play any card in his hand. The dealer may play to it any card he pleases, without restriction as to suit or value, and the two cards played constitute a trick. The highest card of the suit led wins the trick, but trumps beat all inferior suits.

The player who wins the trick places it, face down, in front of himself, and then draws the top card from the stock. His opponent draws the next card; this restores the cards in hand to six, as before the lead.

When all of the cards are played out, the player who wins the last trick receives 10 extra points toward 66. In the course of play, if either player reaches 66 points or more, he declares it at once. If the hand is played to its conclusion, and both players count only 65, neither can score, but the winner of the next hand scores 1 point extra.

A cut must consist of at least two cards. When cutting for deal, the player cutting first must leave sufficient cards for the player cutting last to make a legal deal. The player who cuts last must not leave less than two cards in the remainder of the lower packet.

Do not play any more cards after 66 has been declared; the unplayed cards in hand are void and have no value. When a player announces 66, his adversary may examine the tricks to ascertain whether the announcement is correct.

Closing

If, at any time before the stock is exhausted, a player thinks he can make 66 without further drawing, he may, when it is his turn to lead, turn down the turned-up trump. This is called *closing*. A player may close before a card is led, and consequently before a trick has been taken.

If a player draws out of turn, and his opponent does not discover the error before drawing himself, there is no penalty. If the opponent discovers the error before drawing, he may draw and proceed with the game, or he may end the hand and score 1 point.

The leader has the option of closing either before or after drawing from the stock. His opponent has no choice about the matter, and must play either with or without drawing, as the leader elects.

As soon as the leader closes, discontinue all drawing. The last cards are played subject to the same rules and conditions as those in operation when playing the last six tricks after the stock is exhausted, with the exception that the winner of the last trick does not count 10 points.

If the player who closes fails to count 66, his adversary scores 2 points.

If a player closes before his adversary has won a trick, and fails to count 66, his adversary scores 3 points.

Rules of the Game

1. Each player has the right to shuffle, and it is the dealer's right to shuffle last, but if the dealer shuffles after the pack is cut, there must be a fresh cut.
2. The players deal alternately throughout the game.
3. The dealer must deal six cards to each player, three at a time, and turn up the next or thirteenth card for trump.
4. If the dealer fails to give the proper number of cards and the error is discovered before the trump card is turned, there must be a fresh deal.
5. If there is a faced card in the pack, or if the cards have been dealt without having the pack cut, there must be a fresh deal.
6. If a player deals out of turn, his adversary may stop him at any time before the trump card is turned; but if the trump card is turned, the deal stands good.
7. If a player forgets to draw, and plays a card before discovering the error, his adversary may allow the offending player to draw, and proceed with the game, or he may end the hand and score 1 point.
8. If a player draws when he has six cards in his hand, his adversary may require the delinquent player to play next time without drawing, or he may end the hand and score 1 point.
9. If a player lifts two cards in drawing, his adversary may have them both turned face up, and then choose which the player may take.
10. If a player leads out of turn, or leads a wrong card, there is no penalty. If the adversary plays to the card led, the error cannot be rectified.
11. If, after the stock is exhausted or there is a close, a player does not follow suit or win the trick when able, he can score no point that hand, and his adversary scores 2 points, or 3 if the offender has no points toward 66.

12. If a player announces 66, and on examination it appears that he has fewer points, his adversary scores 2 points, and the hand is ended.
13. The turned and quitted tricks must not be searched during the play of the hand.

Slapjack
Rating: 5+

This game is played by two people, with a standard deck of fifty-two cards. The object of the game is to end up with all fifty-two cards.

One person is chosen to deal the entire deck between the two players, face down. Neither player is allowed to look at his cards. The player who did not deal starts the game by taking a card from the top of his pile and throwing it, face up, onto the table. The other player throws another one, on top of the first card, and so on, until one of the players end up throwing down a Jack.

When you see a Jack on the table, you try to slap your hand over it. The first person to slap it gets all the cards underneath, including the Jack. This process continues until one player holds all the cards, and is declared the winner of the game.

War
Rating: 8+

This game is played with two players, using a pack of fifty-two cards. Evenly divide the deck between the two players.

Hand one stock to each player, face down. The players are not allowed to look at the cards. At the same time, both players expose the top card from their stock. The player who shows the highest card takes both of the cards into his deck, a King being the highest card.

If both players show the same card, each player puts out three cards face down, and one card face up. The person with the highest card as their face-up card wins all of the cards. The game is won when one person holds the entire deck.

Chapter 5

Easy Group Card Games

This chapter is composed of several card games that are suitable for the younger members of the family, thus providing an opportunity for quality family time or good-natured competitiveness among siblings. As an added bonus, these card games will help your children learn numbers as well as how to form strategies.

Concentration

Rating: 5+

Concentration is played by two or more people, with a deck of fifty-two cards. The players cut for the chance to go first. Place all of the cards face down and spread out on a table, in neat rows. The first player turns any two cards over, and tries to remember which cards he turned. The second player (to the left of the first player) and all subsequent players follow in order, trying to locate a pair of matching cards. The first player to succeed removes the cards from the table, and takes another turn.

The game is over when all of the cards have been removed from the table. The player who makes the most matches wins, regardless of the value of the cards.

Crazy Eights

Rating: 8+

This game is usually played by two to four players, but any number can play. When more than four play, it is best to use two complete decks of fifty-two cards.

One player shuffles the deck and, after having it cut by the player to his right, deals one card face up to each player, beginning with the player to his left. The lowest card has the deal. The dealer then deals one card at a time to each player, until all the cards are dealt.

ALERT!

Some variations of Crazy Eights have a rule that you must notify the other players when you have only one card left. If you fail to do so, you must draw two cards as a penalty.

The players arrange their cards in order of suits. The eldest hand (the player to the left of the dealer) puts down a card, face up, on the table. The next player must put down a card from his hand that matches either the pip or the suit of the first card. If you cannot make a match, you can choose to either skip your turn or throw down an Eight. Eights are wild, and you can announce a change of suit to whatever you have the most of in your hand, regardless of the suit of the Eight you have thrown. The game continues in rotation. The first player to get rid of all of his cards wins the game.

Go Fish

Rating: 8+

Go Fish is played by two or more players, with a pack of fifty-two cards. The dealer deals one card to each player in rotation, until the entire deck is dealt. While doing this, the dealer also creates an additional pile that is called the *fish pile*, placed face down in the center of the table. The object of the game is to collect all four suits of every card denomination, called *books*. Before the play begins, each player removes all existing books from his hand, and puts them face down in front of him.

The first player asks any one opponent for a card he needs. For example, if the first player is holding two Fours, one Six, one Jack, one Seven, and two Eights, he may say to one opponent, "Do you have any Sixes?"

FACT

A variation of the Go Fish game is called Authors. In Authors, all cards are dealt and there is no stock pile. If you ask an opponent for a card, and he gives it up, you continue with your turn until he does not have a card that you ask for. The turn then passes to that person.

If that person has the card requested, he must give it to the player, and if he has more than one he must hand over all of them. The player then continues in this fashion, by asking the same opponent, or any other opponent, for another card. This continues until an opponent denies a request. If an opponent does not have the card requested, he says "Go fish," and the player takes one card from the fish pile. If, by chance, he picks the card he asked for, the player gets to continue his turn. Otherwise the turn is over.

The next player to take a turn is the one who rejected the first player, and the game continues in much the same fashion. Each time you make a book, remove the cards from your hand and place them with the other books face down in front of you. The game continues until one player has played through his hand. All of the players then count up the number of books they have created. The player who has the most books at the end of the game wins.

Hearts

Rating: 8+

Hearts is played by four players (playing independently), with a pack of fifty-two cards. Cards rank in the following order: Ace (highest), King, Queen, Jack, Ten, Nine, Eight, Seven, Six, Five, Four, Three, and Two (lowest). The object is to avoid taking any trick (set of cards) that contains a Heart.

As a general rule, it is better to avoid taking a trick in a suit that has been led the second time. There is no harm in the last player in a trick capturing it—provided it contains no Heart—particularly if he takes the trick with a commanding card of the suit, and has a good card for the next lead.

Dealing

The deal is determined by giving a card to each player, face up. The player with the lowest card deals. After shuffling and cutting the cards, the dealer deals the cards to each player in rotation, beginning with the player to his left. Deal one card at a time, face down, until the whole pack is dealt out, thus giving thirteen cards to each player.

Playing

When the deal is complete, the eldest hand (the player to the left of the dealer) leads any card he pleases. Each player plays a card to the lead, and the highest card of the suit led wins the trick.

Each player must follow suit if he can, but if he is not able to follow suit, he may play any card he chooses. The winner of the trick leads to the next, until all thirteen tricks are played.

Rules of the Game

1. There is no trump suit.
2. Tricks do not count, but each trick must be kept intact until the close of the game, to verify a possible revoke.
3. At the close of the game each player reports how many (if any) Hearts he has taken.
4. Any player who has taken tricks containing Hearts must deposit in the pool one chip for each and every Heart captured. If one player takes the whole thirteen Hearts, he must pay thirteen chips into the pool, which is then divided: the other three players receive four chips each, and the odd chip goes to the winning player who sits nearest the left of the dealer.
5. If only one player does not have any Hearts, he takes all the chips in the pool. If two or more players have not captured Hearts, the pool is divided among them as equally as possible, any odd chips remaining after the division going to the winning player nearest to the left of the dealer. When all four players capture Hearts, the player who takes the least number of Hearts is paid by the other three.
6. If a card is exposed during the deal, the dealer must deal over again, unless the exposed card belongs to the dealer.
7. If a misdeal occurs, the dealer must deal over again.
8. A card exposed in the course of play cannot be called.
9. In case of a revoke, the delinquent must pay into the pool as many chips as the pool then contains (if any), plus thirteen additional chips.
10. A revoking player cannot win anything in the round in which the revoke occurred. After the penalty has been paid, the entire pool is divided among the other players.
11. Any player has the right to look at the last trick turned.
12. Every trick must be gathered and turned before a card can be led for the next trick.

I Doubt It

Rating: 8+

This game can be played with two or more people, with a regular deck of fifty-two cards. The object of the game is to dispose of the player's entire hand.

The dealer deals one card to each player in rotation, until the entire deck is dealt. As soon as the players have examined their hands, the eldest hand (the player on the left of the dealer) plays the lowest card or cards he has, beginning with an Ace. He must place the card or cards face down on the table, at the same time calling out what it is. The next player must put down the next-highest card or cards, face down, and so on. For instance, if the first player puts down a card and says "One Ace," the second player says "Two Two's," and so on.

ALERT!

It is not necessary to be honest about your turn. The fun of the game is to put down the wrong card without anyone suspecting you. Naturally, it is not often that the cards run straight on, because no one may play out of turn.

If any other player thinks someone has put down the wrong card, he calls the bluff by saying, "I doubt it." The player must then show his card, and if it is not the one he said, he must take all the cards laid down and add them to his pack. If the card(s) happens to be the right one, then the accuser must take the pile of cards. The player who first succeeds in getting rid of his cards wins the game.

Old Maid

Rating: 8+

Old Maid is played with two or more players, using a full deck of fifty-two cards. The object of the game is to not be stuck holding the Queen of Diamonds (the Old Maid).

Take the Queen of Hearts out of the deck, and deal all the cards among the players. Each player takes out all the pairs of cards in hand and places them face down in a pile in front of him. If you have three cards of the same value you can only put down two, but if you have four of the same value you can put all four down as two pairs.

In a clockwise fashion, the players take turns picking from each other's hands to try to create a match with their own cards. If you create a pair, remove it from your hand and place it in your pile. Your turn then continues. If you don't create a pair, the new card becomes part of your hand and the next player takes a turn. The game continues in this manner until all the cards are played out and only the Queen of Diamonds is left. The player with that card is the Old Maid.

FACT

At most toy stores, you can find Old Maid cards that have pictures of characters on the cards, including the Old Maid herself, instead of the standard suits and numbers. This deck is good to use if you want to include younger players.

Phase Ten

Rating: 8+

This game requires two or more players and is played with a Phase Ten deck of cards. The object is to make it through all ten phases with the lowest score. There are two basic variations of this game, a shorter and a longer one. Both variations are explained later in this section.

The Phases

1. Two sets of 3s
2. One set of 3s plus one run of 4s
3. One set of 4s plus one run of 4s
4. One run of 7s
5. One run of 8s

6. One run of 9s
7. Two sets of 4s
8. Seven cards of one color
9. One set of 5s plus one set of 2s
10. One set of 5s plus one set of 3s

A set is one or more cards with the same number. The cards can be any color. A run is one or more cards in numerical order; for example, 1, 2, 3, 4. The deck also includes special cards. The wild card can be used in place of any card in the deck, and the skip card allows the player to skip another player of his or her choice for the next round.

To begin the game, the dealer shuffles the cards and deals ten cards to each player. Place the remaining cards in the center of the table with the card from the top of the pile turned up and placed in the discard pile. With each round there is a new dealer.

Playing

Play is started by the player to the left of the dealer. The players attempt to collect the cards of the phase. During your turn, you may either take the card off the top of the discard pile or draw from the stack. You must then discard one card. The next player may take that card or draw from the pile, and so on. When you acquire all of the cards for the phase, lay those cards on the table and attempt to get rid of the remaining cards in your hand. Once you have laid the phase out, you may play off the cards that have been laid out by other players who have also completed the phase. When you discard or lay out your last card, you are out and the round is over. Points are assessed on the cards remaining in other players' hands as follows:

Number cards 1–9 count for 5 points each
Number cards 10+ count for 10 points each
Skip cards count for 15 points each
Wild Cards count for 25 points each

At this point, players may play either the shorter or longer version:

- **Shorter version:** All players move to the next phase. The player at the end of phase ten with the lowest score wins.
- **Longer version:** Players who did not complete the phase must remain on that phase until they complete it. The player who completes phase ten first wins. If there is a tie, the player with the lower of the scores wins.

Rummy

Rating: 8+

There are several versions of this very popular game. The difference is usually the number of cards originally dealt. The object of the game is to create sets of three or more cards to gain points, eventually adding up to 500. This section explains two versions of the game: rummy 500 and gin rummy.

Rummy 500

This game can be played by two or more people, using a standard deck of fifty-two cards.

The dealer deals each player seven cards, one at a time. Place the remainder of the deck (the stock) face down on the table. Flip over the top card to create a discard pile.

ALERT!

As soon as you can group cards together, take them out of your hand and lay them on the table in front of you. If you hold them in your hand and another player goes out, you won't be able to add those points to your score; instead, you will have to subtract the cards in your hand from your points on the table.

The players look over their hands and, if possible, group the cards in sets of threes. The cards can be grouped as a *run* or a *lay*. A run consists of three or more cards of the same suit in consecutive order; a lay consists of three or more cards of the same rank (for example, three Kings). If you begin the game with either a run or a lay, remove those cards from your hand and place them on the table face up.

The eldest hand (the player to the left of the dealer) goes first, and picks a card from either the stock or the discard pile. If you can use the card you pick up to form either a run or a lay, keep it, put the run or lay face up on the table, and discard another card from your hand face up into the discard pile. If you can use a card that is in the discard pile, you may pick that up instead, but you must take *all* the cards in the pile, and you must use the top card immediately to form a lay or a run. As soon as you discard, your turn is finished, and the next player goes.

The game ends when the first player has created sets with all of his cards. Any player who still has cards in his hand after the first person goes out must subtract the total number of points he is holding from his score. If he does not have enough points laid down in front of him to cover what is in his hand, he must subtract this score from a previous hand. There are no additional points given for going out first.

The cards are worth the following number of points:

Ace counts for 15 points
Picture cards count for 10 points each
All other cards count for 5 points each

Gin Rummy

This game is played by two or more people. If you are playing with two people, use one standard deck of fifty-two cards. If playing with more than four people, you might want to use two complete decks to make the game more interesting. The object of the game is to form matched sets of runs and lays consisting of three or four cards each.

The dealer deals ten cards to each player, and to himself. Turn over the top card from the stock to create a discard pile.

The eldest hand plays first, and must pick a card from either the stock or the discard pile. If he chooses to take a card from the discard pile, he only has to take the top card. He then tries to use the new card in either a run or a lay, and discards one card that he will not need. Once the first player has discarded, his turn is over and the player to the left of him continues the game.

In this version of rummy, you hold on to the sets in your hand instead of laying them on the table. Whoever can use all of his cards except for one in matched sets wins. The single card left is thrown onto the discard pile, face down, and the player announces, "Gin," to signify that the game is over.

FACT

Gin rummy is so popular that there is a Gin Rummy Association. This association sponsors gin rummy tournaments, including the World Series of Gin Rummy.

Each hand that wins is worth 25 points. Complete games are usually played to reach 100 points.

Slobberhannes

Rating: 8+

This is a game for four players, each playing for his own hand. Use a euchre pack for this game. The cards rank in value from Ace (highest) to Seven (lowest).

Players cut, not for the deal, but for the lead, the highest having preference, and the player on his right dealing. After you play the first hand, the deal passes in rotation to the left. The deal is no advantage so a misdeal involves no penalty. The dealer gives cards to the other players, rotating to the left, two cards at a time. There is no trump, all suits being alike in value.

Each player is bound to follow suit if he can. The highest card wins the trick, and the winner leads to the next. The object is to *avoid* making tricks, because the player who first makes 10 points loses the game, and has to pay an agreed stake to each of the other players.

Points are scored as follows:

First trick counts for 1 point.
Last trick counts for 1 point.
Trick containing the Queen of Clubs counts for 1 point.

The main interest of the game lies in the general struggle not to be sad-
dled with the Queen of Clubs, which the holder will try to play to a Club
trick, or discard to some other lead when he happens to be short.

If, in the same hand, any one player wins all three of the tricks listed
here, he is said to make slobberhannes, and scores an extra point. The penalty of a revoke is also 1 point added to the score of the offender.

Spades

Rating: 8+

Spades can be played by two, three, or four players. Players use a fifty-two-
card deck in which suits are ranked from highest (Ace) to lowest (Deuce).
In four-player spades, players pair off into partners, who then sit across from
each other. The players choose a dealer. After the first dealer, turns and dealing are clockwise. The dealer shuffles the cards and then deals the entire
pack. Each player should have thirteen cards.

Bidding

Each team makes a bid that estimates how many tricks they think they
will take. Write down the bids. You may make a bid of nil if you do not
expect to take any tricks. If your side is behind by at least 100 points, you
may make a bid of blind nil before looking at your cards. You may exchange
two cards with a partner by laying two down and picking up the two laid
down by your partner.

Playing

For the first trick, each player must play her lowest Club. If a player has
no Clubs, she must discard either a Diamond or a Heart. The player with the
highest Club wins the trick. The winner of the first trick starts the second
trick by playing any card except a Spade. The other players follow suit if they

can; if they cannot, they may play any card. If a Spade is played in a trick, the highest Spade wins. If there are no Spades, the highest card of the suit played wins. The winner of the trick leads the next trick. The leader of a trick may not play a Spade until either a player has played a Spade in another trick, or she has nothing but Spades left to play. This is called "breaking Spades."

FACT

Spades, which is a very popular card game, originated in the United States in the 1930s. It isn't yet popular in Europe; however, it is catching on somewhat in those areas in which American troops are stationed.

The Score

If a side takes at least as many tricks as it bids, it gets a score that is ten times the number of the bid. Tricks won in addition to the number of the bid (overtricks) count as 1 point apiece. However, there is a "sandbagging rule," which states that a team that has ten or more overtricks over more than one hand loses 100 points. If there are more than ten overtricks, the remaining overtricks carry over and start counting toward the next ten overtricks, after which another 100 points are deducted. If a nil bidder wins no tricks, the team receives 50 points. If the nil bidder does win a trick, the side loses 50 points. A blind nil bidder's team receives 100 points if the bidder wins no tricks, and loses 100 if she does win at least one trick.

If a side does not win as many tricks as it bid, it loses 10 points for each trick bid. The first side to reach 500 points wins the game.

Uno

Rating: 8+

Uno is played by two or more people, and a special Uno deck is required. Deal seven cards to each player and place the remaining cards face down in the center of the table in a "draw" pile. The object of the round is to get rid of all of your cards.

To start the game, turn the first card in the draw pile face up and lay it down next to the draw pile. The first player must then match the card either by color or by number. For example, if the first card is a blue Nine, you may either discard a blue card or a Nine of any color. You also may use a wild card. If you cannot play anything, you must draw from the pile. If you can play the card you drew, you must play it. If not, the next player takes her turn. When a player has one card left, she must declare "Uno!" If the player does not declare "Uno!" before the next player's turn and the other players catch the mistake, the player must draw two cards.

Special Terms

There are several special terms that are used when you play Uno.

- Wild Card—Wild cards may be played on any card. The person playing the card determines the color of the card.
- Wild Draw 4—The player who plays the card determines the color of the card, and the next player must draw four cards without playing any. However, you may play this card only if you do not have any cards that you can play.
- Draw 2 Card—The next player must draw two cards.
- Reverse—The direction of play is reversed.
- Skip—The next player is skipped.

Scoring

One through Nine count at the face value
Draw 2 counts for 20 points
Reverse counts for 20 points
Skip counts for 20 points
Wild card counts for 50 points
Wild Draw 4 counts for 50 points

And the Winner Is . . .

There are two ways to determine the winner. One method determines that the first player to reach 500 points wins. When a player goes out, the other players must add up their scores, which are then added together to become the score for the player who has gone out. The other method is for each player to keep his or her own score. When one player reaches 500 points, the game is over, and the player with the lowest score wins.

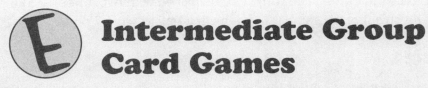

Chapter 6

Intermediate Group Card Games

Though we will never outgrow the games of our childhood, it is always fun to advance to higher levels of play. The games within this chapter are suitable for kids ages eight and up. Though the games may be more advanced and require a bit more skill and strategy, that doesn't mean they are any less fun!

All-Fours

Rating: 8+

The game of all-fours, sometimes called old sledge or seven-up, is played with a full pack of fifty-two cards, with the Ace being the highest and the Deuce the lowest. The game can be played with two, three, or four players. The object of the game is to be the first one to score 7 points.

Dealing

The players cut for the chance to deal, and the person who draws the highest card becomes the dealer. The dealer then gives six cards to each player, three at a time, and turns up the next card when he has finished dealing. The turned-up card is the trump.

Begging

The nondealer then looks at his hand and determines whether he will hold it for play, or *beg*. If he is satisfied with his hand, he says "I stand." If he is not satisfied with his cards, he says "I beg." In that case, the dealer must choose to either grant his adversary 1 point, saying "Take one," or give each player three more cards from the pack, and then turn up the next card, for trump. If the new trump turned up is of the same suit as the first, the dealer must go on, giving each player three more cards and turning up the next, until a change of suit for trump takes place.

Playing the Hand

After these preliminaries are settled, the eldest hand (the player to the left of the dealer) leads a card, and the dealer plays a card to it. These two cards constitute a trick. The player who plays the highest card of the suit led, or trump, wins the trick, and has the next lead. The play proceeds in this way until all the tricks are played. Each player must follow suit, if he can, unless he chooses to trump.

Scoring

The following is a list of points that may be scored, in order of their precedence:

- *High*—The highest trump out; the holder scores 1 point.
- *Low*—The lowest trump out; the original holder scores 1 point, even if it is taken by an adversary.
- *Jack*—The Jack of trumps. The winner of the trick containing it scores 1 point. When the Jack is turned up for trump it counts 1 point for the dealer, and in that case takes precedence over every other point in the score.
- *Game*—The greatest number of points that, in the tricks gained, can be shown by a player. The cards are valued as follows:
  Each Ace: 4 points toward game
  Each King: 3 points toward game
  Each Queen: 2 points toward game
  Each Jack: 1 point toward game
  Each Ten: 10 points toward game

The other cards do not count toward scoring points. It may happen that a deal may be played without either party having any cards worth a score, if no one is holding picture cards or Tens. When the players hold equal numbers (ties), the eldest hand scores the point for game.

One card may count all fours. For example, suppose the eldest hand holds only the Jack of the trump suit, and stands his game; if the dealer has neither trump, Ten, Ace, nor picture card, it will follow that the Jack will be both high, low, Jack, and game.

The player who scores 7 points first wins the game.

All-Fours for Four Players

The parties usually decide who shall be partners by cutting the cards, the two highest and the two lowest being partners. Each player sits opposite his partner. Decide the first deal by cutting the cards, with the highest cut having the deal. After the first deal, players take turns as dealer in rotation to the left.

The dealer and the player on his left are the only players permitted to look at their cards prior to the player deciding how he will play out his hand. The other parties must not raise their cards if the player begs until the dealer announces whether he will *give one* or run the cards for another trump.

FACT

Each Jack turned up by the dealer counts 1 point for him in the game, unless a misdeal should occur before the Jack is turned. The dealer is not excluded from scoring the point if he turns over a Jack and a misdeal occurs afterward, or if he turns over a Jack and the cards run out because the same suit turned.

Rules of the Game

1. In cutting, the Ace is the highest card, and ties cut again. (In the four-handed game, the two highest play against the two lowest.)
2. Less than four cards is not a cut, and the player cutting must leave at least four cards at the bottom of the pack.
3. If a card is exposed, a new cut may be demanded.
4. The dealer must give each player six cards, three cards at a time. If four are playing the dealer begins with the player to his left, and continues in rotation.
5. If the dealer deals without having the cards properly cut, or if a card is faced incorrectly in the pack, or if the dealer in any way exposes any of his adversary's cards, or if he gives out to any player too few or too many cards, there must be a fresh deal. The cards are reshuffled and recut, and the dealer deals again. If the dealer exposes any of his own cards, the deal stands good.
6. After the first hand the players deal alternately, if only two play. If more than two play, the players deal in rotation to the left. When playing for money, the players cut for deal at the commencement of each game.
7. Points are scored in the following order of precedence: high, low, Jack, and game.
8. Should there be a tie for game, the nondealer scores the point. If three or more are playing and there is a tie, the eldest hand scores the point.

9. If a player begs, it is at the option of the dealer to give him 1 point or run the cards for a new trump. When playing three-handed, if the dealer gives one player new cards, he must give them to both.

10. No player may beg more than once in each hand. However, there is nothing to prevent the dealer and the eldest hand from bunching the cards; that is, having a fresh deal, after the eldest has begged, and the cards have been run by the dealer, provided they mutually agree to do so. If the new trump is unsatisfactory to both, they may agree to run them again instead of bunching. However, a suit cannot become trump if it has once been turned down during the deal. This is more a matter of agreement than of actual law.

11. Should the same suit be turned until the cards run out, then the cards must be bunched and dealt again.

12. Each player must follow suit, if he can, unless he chooses to trump. If a player can follow suit (or trump) but fails to (revoke), he becomes liable to the following penalty:

    A. If the player making the revoke plays Jack and game, he cannot score either point, but his adversary may take both points.
    B. If the player making the revoke plays either Jack or game when both points are out, he cannot score the point, but his adversary may add 2 points to his score.
    C. If both Jack and game are out and the revoking player holds a Jack but does not play it, his adversary may score 2 points.
    D. If a Jack is not out, the adversary scores 1 point for the revoke.

13. A revoke is established as soon as the trick in which it occurs is turned and quitted, or a card has been led for the next trick.

Calabrasella

Rating: 8+

Calabrasella is one of the few games that are really interesting for three players. The game is played with a pack of forty cards, which results from removing the Tens, Nines, and Eights from a complete deck before the deal.

Dealing

The players cut for the deal; the lowest card wins. The player to the dealer's right cuts the deck. The dealer reunites the deck and distributes the cards two at a time to each player, starting at his left, until each player has twelve cards. Four cards (the stock) remain. These are placed face down in the middle of the table.

Order of the Cards

The cards rank in the following order from lowest to highest: Three, Two, Ace, King, Queen, Jack, Seven, Six, Five, Four. Their value in scoring is different from their rank in play.

Declaring to Play

When the deal is complete, the eldest hand (player to the dealer's left) looks at his hand and declares whether he will play along or not, saying "I play" or "I pass." If he passes, the next player has the option to play or pass; if the second player also passes, the dealer has the option. If all three pass, the hand is discarded and the deal goes to the eldest hand.

If a player declares to play his hand, the other two become allies and play against him. The single player is entitled, before he plays, to strengthen his hand by exchanging cards with other players or the stock:

1. The single player may ask the other players for a Three in the suit he chooses. The player holding that card must surrender it, receiving a card in exchange from the single player's hand. If no one is holding that specific Three (if it remains in the stock), the single player cannot demand any other card. If the single player already happens to hold all the Threes, he may then ask for a specific Two.
2. The single player then declares how many cards he will exchange for cards in the stock. He must exchange at least one, and of course, cannot exchange more than four. He discards from his hand the number he desires to exchange, and places them face down on the table. He then turns the stock face up, and selects from it the number required to supply the places of the discarded cards.

The other players have a right to see the stock when it is turned up, but they must not look at the cards discarded by the single player.

The cards discarded, together with those not taken from the stock (if any), form a second stock, called the *discard*. The discard remains face down, and belongs to the winner of the last trick.

Discarding more than two cards is not recommended. Chances are that two of the cards in the stock will be of little value. Remember that the Ace, which is the highest scoring card, is not the highest in play. Try to use Aces in your own tricks, and to entrap the Aces of your opponents.

Playing

The eldest hand (whether single player or not) has the first lead. Each player plays one card in turn, the dealer playing last. The three cards played constitute a trick. The highest card of the suit led wins the trick (refer back to the order of the cards earlier in this section). There are no trumps. The players are bound to follow suit if able, but if not, may play any card. A player is not bound to take a trick. The winner of one trick leads to the next, and so on, until all the twelve tricks are played out.

The single player makes a pile of all the tricks he takes, and the allies make a pile of theirs, each trick being turned face down. The winner of the last trick takes the discard and adds it to his heap.

Scoring

When all the cards are played out, each side counts the points in its respective pile. The points accrue as follows:

Ace counts for 3 points
Each King counts for 1 point
Queen counts for 1 point
Jack counts for 1 point
Three counts for 1 point

Two counts for 1 point

The winner of the last trick counts 3 points

FACT

The last trick is by far the most important. It is worth 3 points in itself, is generally rich in good cards, and takes the discard and all points in it. It is therefore a good idea to reserve good cards in order to secure the last trick.

The total number of possible points is 35, but the number reckoned is the difference between the respective scores. For example: If the single player has 20 points and the allies 15, the former wins 5 points from each of the allies. On the other hand, if the single player has 15 points and the allies 20, the single player loses 5 points to each of the allies. Each hand is a complete game in itself.

Rules of the Game

1. The players cut for deal; the lowest card deals.
2. Each player deals in turn, the order of dealing going to the left.
3. There is no misdeal. If there is any irregularity in dealing, on discovery, there must be a fresh deal, even though the hand has been played out.
4. The allies have a right to count the discard face down, and if they find that it contains too few cards they have the option of requiring the single player to make up the difference from his hand, or of ending the game. If the discard is found to contain too many cards, the single player has to suffer the loss of his first available trick.
5. If the single player asks for a Two, when he has not had all the Threes dealt him, his opponents have the option of ending the game.
6. If a card is asked for and is not surrendered, and it is not in the stock, the single player may again require its surrender, and may alter his discard, notwithstanding that he has seen the stock.
7. A round is finished when the deal returns to the original dealer.
8. If the single player exposes a card there is no penalty.
9. If the single player plays out of turn there is no penalty. The card led in

error must be taken back, and the right player must lead. If the second player has played to such lead he must also take back his card; but if all three players have played, the trick is complete, and the hand proceeds as though no error had been committed.

10. If either of the allies exposes a card, the single player may call it (except as provided in Rule #9). The call may be repeated at every trick until the exposed card is played.

11. If either of the allies leads out of turn, and the error is discovered before the trick is complete, the single player may call a suit from the right leader (or, if it is his own lead, may call a suit the first time he loses the lead), or he may refrain from calling a suit, and treat the card led in error as an exposed card. If a suit is called and the leader has none of it, he may play any card he pleases, and no further penalty can be demanded.

12. When the single player leads, it is unfair for the third player to play before the second.

13. If a player does not follow suit when able, the opponents may take 9 points from the score of the side offending and add them to their own.

14. When a trick is complete it must be turned over and put aside. No one has a right to see it again during the play of the hand.

Commerce

Rating: 8+

Commerce is played with one or two decks of fifty-two cards. Up to nineteen people can play if you use two decks. One player shuffles the pack, and after having it cut by the player to his right, deals one card face up to each player, beginning with the player to his left. The lowest card has the deal.

The dealer deals the cards face down, two at a time and then three at a time, to each player in rotation, beginning with the player to his left. When each player holds five cards, the dealer places five cards face up on the table.

Playing

The player to the left of the dealer begins play by doing one of two things. He may exchange up to five cards for those on the table, placing his discarded cards face up on the table with those he leaves, or, if content with his hand, he may pass. The next player to the left may similarly exchange cards or pass, and so on. A player having once passed cannot exchange cards again. The exchanging goes around twice, after which all players show their hands, and the two players with the lowest hands retire from the game.

When playing with two decks, you might want to remove some of the lower cards, so that you can deal out most of the remaining cards. When the active players are reduced to fewer than ten, you should resume using a single pack.

Another round then begins, and the player to the left of the previous dealer deals. The second round proceeds precisely as the first, except that the retired players are excluded. Again, the two players showing the lowest hands at the end of the round retire from the game.

The rounds continue in this manner, retiring two players at a time, until only two players remain. Of these two, the player who shows the highest hand wins the game. The winner receives a chip from each of the other players. In case of an absolute tie, the winner is decided by cutting the cards. The player who cuts the lowest card loses.

If the game is played with an odd number of players, the two lowest hands retire after each round, until only three players remain. At the end of the round played by the three players, only one (the lowest hand) retires, leaving two competitors for the final round.

Rank of the Hands

The hands rank in the following order of precedence, beginning with the highest:

1. Straight Flush: a five-card sequence in the same suit
2. Fours: four of a kind, like four tens or four Jacks
3. Full: three of a kind and two of a kind, like three tens and two Jacks

4. Flush: five cards in the same suit but not in sequence
5. Straight: five cards in sequence but not in the same suit
6. Triplets: three of a kind
7. Two Pair: two pairs of two of a kind, like two tens and two Jacks
8. One Pair: two of a kind

Retired Players

After each show of hands, and until the cards have been cut for the succeeding round, all players, including those retired, may talk freely with the others. The moment the cards are dealt, however, and until the hands are shown again, conversation is forbidden between those playing (the *ins*) and those not playing (the *outs*). A retired player or out may make as many remarks as he pleases to try to trap an in; but if an in replies, the in and the out must immediately exchange their positions in the game. In such a case the in must give up his cards, plus a chip, to the out, and retire from the game until he succeeds in trapping some other active player.

Division Loo

Rating: 8+

Division Loo can be played by any number of people, but five or seven make the best game. Play this game with a pack of fifty-two cards, with the Ace being the highest and the Deuce the lowest.

Dealing

Before dealing, the dealer deposits three chips into the pool, the value of which has previously been agreed upon. It is necessary to make the pool a number that can be exactly divided by three. The chips deposited by the dealer are called a *single*.

After shuffling and cutting the cards, the dealer proceeds to deal three cards, one at a time to each player, beginning at the eldest hand (the player to the left of the dealer), and going around to the left. He also deals an extra hand, called a *dummy,* to the center of the table, and turns up the next card for trump.

In the first deal, or whenever a single occurs, a *bold stand* is played. A bold stand compels every player to play his hand. The eldest hand has the sole privilege of immediately exchanging the hand that was dealt to him for the dummy. A bold stand can occur only in three instances: at the first deal; when three players declare to play, and each takes a trick; or when only two play, and one takes two tricks and the other one trick. Sometimes it is agreed to omit bold stand. In that case, at the first deal, or whenever a single occurs, each player deposits three chips in the pool, and the dealer six chips.

ALERT!

If the dealer deals without having the pack cut, or shuffles the pack after it has been cut with his consent, or deals out of order, he forfeits a single (three chips) to the pool. This penalty goes to the present pool. Then the dealer reshuffles, recuts, and deals again.

Declaring

After the deal is complete each player looks at his cards and declares whether he will play his hand or pass. If he plays, he says "I play"; if he resigns, he says "I pass," and his interest in that pool ceases, unless he elects to exchange his hand for the dummy. The first player to declare has the first right of taking dummy, and if he declines, the next player has that privilege, and so on; but whoever takes the dummy must play it.

No player is permitted to look at his hand before it is his turn to declare. Once he declares, he is compelled to adhere to his decision. When a player resigns his hand he gives it to the dealer, who places it in the stock.

Playing

The remaining players now begin the game. The first player leads a card, and each player in rotation plays one card to it, constituting a trick. The trick is won by the highest card of the suit led or, if trumped, by the highest trump. The winner of the trick then leads to the next, and so on until the hand is played out. The cards are not played on the center of the table, but face up in front of each person playing them.

If the leader has more than one trump, he must lead the highest, unless his trumps are in sequence. If he does not hold two or more trumps, he may lead with whichever card he chooses. The other players, in rotation, must follow suit. If a player holds none of the suit led, he must head the trick with a trump. If a player is unable to follow either suit or trump, he may play any card he chooses.

Sometimes it is agreed that when only one declares to play and the dummy remains on the table, the dealer has the option of taking it and playing for the good of the pool. When this variation is played, the dealer must declare, before taking the dummy, whether he plays for himself or the pool. Otherwise, he is assumed to be playing for himself.

The winner of the first trick must lead a trump, and if he holds two trumps, he must lead the higher of the two. If the leader holds the Ace of trumps (or the King if the Ace is turned up), he must lead it whether he has another trump or not. It is sometimes agreed that when there are more than two players, the leader is not obliged to play his highest trump unless it is the Ace (or King if the Ace is turned up).

After the hand is played to its conclusion, the winner or winners of the tricks divide the amount in the pool, one-third for each trick. If a player wins one trick he gets one-third of the pool; if he wins two tricks he takes two-thirds of the pool; and if he wins all the tricks, he captures the whole pool.

If a player declares to play and fails to take a trick, he must contribute three chips to the next pool. When none of the players who declared to play owe chips to the pool, a bold stand occurs. After the pool has been divided and the new payments are made, the dealer deposits three chips into the pool, and the game proceeds as before.

Rules of the Game

1. The deal is determined by dealing a card, face up, to each player, beginning at the left of the person dealing the cards. The player holding the lowest card deals.

2. The player to the dealer's right cuts the cards. At least four cards must be cut, and at least four must be left in the lower packet.

3. When cutting to the dealer, if a card is exposed, there must be a fresh cut.

4. If, in reuniting the separated cards the dealer exposes a card, you must recut.

5. Each player has the right to shuffle, and it is the dealer's right to shuffle last.

6. The dealer must give to each player one card at a time, beginning with the player to his left, and at the end of each round he must deal one card to the dummy prior to beginning the next round. In this order, the dealer must deliver three cards to each player, and three to dummy.

7. After completing the deal, the dealer must turn up the next card for trumps.

8. If a card is faced in the pack and it is discovered before the deal is completed, there must be a fresh deal.

9. After the first deal, each player takes the deal in rotation, beginning with the player to the left of the dealer. The game should not be abandoned until the deal has returned to the original dealer.

10. If a player deals out of turn, and is not stopped before the trump card is turned, the deal stands good.

11. Each player must declare whether he will play or not, in rotation, beginning with the player to the dealer's left.

12. If a player looks at his cards before it is his turn to declare to play, he forfeits a single to the pool. This penalty goes to the present pool.

13. If a player exposes a card before declaring to play or declares to play before his turn, he forfeits a single to the pool. This penalty goes to the present pool.

14. If a player takes the dummy, and no one plays against him, he takes the pool. If no one declares to play, the dealer takes the pool.

15. If a player, having declared to play, exposes a card before it is his turn; or plays a card out of turn; or before all have declared; or exposes a card while playing so as to be named by any other declared player, he must leave in the pool any tricks he may make, and forfeit twelve chips. If he fails to take a trick he must pay into the pool, up to the limit (if any) in lieu of penalty. These tricks and forfeitures go to the next pool.

16. If a player holds the Ace of trumps and does not lead it, or if he holds King (Ace being turned up) and does not lead it, he must leave in the pool any tricks he may make, and forfeit twelve chips. This forfeiture and the tricks go to the next pool.

17. If a player does not lead the higher of two trumps, unless his trumps are sequence cards, that is, cards of equal value; or does not head the trick when able, or revokes; or holding a trump does not lead trump after trick, he must leave in the pool any tricks he may make, and forfeit twelve chips. This forfeiture and the tricks go to the next pool.

18. When a revoke or any error in play occurs, the cards must be taken up and the hand replayed, if so desired by any player except the offender.

19. If a deck is discovered to be incorrect, the deal in which the discovery is made is void. All preceding deals stand good.

Euchre

Rating: 8+

Euchre is played with a pack of thirty-two cards—the Sixes, Fives, Fours, Threes, and Twos are removed from a complete pack. Two, three, or four persons may play, but the four-handed game is the most popular and will be discussed here (two pairs of partners). The object is to win a minimum of three tricks.

Dealing

After the players cut for the deal, the dealer shuffles the cards, and the player to the right of the dealer cuts. The dealer then gives five cards to each player—first two cards at a time to each in rotation, beginning with the player to his left, then three cards at a time. After each player receives five cards, the dealer turns up the next card for trump, and places it face up on top of the stock.

Ordering Up, Assisting, Passing, and Taking Up

When the trump is turned, the eldest hand (the player to the left of the dealer) examines his hand to see what he will do. He may either order up the trump or pass. If he thinks his cards are strong enough to win three tricks, he says "I order it up." The dealer then discards one card from the player's hand and puts it under the stock, face down, and takes the trump card, instead of the card the player discarded. But if the player is not satisfied with his cards, he says "I pass."

FACT

When playing euchre, the cards in suits, not trumps, rank as in whist: the Ace is the highest and the Seven the lowest. In trumps, the cards rank differently. The Jack of the suit turned up is called the *right bower,* and is the highest trump. The other Jack of the same color (black or red, as the case may be) is called the *left bower,* and is the next highest trump.

If the eldest hand passes, the partner of the dealer then has the option of saying what he will do, and he may either assist his partner or pass. If his hand is strong enough to win three tricks with the help of the trump his partner has turned, he says "I assist"; his partner discards as before, and the trump card belongs to him. If the partner of the dealer has a weak hand, he says "I pass," and the third player has the option of saying what he will do. The third player proceeds exactly as the eldest hand, and, if that player passes, the dealer has the next say.

If all the other players pass, the dealer may either take up the trump or pass. If his hand is strong enough to take three tricks, he says "I take it up." The dealer then discards the weakest card from his hand, and takes the trump card. If the dealer has a weak hand, he says "I turn it down" and, at the same time, places the trump card face up under the stock.

If the dealer turns down the trump, the eldest hand has the option of naming any suit (except the one turned down) for trumps, or of passing again. If he passes, he says "I pass the making." If the eldest hand passes the making, the partner of the dealer then has the option of making the trump, and so on in rotation up to and including the dealer. If all the players, including the dealer, decline to make the trump, a fresh deal ensues, and the eldest hand deals.

If either side adopts (plays with the suit turned up for trump) or makes the trump, the play of the hand begins. When the trump is made of the same color as the turnup (that is, black if the turnup is black, or red if it is red), it is called *making it next in suit.* If the trump is made of a different color from the turnup, it is called *crossing the suit.*

ALERT!

Be careful how you make the trump when your adversaries have scored 3 points, and do not make or order up a trump unless you are the eldest hand, or the dealer's partner.

Playing Alone

If a player holds a hand so strong that he has a reasonable hope of taking all five tricks without the assistance of his partner, he may play alone. If he plays without his partner, he says "I play alone." His partner then places his cards face down on the table, and remains silent during the play of the five tricks.

If the eldest hand orders up or makes the trump, either he or his partner may play alone. If the dealer's partner assists or makes the trump, either he or the dealer may play alone. If the player to the right of the dealer orders up or makes the trump, he may play alone (but his partner cannot). If the dealer takes up or makes a trump, he may play alone (but his partner cannot).

When your opponent is playing alone and trumps a suit that you or your partner leads, be sure to throw away all cards of that suit upon his subsequent leads, provided you do not have to follow suit.

A player cannot play alone after having passed a trump or passed the making of a trump. A player cannot play alone when the opposing side adopts or makes the trump; nor can he play alone unless he announces his intentions to do so before he, or the opposing side, makes a lead.

Playing

The eldest hand leads a card and each player in rotation plays a card to the lead. The four cards thus played constitute a trick. A player must follow suit if he can, but if not able to follow suit, he may play any card he chooses. The highest card of the suit led wins the trick; trumps win all other suits. The winner of the trick leads to the next, and so on until the five tricks are played.

Scoring

The game is 5 points. If the side that adopts or makes a trump wins all five tricks, the partners make a *march* and score 2. If they win three tricks, they make the *point* and score 1. Four tricks count no more than three tricks. If they fail to take three tricks they are *euchred,* and the opposing side scores 2 points. When a player plays alone and takes all five tricks he scores 4 points. If he takes three tricks he scores 1 point. If he fails to take three tricks, he is euchred, and the opposing side scores 2 points. The Three and Four are used in marking game. The face of the Three being up, and the face of the Four down on it, counts one, whether one, two, or three pips are exposed; the face of the Four being up, and the Three over it, face down, counts two, whether one, two, three, or four of the pips are shown. The face of the Three uppermost counts three, and the face of the Four uppermost counts four.

Rules of the Game

1. At the outset of the game each player cuts for the deal, and the lowest cut deals. If there is a tie, the parties tied cut again. The players cutting the two highest cards play against those cutting the two lowest.
2. In cutting, the Ace is lowest, and the other cards rank as in whist.
3. Should a player expose more than one card, he must cut again.
4. The cards may be shuffled by any player who demands that privilege, but the dealer always has the right to shuffle last.
5. The cards must be cut by the right-hand opponent before they are dealt. A cut must not be less than four cards removed from the top.
6. After the first deal, the right of dealing goes to the left.
7. A misdeal forfeits the deal. The following are misdeals: Too many or too

few cards given to either player; dealing the cards when the pack has not been properly cut. The claim for a misdeal must be made prior to the trump card being turned, and before the adversaries look at their cards.

8. Whenever a misdeal is attributable to any interruption by the adversaries, the deal will not be forfeited. If an adversary touches his cards during the deal, and the dealer's partner has not done so, no misdeal can be claimed.

9. If a card is exposed by the dealer or partner, should neither of the adversaries have touched their cards, a new deal may be claimed, but the right to deal is not lost.

10. If, during the deal, the dealer's partner touches any of his cards, the adversaries may do the same without losing their privilege of claiming a new deal.

11. If an opponent displays a card dealt, the dealer may make a new deal, unless he or his partner have examined their own cards.

12. If a deal is made out of turn, and it is not discovered before the dealer has discarded and the eldest hand has led, it is good.

13. If a card is faced in dealing, unless it be the trump card, a new deal may be demanded, but the right to deal is not lost.

14. If the pack is discovered to be defective, by reason of having more or less than thirty-two cards, the deal is void; but all the points made before are good.

15. The dealer, unless he turns down the trump, must discard one card from his hand and take up the trump card.

16. The discard is not complete until the dealer has placed the card under the pack; if the eldest hand makes a lead before the discard is complete, he cannot take back the card thus led, but must let it remain. The dealer, however, may change the card he intended to discard and substitute another, or he may play alone, when a card has been prematurely led.

17. After the discard has been made, the dealer may let the trump card remain upon the stock until it is necessary to play it on a trick. After the trump card has been taken in hand, no player has a right to demand its denomination, but he may ask for the trump suit and the dealer must inform him.

18. Should a player play with more than five cards, or if the dealer forgets to discard or omits to declare the fact before three tricks have been

turned, the deal is lost. However, should the adverse side win, they may score all the points they make.

19. All exposed cards may be called, and the offending party compelled to lead or play the exposed card or cards when he can legally do so, but in no case can a card be called if a revoke is thereby caused. The following are exposed cards: two or more cards played at once; any card that a player indicates he holds in his hand; any card dropped with its face upward; all cards exposed, whether by accident or otherwise, so that an opponent can distinguish and name them.

20. If any player leads out of turn, his adversaries may demand of him to withdraw his card, and the lead may be compelled from the right player; the card improperly led may be treated as an exposed card and called at any time during that deal, provided it causes no revoke.

21. If any player leads out of turn and the mislead is followed by the other players, the trick is completed and stands good; but if only the second, or the second and third, have played to the false lead, their cards, on discovery of the mistake, are taken back, and there is no penalty against anyone except the original offender, whose card may be called.

22. If any player trumps a card in error, and thereby induces an opponent to play otherwise than he would have done, the latter may take up his card without penalty, and may call upon the offender to play the trump at any period of the hand.

23. If two cards are played or if a player plays twice to the same trick, his opponent can elect which of the two shall remain and belong to the trick, provided, however, that no revoke be caused.

24. If a player, thinking that he can take every trick, or for any other reason, throws down his cards upon the table with their faces exposed, the adverse side may call each and all of the cards so exposed, and the delinquent party must play the exposed cards accordingly. This cannot be done, however, in the case of a lone hand.

25. When a revoke occurs, the adverse parties are entitled to add 2 points to their scores.

26. If a suit is led and any one of the players, having a card of the same suit, shall play another suit to it, a revoke is committed. But if the error is discovered before the trick is quitted or before the party having so played a

wrong suit (or his partner) shall play again, the penalty amounts to only the cards being treated as exposed, and being liable to be called.

27. When the player who has made a revoke corrects his error, his partner, if he has played, cannot change his card played; but the adversary may withdraw his card and play another.

28. When a revoke is claimed against adversaries, if they mix their cards, or throw them up, the revoke is taken for granted, and they lose the 2 points.

29. No party can claim a revoke after cutting for a new deal.

30. A revoke on both sides forfeits to neither, but requires a new deal.

31. If a player makes a revoke, his side cannot count any points made in that hand.

32. A party refusing to play an exposed card on call forfeits two cards to his opponents, as in a revoke.

33. Any player making a trump cannot change the suit after having once named it. If he should by error name the suit previously turned down, he forfeits his right to make the trump, and such privilege must pass to the next player.

34. A player may only play alone when he orders up, takes up, or makes a trump, or when his partner assists, orders up, or makes a trump. He cannot play alone with a trump he has passed, or with a trump the making of which he has passed; nor can he play alone after a lead has been made.

35. A player cannot play alone when he or his partner is ordered up by an opponent, or when the opposite side adopts or makes the trump.

36. When a player elects to play alone, his partner cannot supersede him and play alone instead.

37. When a player announces that he will play alone, his partner must place his cards upon the table face down. Should he accidentally expose the face of any of his cards, his opponents may compel him to play or not to play with his partner, at their option.

38. A player who goes alone must clearly announce his intention. If he is not clearly understood by his adversaries and he or they make a lead, he forfeits his privilege and must play with his partner.

39. If a partner indicates his hand by words or gestures to his partner, including telling him to follow the rules of the game, the adversary scores 1 point.

40. No player has a right to see any trick but the last one turned.

Grabouche

Rating: 8+

Grabouche may be played by two, four, six, or eight people. You need three complete decks of fifty-two cards each if two, four, or six people play; when eight play, you need four decks. The cards rank as follows: Ace (highest), King, Queen, Jack, Ten, Nine, Eight, Seven, Six, Five, Four, Three, and Two (the lowest).

When four people play, they divide into two teams, each player sitting opposite his partner. When six people play, they form two teams of three, and the players composing the two sets sit in alternate order. When eight people play, two teams of four each are formed, and the players are similarly seated alternately.

Dealing

The player who cuts the lowest card deals. Ties are cut over. The dealer counts out twenty cards for each team face down. The top card of each pile is turned up. When six or eight people play, the number of cards in the two piles is sometimes increased.

The dealer then deals a second set of cards: five to each person, beginning with the player to the left of the dealer. Make up the remaining cards into groups of five, to be given to each player when his hand is played out.

Playing

The player on the left of the dealer opens the play and may begin by placing an Ace (if he has one) face up in the center of the table. A player is entitled to use cards from his hand, the top cards of own or his partners' table piles (explained later in this section), or the top card of his twenty pile. He may build upon the Ace in sequence with all the suitable cards contained in his hand. For example, he may then put out the Two, the Three, and so on, in their regular upward sequence. He may do this not only to get rid of his hand and take a fresh one, but, if possible, to reach the denomination of the card turned up on his pile of twenty, so that he or his partner may play it off.

The Aces must always be placed in the center, and cards built upon the

Aces are known as the *center piles*. When a player plays his last card in the center, he may take a fresh hand and continue playing. When finished playing in the center, he lays one card, face up, in front of him. This is known as a *table card*. No more than four piles of table cards are permitted in front of each player; it is therefore best to arrange them in sequence, placing the lower cards on the higher or, when possible, making one pile all of the same denomination.

You do not have to play the Ace at once, and you should not to be too hasty in playing it when the exposed card on the adversaries' pile is a low one and you have no cards to build up the Ace to the denomination of their card, or beyond it. If you hold no cards in sequence with the Ace, it is better to first play your other cards upon the table, retaining your Ace to the last. This is particularly beneficial when your last two cards are both Aces, as it affords you an opportunity of getting a fresh hand that may contain cards that will continue your play advantageously.

ALERT!

No remarks of any kind are allowed between partners regarding a play. Should a player, by word or gesture, express disapproval or approval of a partner's play, the opposing players may each place a card from their hand in the center of the pile of the offending side.

After the first player has completed his play, the next player similarly plays, and so on all around. When a player cannot or does not choose to play upon the center piles, he deposits a table card in front of himself.

A player is not obliged to build upon the center piles unless he chooses to do so. When it comes his turn, he may play a card on either of his table piles as often as he likes, whether such card is in sequence with the cards in the center piles or not.

The object of the game is to play off the cards from the twenty pile; therefore, if by playing on the center piles you lead up to the denomination of the card on your own pile, do so. However, you should refrain from playing on the center when it will help your opponents to accomplish the same object. Instead, play upon the table piles, because your adversaries cannot use the cards on your table, and the cards thus exposed may be employed by your partners to prevent the opponents from playing off their pile. This is called *blocking*.

It is sometimes a good idea to play up to the adversaries' card when doing so allows you to get rid of all your cards and take a fresh hand.

Get rid of your hand as quickly as possible, and always play from your hand, in preference to playing the same card from the table, unless, of course, the corresponding card is the top one on your pile of twenty; always give that the preference.

You can build upon the Aces without any regard to suit. When the King is finally put on, remove the pile from the center, shuffle it, and make it up into books of five each, ready for use when needed.

When you play off the top card of a twenty pile, immediately turn up the next card. Continue in this way until the last card of the pile is played. The side that first plays off all the cards in their twenty pile wins the game.

Rounce

Rating: 8+

Rounce may be played by up to nine people, but five or seven make a good game. The game is played with a pack of fifty-two cards, which rank as follows: Ace (highest), King, Queen, Jack, Ten, Nine, Eight, Seven, Six, Five, Four, Three, and Two (the lowest).

The dealer gives five cards to each player in rotation, beginning with the player to his left, by alternate rounds of two and three at a time. He also deals an extra hand of six cards in the center of the table, called a *dummy*.

The dummy must be dealt before the dealer deals to himself, and should be filled immediately preceding his own hand. The dealer then turns up the top card on the pack, which is the trump. After the first hand, the deal passes to the left.

Declaring to Play

After the deal is complete, each player in rotation, beginning with the eldest hand, looks at his cards and declares whether he will play his hand, take the dummy, or resign. If he is satisfied with his cards, he says "I play"; if he resigns, he says "I pass," and throws down his cards.

ALERT!

If a player, having declared to play, exposes a card before it is his turn to play, or plays a card out of turn or before all have declared, or exposes a card while playing so as to be named by any other declared player, he is rounced, meaning 5 points are added to his score.

The eldest hand has the first privilege of taking the dummy. If he wants it, he places his original hand in the center of the table, face down, and discards one card from his new hand. If he declines to take the dummy, the option passes to the next player to his left. Whoever takes the dummy must play it.

When all refuse to play, the player to the right of the dealer must play his hand, take the dummy, or, if he does neither, give the dealer 5 points. The dealer, when he elects to play, may discard any card in his hand, and substitute for it the card turned up for trump.

Playing the Hand

After all have declared, the first player leads a card, and each person in rotation (to the left) plays a card to the lead. The cards that are played constitute a trick. The trick is won by the highest card of the suit led, or, if trumped, by the highest trump played. Suit must be followed, but if this is not possible, a player may trump or not, at his option. The winner of a trick must lead a trump; however, if he holds no trump, he may lead any card he chooses.

Scoring

Each player begins the game with 15 points. The player who is the first to reduce his score to nothing wins the game. Each trick taken counts as

1 point taken off your score, and if you fail to take a trick after entering to play your hand, you are *rounced,* and 5 points are added to your score at once.

Rules of the Game

1. One of the players shuffles the pack, and, after having it cut by the player to his right, deals a card face up to each player in rotation, beginning to his left. The player who receives the lowest card deals. If two or more players receive the same low card, they must cut the pack, and again the lowest deals. Ace is low.

2. Each player has a right to shuffle the deck. The dealer has the right of shuffling last.

3. The player to the dealer's right cuts the cards, and if there is a card exposed in cutting, the pack must be reshuffled, and cut again.

4. The dealer must deliver the cards face down, two at a time, and then three at a time to each player in rotation, beginning with the player to his left; and before giving any cards to himself he must deal six cards to the dummy. After he deals to himself, the dealer turns up for trump the card remaining on top of the pack.

5. If, before the deal is completed, it is discovered that a card is faced in the pack, there must be a fresh deal.

6. If the dealer deals without having the pack cut; or shuffles the pack after it has been cut with his consent; or deals out of order—for instance, misses a hand or deals too many or too few cards to any player (even though the hand has been partly played out when the error is discovered); or exposes a card in dealing, he is rounced. The cards are reshuffled and recut, and the deal passes.

7. The player to the left of the dealer has the next deal.

8. If a player deals out of turn, and is not stopped before the trump card is turned, the deal stands good, and the player to the left of the player who dealt out of turn has the next deal.

9. Players must declare in rotation, beginning to the dealer's left.

10. If a player exposes a card before declaring to play, or declares to play before his turn, he is rounced.

11. Any player who thinks he cannot take a trick may decline to play his hand.

12. If the dealer elects to play, he may discard any card in his hand and substitute for it the card turned up for trump. (If the dealer plays the dummy, he cannot take the turned-up trump.)

13. If a player, having declared to play, fails to win a trick, he is rounced.

14. If a player fails to follow suit when he has a card of the suit led; or if he fails to lead a trump after taking a trick, when it is possible for him to do so, he is rounced.

15. When a revoke or any error of play occurs, the cards must be taken up and the hand replayed, if so desired by any player except the offender.

16. If a pack is discovered to be imperfect, the deal in which the discovery is made is void. All preceding deals stand good.

Chapter 7

Challenging Group Card Games

C ard games can provide an enjoyable social atmosphere, so much so that many people get together for games on a weekly basis. This chapter offers a variety of advanced-level card games that will challenge players, while strengthening friendships at the same time.

Solo

Rating: 12+

Contrary to its name, solo is played by three or four (usually four) players, with a euchre pack of thirty-two cards. Five players may play, but then you'll need to increase the number of the cards to forty, by adding the Fives and Sixes of each suit. The game as described here is for four players.

Before dealing the cards, the dealer puts a stake into the pool. The amount of the stake is agreed upon before the game, and is usually two or four chips. The pool is increased by the forfeits (or *béte*) that occur in the game. A béte can never exceed sixteen chips, and when the pool contains sixteen, it is called a *stamm*.

Shuffle the cards. After the player to the dealer's right has cut, deal eight cards to each player, in groups of three, two, and three at a time. After the first round, the deal passes to the left in rotation.

Solo has a lot of rules and vocabulary to learn. However, don't be discouraged. While it may seem complicated as you read through the instructions, the best way to learn is by getting hands-on experience. Just play!

Object of the Game

The object of the game is for a player to get the privilege of naming the trump, while either playing alone against the other three, or with the assistance of a friend against the remaining two players. This privilege is accorded to the bidder or announcer of the highest play. A successful bidder must take five tricks in order to win the value of his bid from the opponents; if he fails to take five tricks, he must pay the same price to each of the opponents.

Rank of the Cards

The Queen of Clubs is called *Spadilla,* and is always the best trump. The Seven of the trump suit (whatever it may be) is called *Manilla,* and ranks second, or below Spadilla. The Queen of Spades is called *Basta*, and is always the third trump. These three cards are natural *Matadores*. When Clubs or Spades are trumps, they are termed *short suits*, because they contain nine trumps; when Hearts or Diamonds are trumps, they are *long suits*, because they contain ten trumps.

Rank of Bids

One of the suits is selected—this is termed *couleur*—and bids in that suit are worth twice as much as in either of the other three suits. Couleur is generally Clubs or, after the first game, that suit in which the first game was won. The rank and value of the bids is as follows:

Simple game, in suit	2 chips
Simple game, in couleur	4 chips
Forcée partout, in suit	4 chips
Forcée partout, in couleur	8 chips
Solo, in suit	4 chips
Solo, in couleur	8 chips
Tout, in suit	16 chips
Tout, in couleur	32 chips

Forcée partout outranks a simple game; solo outbids forcée partout, and tout outranks any solo.

Matadores or Honors

Higher Matadores. Spadilla, Manilla, and Basta are called *higher Matadores*. When all three are in a player's hand (or in his and his friends' hands), they count as one chip for the three in the payment of the game.

Lower Matadores. When all three of the higher Matadores are held by either side, all trump cards that are also held in uninterrupted succession from Ace downward are also counted as Matadores. Each lower Matadore counts as one chip.

Reservation or reneging is allowed when a trump or lower Matadore is led; in that case a higher Matadore unguarded may be *reserved* without penalty for a revoke.

FACT

You do not need to play a Matadore to a lead of trumps, even if a higher Matadore has been played, unless the higher Matadore has been led. A higher Matadore, when led, forces a lower Matadore unguarded; a lower Matadore or any trump card led does not force a higher Matadore. Sometimes solo is played without the element of reservation being introduced.

Simple Game

A *simple game* occurs when the player is unwilling to play a solo. He names the trump suit, and calls for an Ace. The holder of the called Ace then acts as his partner or friend. Until the called Ace falls in play, it is not necessarily known who the friend really is; but, acting on his own knowledge, the friend is bound to assist the player to the best of his ability.

The payment for a simple game in suit is two chips, or, if in couleur, four chips. If the player and friend win five tricks, each receives the value of the game (including the price of the Matadores, if any), from his left-hand neighbor.

If the player holds all four Aces and is not willing to play a solo, he can call for a King instead of an Ace.

Forcée Partout

The holder of Spadilla and Basta must always announce it, unless a higher bid has already been made by that player or a previous bidder. It may be played as a solo or with a called Ace. The holder of the called Ace then names the trump, but not in the suit of the called Ace.

Forcée Simple

When all players have passed, the holder of Spadilla is forced to call for an Ace and play with his friend against the other two players. The holder of the called Ace then names the trump, but not the suit of the called Ace.

Forcée simple is not a bid; but, in the absence of any bid, it is a compulsory play of at least a simple game, with corresponding payments.

Solo

A *solo* occurs when the player attempts to take five tricks unaided. He names the trump, and plays alone against the other three. The payment of a solo in suit is four chips; in couleur, eight chips. The player alone receives payment for the game (and Matadores, if any) from the other three. If he loses, he pays each of them the same amount. If the solo is in couleur, and he wins it, he also draws a stamm from the pool. If he loses the game, he puts a béte into the pool, in addition to the regular payments.

A *tout* occurs when the bidder proposes to take all the tricks, either playing solo or with a called Ace. The payment for a tout is sixteen chips if in suit, or thirty-two chips if in couleur.

If in the course of playing a solo or a simple, the player succeeds in taking the first five tricks, and believes it possible to make all eight, he should lead his sixth card. This act signifies that he proposes incidentally to play for tout. By doing this, he forfeits his right to any payment to which the winning of the five tricks would have entitled him. If he succeeds, he wins double the value of the game if in suit, or four times the value if in couleur, from each of the others, and also the price of any Matadores. If he fails to take all the tricks, he must pay in the same proportion.

If no bid is made, the holder of Spadilla is obliged to assume the play.

Playing by Bidding

After the hands are dealt, the eldest hand has the first say. If his hand is not good, he can pass, and the next player can do the same, and so on. If the eldest hand considers his cards good enough (with the assistance of an Ace) to make five tricks, he says "I ask." The next player can outbid him, or pass. The other two players have the opportunity in turn to bid higher or pass. The highest bidder then plays alone against the other three, or, with the assistance of a friend, against the other two. In either case, the bidder names the trump. If the called Ace is in the caller's own hand, the game then ranks in value as a solo. If the caller holds all four Aces, and will not play solo, he can call for a King in the same manner as for an Ace.

If all pass, then the player who holds Spadilla is compelled to play a forcée simple; that is, to call for an Ace, the holder of which becomes his partner or friend.

ALERT!

If, when a solo is played, any of the three opponents lead or play a card out of turn, or expose a card, they all equally lose the game. There is no penalty for the solo player if he commits any of these errors.

The bidding is done in this manner: Suppose A has a hand good for playing a solo in Hearts. He says "I ask." B asks "Is it in couleur?" A answers "Yes." B says "Is it solo?" A answers "Yes." B again asks "Is it solo in couleur?" A replies "No," and therefore passes. B then has the say, and unless either C or D can bid a tout, B must play solo in couleur. A player is compelled to play at least the game he bids.

Following the Bidding

After the bidding has been concluded, the eldest hand leads any card he chooses. The player to his left plays a card to it, and so on in rotation until each player has played a card to the lead. The four cards thus played constitute a trick. The highest card of the suit led wins the trick. Trumps win other suits. Suit must be followed, except with Matadores. If suit cannot be followed, trumping is optional. The winner of the trick leads to the next, and so on.

Rules of the Game

1. The deal is determined by one of the players delivering a card face up to each player in rotation, beginning to his left. The player to whom the first Club falls is dealer.
2. After the dealer has shuffled the cards, and the pack has been cut by the player to his right, he delivers to each player in rotation, beginning with the player to his left, eight cards: three and two and three at a time. After the first hand has been played, the deal passes in rotation to the left.

3. If the dealer deals without having the pack properly cut; or if he exposes any of the cards of the other players, or if he gives any player too few or too many cards; or if a card is faced in the pack, there must be a fresh deal.

4. A player who has once passed cannot afterward bid to play that deal.

5. If a player asks, he must play, unless he is superseded by a higher bid.

6. If all the players pass, the holder of Spadilla is forced to call for an Ace, and play with his friend against the other two players.

7. If a player passes, having Spadilla and Basta in his hand, unless solo or a higher bid has already been made, he must pay a forfeit or béte, and a new deal ensues.

8. If a solo player leads a card before naming the trump, it is assumed that he means to play in couleur, and he must so play.

9. If a player, having made the first five tricks, leads his sixth card, he is bound to play for tout, or all the tricks, with all the payments that tout involves. If he make all the tricks, he is paid for all. If he fails to make all the tricks, he loses all.

10. If, when a solo is played, any of the three opponents lead or play a card out of turn, or expose a card, they all equally lose the game. There is no penalty for the solo player if he commits any of these errors.

11. If the game is played with a called Ace, two against two, and any player commits either of the errors enumerated in Rule #10, he and his partner equally forfeit the game, the guilty player alone paying a béte into the pool.

12. If a player calls for the Ace of a suit of which he has none, he must announce that fact before he plays. If he fails to announce it, he loses the game at once.

13. If a player has announced that he has none of the suit of the called Ace, he is at liberty to trump or overtrump the trick to which the called Ace has been played.

14. The holder of a called Ace must play it at the first opportunity.

15. Each player must follow suit, if possible. If a suit is led, and any player having a card of that suit should play a card of another suit to it, and the trick has been turned and quitted, that constitutes a revoke. However, a player is entitled to renege or reserve a Matadore when a lower trump is led, and also to renege a higher Matadore when a lower one is led; but a

higher Matadore when led always forces the lower one, when the latter is unguarded.

16. If a player revokes when not entitled, or reneges when not entitled, his side forfeits the game.

Speculation

Rating: 12+

This game is played with a deck of fifty-two cards. Any number of people may play—if you have a lot of people, you may wish to play with two or more decks. Determine the deal by giving one card to each person. If no one receives a Jack, again give one card to each player. The first person to receive a Jack has the deal. Before the cards are dealt, the players each stake a sum agreed on to form a pool. The dealer stakes double.

The dealer gives three cards, face down, to each player in rotation, beginning with the eldest hand (the player to his left), and then turns up the top card of the stock for trumps.

FACT

Speculation was a very popular parlor game in the nineteenth century. In fact, it is mentioned in several books of the time, including novels by Charles Dickens and Jane Austen.

The eldest hand then turns up one of his cards. If it is not a trump, or is a smaller trump than the turnup, it is of no value. The next player to the left then turns up a card, and so on, until a higher trump than the turnup appears. The cards rank Ace (highest), King, Queen, Jack, Ten, and so on, down to the Two (lowest).

The player who shows a better trump than the turnup may sell it, if a price is offered that he approves. If more than one player desires to buy, the card is sold to the highest bidder. If the player does not approve the offered price, or there are no bidders, the player keeps the card. The others then turn up their cards. The holder of the highest trump shown (whether by purchase, or by not being able to sell) does not turn up again until his card is beaten by a higher trump. This higher trump may be kept or sold, and the holder of it is similarly exempt from turning up. The dealer does not turn up any of his cards until the trump card is beaten. The player who turns up or purchases the highest trump takes the pool.

If a player looks at his card out of turn or when he is not entitled to look at it, he cannot take the pool.

Speculation is not confined to the cards shown. The trump card may be bought or kept either before or after it is turned up. If it is sold, the dealer turns up, and the purchaser is exempt until the card is beaten. Unseen cards or hands may be speculated upon. This is frequently done toward the end of a hand, either when no high trump has been turned, or by the possessor of a high trump, to prevent its being beaten.

Sometimes, when a player turns up a Jack or a Five, he is required to pay a chip to the pool. If this rule is adopted, and the card has been purchased unseen, the buyer has to pay instead of the holder.

When the Ace of trumps is turned, the hand is ended, and the holder or purchaser (if it was an unseen card) takes the pool. When no trump is turned from any of the hands, the dealer or purchaser of the turnup card takes the pool.

Sometimes an extra hand is dealt, which is turned up when all other hands have been shown. If the extra hand has the best trump, the pool remains for the next deal, and the players contribute again, so the pool is doubled.

Spoil Five

Rating: 12+

This game is played with a complete pack of fifty-two cards. Any number may play, from three to ten, but five make the best game. The object of the game is for a player to win a minimum of three tricks, or to block other players from doing so.

The Pool

Before play begins, each player pays to the pool a certain sum or number of chips agreed on. Should the game be won in that deal, the winner takes the pool; but if a spoil occurs, the pool remains, and each player puts an additional sum (generally a half or a third of the original stake) into the pool. This is repeated after every spoil until a game is won.

Dealing

The dealer gives five cards to each player in regular rotation, beginning with the eldest hand (the player to the left of the dealer). The cards must be distributed first two at a time, and then three at a time.

After the dealer serves five cards to each player, one card from the top of the pack is turned face up and placed on top of the stock. This card determines the trump, and is called the trump card. After the first hand is played, each player takes the deal in succession, beginning with the eldest hand.

Robbing

If the turnup card is an Ace the dealer has the privilege of *robbing*, which means he may discard any card from his hand in exchange for the Ace that was turned up. If the dealer chooses to rob, he must discard before the eldest hand plays, but will not pick up the Ace until it is his turn to play the first trick. The dealer places his discard face down on the table or under the pack. The suit to which the Ace belongs still remains the trump suit.

If an Ace is not turned up, and any player holds the Ace of the trump suit in his hand, that player must rob; that is, he must discard a card from his hand, and take in the turnup. A player is not bound to declare that he is about to rob until it is his turn to play, but he must declare the rob before he plays his first card. The usual way of making the declaration is to place the rejected card face down on the table. If the player neglects to do this before he plays, the power of robbing becomes void, and he is liable to a penalty. No one is allowed to inspect the card put out in robbing.

After robbing, the dealer may employ the turn-up card to trump the first trick, or he may use it to follow suit to a trump that has been led by the eldest hand. No other player has this privilege.

ALERT!

You will forfeit the pool if you do any of these things: rob without the Ace, lead or play out of turn, lead without waiting for the completion of the trick, expose a card, omit to play to a trick, revoke when not entitled, renege when not entitled, or play to the first trick with too many or too few cards in your hand.

Each player plays one card at a time in rotation, beginning with the eldest hand. The player of the highest Spoil Five card wins the trick (please see the following section, "Rank of the Cards"). Trumps win other suits. The winner of the trick leads to the next, and so on until the hand is played out, or until one player wins three tricks. A player who wins three tricks in one hand wins the game. If no one wins three tricks, the game is said to be *spoiled.*

Rank of the Cards

The rank of the cards differs in the red and black suits, and again in the trump suit. In *suits that are not trumps,* the order of the cards is as follows, beginning with the highest:

Red Suits When Not Trumps: King, Queen, Jack, Ten, Nine, Eight, Seven, Six, Five, Four, Three, Two, Ace. The Ace of Hearts always ranks as a trump. Therefore, in the above-mentioned order for red suits when not trumps, the Ace of Hearts must be omitted from the Heart suit.

Black Suits When Not Trumps: King, Queen, Jack, Ace, Two, Three, Four, Five, Six, Seven, Eight, Nine, Ten. The order of the cards below the Jack is thus commonly expressed as "The highest in Red and the lowest in Black."

In the trump suit, which includes the Ace of Hearts, the rank of the cards is as follows, beginning with the highest:

Red Suits When Trumps: Five, Jack, Ace of Hearts, Ace of trumps, King, Queen, Ten, Nine, Eight, Seven, Six, Four, Three, Two.

Black Suits When Trumps: Five, Jack, Ace of Hearts, Ace of trumps, King, Queen, Two, Three, Four, Six, Seven, Eight, Nine, Ten.

The order of the cards in trumps below the Jack adheres to the rule "The highest in Red and lowest in Black." Of course when Hearts are trumps there is only one Ace in the trump suit. It is as though the Ace of Hearts were thrust into all other trump suits, between the Jack and the Ace of that suit.

Reneging

The Five of trumps, Jack of trumps, and Ace of Hearts may *renege;* that is, they are exempt from following suit when an inferior trump is led.

The Five of trumps may renege to any trump led. No trump can renege when the Five is led.

The Jack of trumps can renege to any trump led except to the one superior to it, the Five. If the Five is played (not led) the Jack can renege. If the Jack is led, no trump can renege except the Five.

FACT

Similarly, the Ace of Hearts can renege to any trump led, except to the trumps superior to it, including the Five and the Jack. If the Ace of Hearts is led when Hearts are trumps, the Five and Jack are entitled to renege. If the Ace of Hearts is led when hearts are not trumps, a player holding no trump need not play a Heart.

Jinking

Sometimes, by mutual agreement, *jinking* is allowed. A jink is when a player plays for and wins all five tricks. The winner is paid not only the pool, but also the amount originally staked by each player.

When jinking is allowed, and a player, having won three tricks, continues to play for a jink but fails to win every trick, he scores nothing that hand. Therefore, he cannot win the game that deal. It is optional on the player's part whether he will run the risk of scoring nothing for the chance of obtaining a jink.

Whist

Rating: 12+

Whist is played by four people, with a pack of fifty-two cards, which rank as follows: Ace (highest), King, Queen, Jack, Ten, Nine, Eight, Seven, Six, Five, Four, Three, and Two (the lowest). The four players divide themselves into two teams, each player sitting opposite his partner. The teams are determined by cutting; the players who hold the two highest and the two lowest cards become partners.

Beginning with the player to his left, the dealer delivers one card at a time to each player in rotation, until the whole pack is dealt out (each player will be holding thirteen cards, and the dealer will have twelve). The last card, which is the trump card, is turned face up on the table, where it remains until the dealer plays the first trick. The dealer should then, before playing, take the trump card into his hand.

Playing

When the deal is completed, and the players have arranged their cards, the eldest hand (the player to the left of the dealer) leads any cards he pleases. Each player plays a card to the lead, and the highest card of the suit led wins the trick. Trumps win all other suits. Each player must follow suit if he can, but if unable to follow suit, may play any card he chooses. The winner of the trick leads to the next, and so on, until the thirteen tricks are played. A second deal then occurs, the eldest hand having the deal, and so the game proceeds.

The Rules of the Game

1. The rubber is the best of three games. If the first two games are won by the same players, the third game is not played.
2. A game consists of 7 points. Each trick above eight counts for 1 point.
3. Honors (Ace, King, Queen, and Jack of trumps) are counted as follows: If a player and his partner, either separately or conjointly, hold the four honors, they score 4 points; any three honors, they score 2 points; only two honors, they do not score.

4. Players who, at the beginning of a deal, have 6 points, cannot score honors.

5. The penalty for a revoke takes precedence over all other scores. Tricks score next; honors last.

6. Honors, unless claimed before the trump card of the following deal is turned up, cannot be scored.

7. Honors must be called at the end of the hand; if so called, they may be scored at any time during the game.

8. The winners gain 3 points when their adversaries have not scored; 2 points, when their adversaries have scored less than 3 points; or 1 point, when their adversaries have scored 3 or 4.

9. The winners of the rubber gain 2 points (commonly called the rubber points), in addition to the value of their games.

10. Should the rubber have consisted of three games, the value of the losers' game is deducted from the gross number of points gained by their opponents.

11. If there are more than four candidates, the players are selected by cutting, those first in the room having the preference. The four who cut the lowest cards play first, and again cut to decide on partners; the two lowest play against the two highest. The lowest is the dealer, who has choice of cards and seats, and, having once made his selection, must abide by it.

12. When there are more than six candidates, those who cut the two next lowest cards belong to the table, which is complete with six players; on the retirement of one of those six players, the candidate who cuts the next lowest card has a prior right to any latecomer to enter the table.

13. At the end of a rubber, should admission be claimed by any one or by two candidates, he who has (or they who have) played a greater number of consecutive rubbers than the others is (or are) out; but when all have played the same number, they must cut to decide who will go out. The highest are out.

14. Any one quitting a table prior to the conclusion of a rubber may, with consent of the other three players, appoint a substitute in his absence during that rubber.

15. The pack must be shuffled neither below the table nor so that the face of any card be seen.

16. The pack must not be shuffled during the play of the hand.

17. Each player after shuffling must place the cards, properly collected and face down, to the left of the player about to deal.

18. The dealer always has the right to shuffle last; but should a card or cards be seen during his shuffling or while giving the pack to be cut, he may be compelled to reshuffle.

19. The player on the dealer's right cuts the pack, and in dividing it must not leave fewer than four cards in either packet; if in cutting, or in replacing one of the two packets on the other, a card be exposed, or if there is any confusion of the cards, or a doubt as to the exact place in which the pack was divided, there must be a fresh cut.

20. If, while dealing, a card is exposed by the dealer or his partner, should neither of the adversaries have touched the cards, the latter can claim a new deal. A card exposed by either adversary gives that claim to the dealer, provided that his partner has not touched a card; if a new deal does not take place, the exposed card cannot be called.

21. If, during dealing, a player touches any of his cards, the adversaries may do the same, without losing their privilege of claiming a new deal, should chance give them such option.

22. If a player, while dealing, looks at the trump card, his adversaries have a right to see it, and may exact a new deal.

23. A misdeal loses the deal. It is a misdeal unless the cards are dealt into four packets, one at a time in regular rotation, beginning with the player to the dealer's left. It is also a misdeal should the dealer place the trump card, face down, on his own or any other pack; should the trump card not come in its regular order to the dealer (but he does not lose his deal if the pack be proved imperfect); should a player have fourteen cards, and either of the other three less than thirteen; should the dealer, under an impression that he has made a mistake, either count the cards on the table or the remainder of the pack; should the dealer deal two cards at once, or two cards to the same hand, and then deal a third; or, should the dealer omit to have the pack cut to him, and the adversaries discover the error, prior to the trump card being turned up, and before looking at their cards, but not after having done so.

24. A misdeal does not lose the deal if, during the dealing, either of the adversaries touches the cards prior to the dealer's partner having done

so; but should the latter have first interfered with the cards, notwithstanding either or both of the adversaries have subsequently done the same, the deal is lost.

25. Should three players have their right number of cards but the fourth have less than thirteen, and not discover such deficiency until he has played any of his cards, the deal stands good; should he have played, he is answerable for any revoke he may have made as if the missing card, or cards, had been in his hand; he may search the other pack for it, or them.

26. If a pack, during or after a rubber, be proved incorrect or imperfect, that hand in which the imperfection was detected is void. All other hands stand good.

27. The dealer, when it is his turn to play to the first trick, should take the trump card into his hand. If left on the table after the first trick be turned, it is liable to be called; his partner may at any time remind him of the liability.

28. After the dealer has taken the trump card into his hand, it cannot be asked for; a player naming it at any time during the play of that hand is liable to have his highest or lowest trump called. However, anyone may inquire what the trump suit is, at any time.

29. If the dealer takes the trump card into his hand before it is his turn to play, he may be desired to lay it on the table; should he show a wrong card, this card may be called, as also a second, a third, etc., until the trump card be produced.

30. If the dealer declares himself unable to recollect the trump card, his highest or lowest trump may be called at any time during that hand, and unless it causes him to revoke, must be played; the call may be repeated, but not changed, i.e., from highest to lowest, or vice versa, until such card is played.

31. All exposed cards are liable to be called, and must be left on the table; but a card is not an exposed card when dropped on the floor, or elsewhere below the table. The following are exposed cards: two or more cards played at once; any card dropped face up, or in any way exposed on or above the table, even if it is snatched up so quickly that no one can name it.

32. If anyone plays to an imperfect trick the best card on the table, or leads

one that is a winning card as against his adversaries, and then leads again, or plays several such winning cards, one after the other, without waiting for his partner to play, the latter may be called on to win, if he can, the first or any other of those tricks, and the other cards thus improperly played are exposed cards.

33. If a player, or players, under the impression that the game is lost or won, or for other reasons, throw his or their cards on the table and expose them, their adversary has the right to call it; if a player retains his hand, he cannot be forced to abandon it.

34. If all four players throw their cards on the table, the hands are abandoned, and no one can again take up his cards. Should this general exhibition show that the game might have been saved or won, neither claim can be entertained, unless a revoke is established. The revoking players are then liable to the following penalties: They cannot under any circumstances win the game by the result of that hand, and the adversaries may add three to their score, or deduct three from that of the revoking players.

35. A card detached from the rest of the hand so as to be named is liable to be called; but should the adversary name a wrong card, he is liable to have a suit called when he or his partner have the lead.

36. If a player who has rendered himself liable to have the highest or lowest of a suit called fails to play as desired, or if when called on to lead one suit, leads another, having in his hand one or more cards of that suit demanded, he incurs the penalty of a revoke.

37. If any player leads out of turn, his adversaries may either call the card erroneously led, or may call a suit from the player or his partner when it is next the turn of either of them to lead.

38. If any player leads out of turn, and the other three have followed him, the trick is complete, and the error cannot be rectified; but if only the second, or the second and third have played to the false lead, their cards, on discovery of the mistake, are taken back. There is no penalty against anyone except the original offender, whose card may be called—or he, or his partner, when either of them next has the lead, may be compelled to play any suit demanded by the adversaries.

39. In no case can a player be compelled to play a card that would oblige him to revoke.

40. The call of a card may be repeated until such card has been played.

41. If a player called on to lead a suit has none of it, the penalty is paid.

42. If the third hand plays before the second, the fourth hand may play before his partner.

43. Should the third hand not have played, and the fourth play before his partner, the latter may be called on to win or not to win the trick.

44. If anyone omits playing to a former trick, and it is not discovered until he has played to the next, the adversaries may claim a new deal; should they decide that the deal stands good, the surplus card at the end of the hand is considered to have been played to the imperfect trick, but does not constitute a revoke.

45. If anyone plays two cards to the same trick, or mixes his trump or other card, with a trick to which it does not properly belong, and the mistake is not discovered until the hand is played out, he is answerable for all consequent revokes he may have made. If, during the play of the hand, the error is detected, the tricks may be counted face down, in order to ascertain whether there are too many cards; should this be the case, they may be searched, and the card restored. The player is liable for all revokes that he may have made.

46. The penalty for a revoke is at the option of the adversaries who, at the end of the hand, may take three tricks from the revoking player, or deduct 3 points from his score, or add 3 to their own score. Penalty can be claimed for as many revokes as occur during the hand; is applicable only to the score of the game in which it occurs; cannot be divided, i.e., a player cannot add 1 or 2 to his own score and deduct 1 or 2 from the revoking player; or takes precedence of every other score.

47. At the end of the hand, the claimants of a revoke may search all the tricks.

48. If a player discovers his mistake in time to save a revoke, the adversaries, whenever they think fit, may call the card thus played in error, or may require him to play his highest or lowest card to that trick, in which he has renounced; any player or players who have played him may withdraw their cards and substitute others. The cards withdrawn are not liable to be called.

49. If a revoke is claimed, and the accused player or his partner mix the cards before they have been sufficiently examined by the adversaries,

the revoke is established. The mixing of the cards only renders the proof of a revoke difficult, but does not prevent the claim, and possible establishment, of the penalty.

50. A revoke cannot be claimed after the cards have been cut for the following deal.

51. The revoking player and his partner may, under all circumstances, require the hand in which the revoke has been detected to be played out.

52. In whatever way the penalty is enforced, under no circumstances can a player win the game by the result of the hand during which he has revoked; and, he cannot score more than 4 points.

53. Anyone during the play of the trick, or after the four cards are played and before they are touched, may demand that the cards be placed before their respective players.

54. If any one, prior to his partner playing, should call attention to the trick—either by saying that it is his, or by naming his card, or, without being required to do so, by drawing it toward him—the adversaries may require that opponent's partner to play the highest or lowest of the suit then led, or to win or lose the trick.

55. In all cases where a penalty has been incurred, the offender is bound to give reasonable time for the decision of his adversaries.

56. Any player may demand to see the last trick turned, and no more. Under no circumstances can more than eight cards be seen during the play of the hand, including the four cards on the table that have not been turned and quitted, and the last trick turned.

Chapter 8

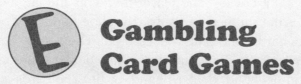

Gambling Card Games

If you're looking for a game that is a little more challenging and has the added element of excitement, look no further. This chapter contains the most common gambling games. Whether you play for money or peanuts, you will feel the thrill of heightening the competitiveness of play. Adults only, please.

Baccarat

Rating: Adult

Baccarat is a casino card game played by high rollers. The object of the game is to get as close to nine as possible. The dealer shuffles the cards (usually about six to eight decks). The player then cuts the large deck in half. The dealer places the shuffled cards into the shoe (a dealing box that holds several decks of cards) and pulls one card out. The dealer then passes the shoe to the players, who draw out cards as the dealer instructs. Each player places a bet on his hand, dealer's hand, or tie. The cards are then shown. The one closest to nine wins. Cards are counted as follows:

Two through Nine count at face value
Ten and face cards 0 points
Ace counts for 1 point

If the total is more than nine, the last digit is what counts; for example, Five of Hearts + Five of Diamonds = 0. If the total is nine, the holder of the cards wins. If the player holds less than six, he draws. The dealer draws when holding zero to 2 points and stands at 7; between 3 and 6, whether the dealer draws depends on what the player does.

Poker

Rating: Adult

There are many varieties of poker, and we've chosen two of the most popular ones to list here: draw poker and straight poker. All are played with a regular pack of fifty-two cards, and by any number of persons from two to six. Many of the games can be easily modified to include more players. The object of the game is for a player to have the best hand at the table.

Draw Poker

Before the dealer begins to deal the cards, the eldest hand (the player to the left of the dealer) must deposit in the pool an *ante* not exceeding one-half the limit previously agreed upon; this is called a *blind*. The dealer then gives five cards to each player, one at a time, beginning with the eldest hand.

Going In on the Original Hand

After the cards are dealt, the players look at their hands. Each player, beginning with the player to the left of the eldest hand, determines whether he will *go in* (to play for the pool) or not. Any player who decides to go in must put into the pool double the amount of the ante, except the eldest hand, who contributes the same amount as his original ante.

Those who pass throw their cards face down on the table in front of the dealer.

ALERT!

If the dealer delivers more or less than five cards, and a player does not realize this before reviewing his hand, no misdeal occurs, and the player must sit out that game.

Any player—when it is his turn, and after contributing his ante—may increase the ante (called a *raise*) any amount within the previously agreed limit of the game. The next player, after making good the ante and raise (depositing those amounts into the pool), may then also raise it any amount within the limit, and so on.

Players who raise the ante must do so in rotation, going around to the left. Any player who remains in to play must put in the pool whatever amount will make his stake equal to the increase, or abandon all that he has already contributed to the pool.

Straddling

Another feature that may be introduced when betting on the original hand is the *straddle*. The straddle is nothing more than a double blind. For example:

A, B, C, D, and E play. A deals. B, the eldest hand, antes one chip. C can straddle B's ante by putting two chips in the pool, provided he does so before the cards are cut for the deal. D may double the straddle by putting in four chips, and so on up to the eldest hand, provided the bets do not exceed the limit.

The straddle gives a player the first opportunity to be the last in before the draw. After the draw, the player to the left of the eldest hand must make the first bet, provided he remains in. A good player very rarely straddles.

Filling the Hands

After the bidding, each player has the right to draw any number of cards he chooses, from one to five, or he can retain his cards as originally dealt to him. If a player draws cards, he must discard a like number from his original hand, and he must place the rejected cards face down on the table near the next dealer.

FACT

None but the eldest hand has the privilege of going a blind. The party to the left of the eldest hand may double the blind. The next player may straddle it, the next double the straddle, and so on, but the amount of the straddle, when made good, must not exceed the limit of the game.

The dealer asks each player in rotation, beginning with the eldest hand, how many cards he wants. When the player has discarded, the dealer gives the number requested from the top of the pack. When the other hands have been helped, the dealer, if he has gone in and wants cards, then helps himself last.

Betting, Raising, and Calling

When all the hands are filled, the player to the left of the eldest hand has the first say, and he must either bet or retire from the game, forfeiting what he has already staked. The other players must do the same in rotation, up to the eldest hand.

When a player makes a bet, the next player must *see him,* by putting an equal amount of chips in the pool, or *better* by raising the bet any amount not exceeding the limit, or he must pass out of the game. This continues either until one player drives all the others out of the game, and takes the pool without showing his hand, or until all the other players who remain in see the last raise (no one going better) and *call* the player who made the last raise. When a call is made, the players remaining in all show their hands, and the strongest hand takes the pool.

Rank of the Hands

The rank of the hands is as follows, beginning with the lowest:

1. *One Pair* (accompanied by three cards of different denominations). If two players each hold a pair, the highest pair wins; if the two are similar, the highest additional card wins.
2. *Two Pair* (accompanied by a card of another denomination).
3. *Triples.* The highest three of a kind win. Triples beat two pairs.
4. *Straight.* A sequence of five cards not all of the same suit. An Ace may either begin or end a straight. For example: Ace, King, Queen, Jack, Ten is the highest straight. Five, Four, Three, Two, Ace, is the lowest straight. If more than one player holds a straight, the straight headed by the highest card wins. A straight will beat three of a kind.

Sometimes straights are not played. At the beginning of the game you should determine whether to admit them. If straights are counted, a straight flush outranks four cards of the same denomination.

5. *Flush.* Five cards of the same suit, not in sequence. If more than one player holds a flush, the flush holding the highest card wins; if the highest cards tie, the next highest cards in those two hands wins. A flush will beat a straight, and three of a kind.
6. *Full House.* Three cards of the same denominations and a pair. If more than one player holds a full house, the highest three of a kind wins. A full house will beat a flush.
7. *Four of a Kind.* Four cards of the same denomination, accompanied by any other card. If more than one player holds fours, the highest fours wins. When straights are not played, fours beat a straight flush.

8. *Straight Flush.* A sequence of five cards, all of the same suit. If more than one player holds a straight flush, the hand headed by the highest card wins. When straights are not played, the straight flush does not rank higher than a common flush, but when straights are played, it is the highest hand that can be held, and beats four of a kind.

When none of the foregoing hands are shown, the highest card wins; if these tie, the next highest in those two hands, and so on. If two or more players hold hands identical in value, and those hands are the best out, the players divide the pool equally.

Rules of the Game

1. The deal is determined by giving one card to each player; the player who gets the lowest card deals.
2. In determining the deal, the Ace is lowest and the King highest. Ties are determined by cutting.
3. The cards must be shuffled above the table; each player has a right to shuffle the cards, but the dealer shuffles last.
4. The player to the right of the dealer must cut the cards.
5. The dealer must give each player one card at a time, in rotation, beginning to his left, and in this order he must deliver five cards to each player.
6. If the dealer deals without having the pack properly cut, or if a card is faced in the pack, there must be a fresh deal. The cards are reshuffled and recut, and the dealer deals again.
7. If a card is exposed during dealing, the player to whom such card is dealt must accept it as though it had not been exposed.
8. If the dealer delivers more or less than five cards, and a player discovers and announces the fact before he picks up his hand, it is a misdeal. The cards are reshuffled and recut, and the dealer deals again. .
9. After the first hand the deal proceeds in rotation, beginning with the player to the left of the dealer.
10. After the deal has been completed, each player who remains in the game may discard from his hand as many cards as he chooses, or his whole hand, and the dealer gives him an equal number from the top of the remaining pack. The eldest hand must discard first, and so on in regular rotation around to the dealer, who discards last.

11. Any player, after having asked for fresh cards, must take the exact number called for; and after cards have once been discarded, they must not again be taken in hand.

12. Should the dealer give any player more cards than the player has demanded, and the player discover and announce the fact before raising his cards, the dealer must withdraw the superfluous cards and restore them to the pack. But if the player looks at the cards before informing the dealer of the mistake, he must retire from the hand. The same rule holds true if the dealer gives fewer cards.

13. If the dealer exposes one or more cards when refreshing any player's hand, the dealer must place the exposed cards on the bottom of the pack and give to the player a corresponding number from the top of the pack, before serving the next player.

14. In opening the pool before the cards are dealt, the eldest hand makes the first ante, which must not exceed one-half the limit. After the cards are dealt, every player in his proper turn, beginning with the player to the left of the eldest hand, must make this ante good by depositing double the amount in the pool, or retire from that hand.

15. After the hands are filled, any player who remains in the game may, in his proper turn, beginning with the player to the left of the eldest hand, bet or raise the pool any amount not exceeding the limit of the game.

16. After the draw has been made, the eldest hand has the privilege of deferring his say until after all the other players have made their bets or passed. The eldest hand is the last player to declare whether he will play or pass. If, however, the eldest hand passes out of the game before the draw, then the next player to his left in play must make the first bet or, failing to bet, must pass out of the game.

17. If a player, in his regular turn, bets or raises a bet any amount not exceeding the limit of the game, his adversaries must either call him, go better, or retire from the game for that hand. When a player makes a bet, he must deposit the amount in the pool.

18. If a player makes good (or sees) a bet and calls for a show of hands, each player must show his entire hand, and the best poker hand wins the pool.

19. If a player bets or raises a bet and no other player goes better or calls him, he wins the pool and is not compelled to show his hand.

20. Upon a show of hands, if a player miscalls his hand, he does not lose the pool for that reason, because every hand shows for itself.

21. Any player betting with more or less than five cards in his hand loses the pool, unless his opponents all throw up their hands before discovering the foul hand. If only one player is betting against the foul hand, that player is entitled to the ante and all the money bet; but if there are more than one betting against him, then the best hand among his opponents is entitled to the pool.

22. If the player to the left of the eldest hand declines to straddle a blind, he prevents any other player from doing so.

ALERT!

Don't forget this rule: If a player makes a bet, and an adversary raises him, and the player who made the previous bet does not have enough chips to see the raise, the player can put up all the chips he may have and call for a show of cards. If the player calling for a show has the best hand, he wins the ante, and an amount from each player who bets over him, equal to the sum that he himself has bet.

Straight Poker

Straight poker, or bluff, as it is sometimes called, is played with a pack of fifty-two cards. The game is governed by the same rules as draw poker, except for the following variations:

1. The winner of the pool has the next deal.
2. Each player antes before the cards are dealt.
3. Any player may pass from the game, but only before the cards are dealt.
4. No player is permitted to draw or discard any cards from his original hand.

Twenty-One

Rating: Adult

Twenty-one, also known as blackjack, may be played by any number of players. Use a pack of fifty-two cards for this game. The Tens and court cards are each worth 10 points, and the other cards according to their pips. The Ace in each suit may be valued as 1 or 11, at the option of the holder, according to the requirement of his hand.

Dealing and Betting

When the players have taken their seats, one player shuffles the pack, and (after having it cut by the player to his right) deals a card face up to each player in rotation, beginning to his left. The player to receive the first Ace becomes the dealer.

After the deal is determined and the cards are shuffled and cut, the players make their stakes into the pool. It is sometimes agreed that the players may all look at the first card dealt to them before making their bets. The dealer also has the privilege of seeing his first card, and may insist on all the players doubling their bets.

The dealer, holding the pack face down, takes the top card and places it upon the bottom of the pack. This is called the *burnt card,* or *brulet.* The dealer then delivers one card, face down, to each player in rotation, beginning to his left. He repeats this operation one more time, giving each player a total of two cards.

Playing

The players all examine their hands, and the dealer asks each in rotation, the eldest hand (the player to the left of the dealer) first, whether he will take any cards. If you are satisfied with your hand, you say "Stay," and place your hand upon the table, face down. If you are not content with your hand, you call for a card, saying "Hit me." The dealer then deals you a card face up on the table, and again asks, "Are you content?" This continues until you are satisfied with your hand. The dealer repeats this operation for each player.

If the count of the pips in your entire hand is more than twenty-one, you throw your hand face down, and are out of the hand. When you overdraw, you *bust*.

After all the players have stood or drawn, or quit, the dealer exposes his hand, and either stands or draws. If he overdraws, he pays, according to the sums staked, to each player who has not overdrawn. If he stands, or draws so that his hand does not exceed twenty-one, he receives from or pays to each player in rotation. The player whose cards amount most nearly to twenty-one wins the game. Players who have to pay the dealer throw their cards in the middle of the table without showing them. Players who claim anything from the dealer show their cards. Ties stand off, meaning no one pays the other.

A player or dealer who has a pair dealt may draw and stake on each separately. Cards worth 10 points can only pair with cards of the same denomination; that is, Kings with Kings.

If a player has an Ace and a court card dealt him, which totals twenty-one (called a *natural twenty-one),* he turns his hand face up on the table and receives double his stake from the dealer. The dealer, however, need not pay until he has looked at his own cards, to see if he also has a natural. When the dealer has a natural, he similarly receives payment (except from the player who also has a natural). In this instance, no one draws, because there is no chance of beating the dealer's hand.

If a player or the dealer has a pair dealt him originally, he may stake and draw on each card separately or not, as he pleases. If he goes on each, he separates the cards and puts a stake on each, and when it comes his turn to draw he says, "I go on each." In this case each party pays and receives on both hands. But if a natural occurs in a double hand, the holder receives only a single stake on each, because to obtain a natural only the first two cards may be counted.

Rules of the Game

1. Only the dealer has a right to shuffle. The cards remaining undealt may not be reshuffled.
2. In cutting, at least four cards must be separated.
3. If a card is exposed in cutting or in reuniting the cut packets, or if there is any confusion of the cards, the pack must be reshuffled and cut again.
4. If two cards are dealt together to one player, the mistake may be rectified before a third card is dealt. But if a third card is dealt before the error is discovered, the player who has the surplus card, having looked at his hand, must reject one card and give it, face down, back to the dealer.
5. If a card is exposed in dealing, the player may keep it or reject it; if he rejects it, the rejected card is given to the dealer. If the dealer exposes one of his own cards, he must keep it.
6. Drawn cards must be dealt one at a time, face up on the table. Each player in rotation must be content before the next can draw a card. In drawing separately on split cards, the player must be content on one card before drawing on another.
7. If two drawn cards are dealt together, the player may keep either or both. If he keeps only one, he cannot draw another card.
8. If the dealer in drawing gives himself two cards together, he must keep them both.
9. If a player is missed in dealing or drawing, he may have his hand completed from the pack, or may give up the hand.
10. If the dealer in dealing misses himself and a player draws cards before the error is discovered, the dealer must pay to each player the amount of his stake, and double to the natural. If the error is discovered before any cards are drawn, the dealer may complete his hand from the top of the pack, and there is no penalty.
11. The burnt card must not be dealt or drawn.
12. If a player (not the dealer) holds a natural twenty-one, it puts the dealer out. The holder of a natural has the next deal, except if it is the first hand of the deal, or the dealer also has a natural.
13. Each player is bound to place his stake in front of him, before a card is dealt. When content with his hand, he puts it face down on the table, and places his stake on top of it. No stake can be withdrawn, added to,

or lessened after it has been made, but must be allowed to remain until the dealer declares his stand.

14. When the dealer and a player tie, the two cancel or stand off, and neither receives from or pays to the other.

15. When all the players have stood or drawn, the dealer exposes his hand on the table.

16. A natural twenty-one must consist of an Ace and a card worth 10 points dealt in the first two rounds. The dealer pays to and receives from a player for a natural, unless a tie should occur. In case of a double hand, an Ace and a tenth card form acquired and not natural twenty-ones, and receive and pay only single stakes.

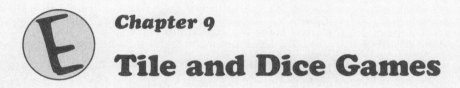

Chapter 9

Tile and Dice Games

The and dice games are a little more obscure than the classic board and card games—and that's all the more reason for you to learn to play them! Introduce these to your friends and family and add a little variety to your regular stockpile of games to play.

Bunco

Rating: 8+

Bunco is a game of dice played by teams. Players divide into groups (usually twelve players divide into groups of four, but you can adjust for the number of players available). Teams sit at three tables (head, middle, and bottom) with teammates sitting opposite one another. Each table gets three dice and a score sheet with pencils. Designate one person to be the scorekeeper. At the end of each round the winners move to the next higher table (bottom goes to middle, middle to head). Losers at the head table go to the bottom.

Playing

The scorekeeper of each table begins play for the round by rolling the dice. Keep rolling until the roll no longer earns points. The player to the left of the scorekeeper then takes a turn, and so on. Play for each round continues until a team at the head table scores at least 21 points. Change partners after each round. Six rounds make up a set, and you play at least two sets. The player with the most wins is the overall winner.

If you find that you enjoy this game, you may want to consider getting a group of friends together and scheduling a regular meeting to play Bunco and socialize. Make the get-together more exciting by offering prizes for games both won and lost.

Scoring

When the number of spots on any of the dice that you roll matches the number of the round you are on, you earn 1 point for each matching die (for example, in round two, a roll such as three, two, two gets 2 points). If you roll three of a kind (of any number), you earn 5 points. If all three dice match the number of the round, you get "Bunco," which counts for 21 points. The scorekeeper declares the winning team at the table after each round.

Dice

Rating: 8+

There are several variations of dice games. Two of the most common variations—classic dice and ace in the pot are explained here. Dice games can usually be played by any number of players. In all dice games the six spot is always high; the one spot is always low. To constitute a fair throw all the dice must be thrown clean from the box and lie flat on the table. The dice, when thrown, must not be touched, until the result of the throw has been noted.

A throw is foul or unfair if one of the dice rolls off the table and falls on the floor; if any of the dice are touched while rolling; if a die is cocked, remaining tilted on edge against another die or other obstruction; or if one die rests flat on the top of another. Foul throws must be thrown over again.

Classic Dice

Each player throws three dice, three times. Add together the sum of the spots to determine your score. If there's a tie, the players may throw another dice and add the new score to the total.

For example: On your first throw the dice show one, four, and six, which added together count eleven. Your second throw is five, two, and three; together, they count ten. Your third throw is two fives and a four, making fourteen. The sum of eleven, ten, and fourteen, which is thirty-five, is your score. The one who scores the highest wins the game.

Ace in the Pot

Give each player two chips (you can also use pennies or checkers). Place some sort of receptacle in the center of the table; this is called the pot. Begin by throwing two dice. If you throw a one, you put one of your chips in the pot. If you throw a six you pass one chip to your left-hand neighbor. None of the other spots have value.

Each player has one throw in regular rotation, provided he possesses a chip, and it goes around until all the chips but one have been played into the pot. At that point, close the pot. The holder of the last chip has three chances to throw a six, which will force him to get rid of his chip by passing it to his neighbor. If the player does that, his neighbor also gets three chances to throw a six, forcing him to pass the chip back. This continues until the last chip holder fails in his three throws to throw a six; he is then declared the winner.

FACT

Another quick and easy dice game to play is twenty-one. The game is played with a single die. Each player throws as many times as necessary to get the sum of the spots equal to or as near as possible to, but not over, twenty-one. The player who gets twenty-one or closest without going over wins.

The pot always has the preference while it is open, so that if you have only one chip and throw a six and a one, you must put the chip in the pot, unless it has been closed.

Dominoes

Rating: 8+

On the face of each domino are two compartments, each of which is either blank or contains a number of black pits, from one to six. The dominoes are called, according to the numbers shown, Double Blank, Blank Ace, Blank Deuce, Blank Trey, Blank Four, Blank Five, Blank Six; Double Ace, Ace Deuce, Ace Trey, Ace Four, Ace Five, Ace Six; Double Deuce, Deuce Trey, Deuce Four, Deuce Five, Deuce Six; Double Trey, Trey Four, Trey Five, Trey Six; Double Four, Four Five, Four Six; Double Five, Five Six; and Double Six—twenty-eight pieces in all. A single pit is called Ace, and Trey means "three"; thus Ace Trey means that one of the compartments has one pit and the other has three. Shuffle the pieces on the table face down. Each player then draws at random the number of dominoes that the game requires. Play the pieces one at a time. Each piece that you play must match the end of a piece that does not join any other.

Most of the games can be played by any number of people. There are various games, but two of the most popular are block and draw.

Block

Each player draws seven dominoes from the pool. The highest double leads in the first hand, and, after that, each player leads alternately until the end of the game. If a player cannot play, the next plays. If neither can play, the set is blocked, and they count the number of spots on the pieces each still holds.

FACT

Dominoes were originally made from pieces of ivory or bone, with ebony backs. Today, you can find them made out of plastic, wood, or other kinds of hard materials.

Whoever has the lowest number of spots adds to his count the number held by his opponents. If there are two players with the same number of spots, and the number is lower than their opponents', there is no count. If anyone is able to play his last piece while his opponents hold theirs, he cries "Domino" and wins the hand, and adds to his count the number of spots that the rest hold. The number required to win the game is 100, but it may be made less by agreement.

Draw

Each player draws seven dominoes. The game has the same rules as block, with one exception: when a player cannot play, he is obliged to draw from the pool until he can play, or has exhausted the stock of pieces.

The player may draw as many pieces as he needs to until he can match. The object of drawing is to enable him to play. Once he has drawn the required piece, play continues as before.

Mahjong

Rating: 12+

A very social game, mahjong can be played by three or four players, each playing individually. Usually, groups of four play this famous tile game. The game is played with dice, 136 symbolic tiles, and chips used for scoring. The object of the game is to collect as many scoring combinations as possible.

The tiles are organized into five suits: Honors, Winds, Bamboos, Circles, and Characters.

Honors	
White Dragon	4 tiles
Green Dragon	4 tiles
Red Dragon	4 tiles
Winds	
East Wind	4 tiles
South Wind	4 tiles
West Wind	4 tiles
North Wind	4 tiles
Bamboos	
Numbered 1 through 9 (4 tiles each)	36 tiles
Circles	
Numbered 1 through 9 (4 tiles each)	36 tiles
Characters	
Numbered 1 through 9 (4 tiles each)	36 tiles

Completing Hands

The object of the game is to complete one's hand (*to mahjong*). A completed hand consists of any four groups of three tiles each and one pair, using fourteen tiles. A group is either *three of a kind* in the same suit or a

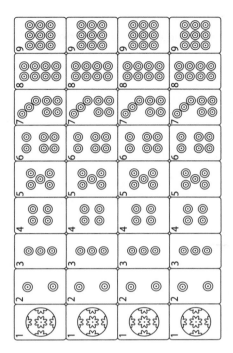

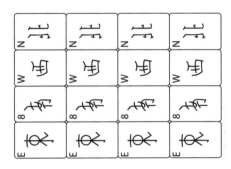

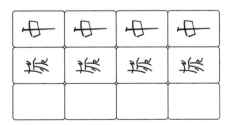

◀ A complete set of mahjong tiles

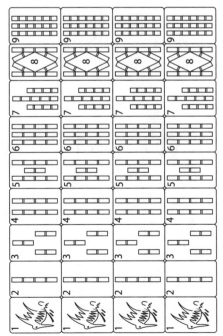

sequence of three tiles in the same suit (Seven, Eight, and Nine Bamboos). The grouping shown is an example of a completed hand. A hand may be completed by *drawing*, *punging*, or *chowing*.

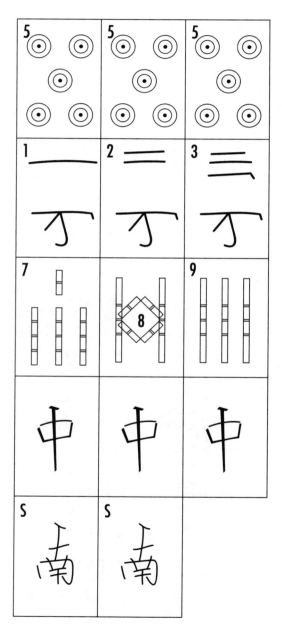

◀ An example of a completed hand

Drawing

This refers to breaking up a wall. Starting with East Wind, each player may draw one tile from the wall, discarding from his hand another tile. Throughout the game, each player must always hold thirteen tiles. Should a tile be drawn that is of no assistance to the player in mahjonging, that tile may be discarded in place of a tile already in the hand.

Punging

This means securing a third tile (or fourth) to any pair (or three of a kind) already held in the hand. Any player, whether in turn or not, who holds a pair (or three of a kind) may *pung* an additional tile immediately after it is discarded by another player. When a player desires a tile just discarded, he calls "Pung!" and positions the two (or three) already in his hand face up to his right along with the newly acquired tile.

After punging, the play continues to the right. The player or players sitting to the right of the player whose discard has been punged lose their turns.

Is it possible to play mahjong with three people?
Yes. In this version of the game, everything stays the same—the players build four walls as usual—but the turn of the absent player is skipped.

Chowing

This refers to securing a third tile to make a sequence group with two already held, when the third tile is discarded by the preceding player on the left. When a player holding two tiles sees he can form a sequence group with the tile just discarded by his opponent to his left, he calls "Chow!" and places the two tiles already held, with the tile discarded, face up to his right. A player may only chow from the player preceding him, unless he requires only one tile to mahjong. In that case he may chow from any player.

Unless a tile is punged or chowed immediately after being discarded, it becomes dead and cannot be used later in the game. Discarded tiles are placed in the center of the table face up, inside the wall, in any random fashion.

Should a player draw a group without punging or chowing, he does not expose these with the groups punged or chowed, but retains them in his hand. This prevents other players from learning how near he is to mahjonging.

Four of a Kind

Any player holding a group of three of a kind in his hand may pung the fourth immediately after it is discarded. This fourth, to the group of three already held, does not count in the thirteen tiles in the hand. It is an extra tile and will increase the score.

When the fourth tile is punged it is placed face up with the other three. However, if any player draws four of a kind during the progress of play he exposes these with the other groups punged or chowed, turning one tile over to indicate that the four tiles were drawn, because groups drawn count for more points than those punged. If the group of four of a kind drawn is not exposed in this manner before someone mahjongs, it will only be counted as a group or three of a kind. When the fourth tile is punged or drawn to a group of three of a kind, this tile does not count in the thirteen tiles held in the hand, and it must be replaced by one of the "loose tiles" on top of the wall.

After punging a third tile to a pair held in the hand, the fourth cannot be punged if discarded by an opponent. However, if the fourth tile is drawn it may be placed with the three already exposed, and a loose tile is then drawn to replace it in the hand.

Precedence

A player who requires only one tile to mahjong has first precedence to a tile discarded, whether this tile is to be used to pung, chow, or make the pair required in a completed hand. This is the only time that a chow has precedence over a pung or that a tile can be chowed from any opponent except the one immediately preceding the player chowing. If two players both desire the same tile discarded, the player who can pung has precedence. If two or three players each require the same tile to mahjong, the player having first turn after the player discarding has precedence.

Draws

Should all tiles be drawn from the wall except the last fourteen tiles, including the loose tiles, all hands are declared dead and of no value. Tiles are reshuffled and a new round or *wind* is dealt. However, the players do not change their seating arrangements.

To Begin

Place the four Winds of Heaven buttons (the small white buttons) face down on the table. Each player selects a button and takes a seat according to the button's designation, East having choice of seats. South then sits to the right of East; West opposite East; and North to the left of East.

FACT

Mahjong is a classic Chinese game. Mahjong literally means *sparrows*. In the past, the Chinese played the game very rapidly, recognizing the various tiles by their feel. The players could discard the tiles so quickly that the playing sounded like a sparrow tapping.

East is always the *banker* for the first table. A *table* consists of four rounds, so that each player has a turn as the banker. When the last player has played East Wind for the fourth time, it is customary to total up chips and settle scores. Any number of rounds may be played, though it is generally customary to allow each player to become and lose East Wind the same number of times.

As the banker, East distributes the chips to all the players, including himself. The value of the chips is arbitrary, but they are usually assigned values according to size.

The banker then follows this method of distribution:

- Two 500-point chips, totaling 1,000 points
- Nine 100-point chips, totaling 900 points
- Eight 10-point chips, totaling 80 points
- Ten 2-point chips, totaling 20 points

After the chips are distributed, each player rolls the dice. The highest throw is the first East Wind. The other players become South Wind, West Wind, and North Wind respectively, according to their seating in reference to the East Wind: South Wind to the right of East Wind, West Wind opposite, and North Wind to the left. The players can then trade their original buttons with each other to remind them of their positions.

Dealing

East Wind and West Wind place the tiles face down on the table and shuffle thoroughly, making sure to remove the extra four blank tiles. Each player then draws thirty-four tiles at random and piles them into a wall that is seventeen tiles long and two tiles high. The interior of the wall becomes the playing field.

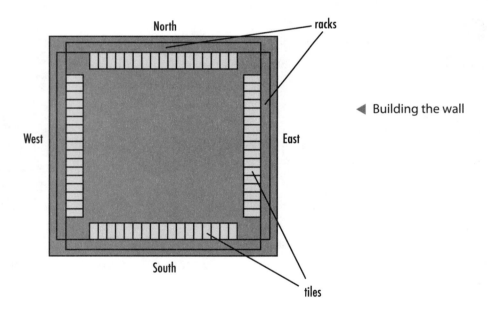

◀ Building the wall

When building the wall, the easiest method is to use two hands. Pick three tiles with the right hand and two tiles with the left, bringing them together to form a row of five. Repeat the same operation, placing the second five on the top of the first five. Then, select three tiles with each hand, this time bringing these together to form a row of six in front of the row of five already built. Repeat, placing the second six on top of the first six. Finally, split this double row of six tiles, carrying three to each end of the five-tile wall, making eleven tiles in this wall. Repeat each step until your wall is complete. This builds a wall of seventeen tiles without making it necessary to count. Push the completed wall forward to position. You may move the entire wall to any part of the table without disturbing its formation by holding the two end bottom tiles and evenly pressing on the bottom tiles inward. Do not press on the top tiles.

Should any player hold more or less than thirteen tiles in his hand during the progress of play and not be mahjong, his hand becomes dead. Play continues, however. When the Wind is finished he must pay all scores and receive nothing. Do not counts any points in his hand.

East Wind then throws the dice. The total number of points thrown designates the player whose wall is to be broken. Starting with himself as one, East Wind counts around the table to his right, stopping at the number of the point thrown. The figure shows the various numbers that may be thrown by East Wind and the corresponding walls to be broken. For example, if the dice added up to seven, then West Wind's wall would be broken.

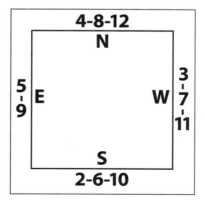

▲ Numbers that may be thrown by the East Wind

The player whose wall is to be broken throws both dice, adding the number thrown to the number previously thrown by East Wind. This designates the point where the break will occur. If East Wind throws seven and then West Wind two, the sum of the two throws designates that the ninth tile (counting from the right) will be the point of break.

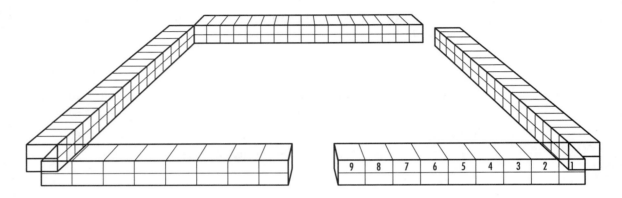

▲ The wall is broken.

These two tiles are known as the loose tiles and are placed on the top of the wall to indicate the end. If, during the progress of the game, these are drawn, the next two tiles are placed on top, and so on.

East Wind draws the first four tiles to the left of the break. South Wind, West Wind, and North Wind (in this order) draw the succeeding four tiles. All players continue to draw four tiles at a time until each has twelve tiles. East Wind then draws the next top tile, South Wind the next bottom tile, West Wind the next top tile, and North Wind the next bottom tile, making thirteen tiles in each hand.

Each player then arranges his hand according to suits, the same as in cards.

East Wind draws the next top tile from the wall and discards from his hand a tile, face up on the table, calling out the number and suit; for example, "Six Bamboo" or "Red Dragon." Each player in turn draws a tile and discards one in place of this until one player completes his hand, or mahjongs.

Scoring

The most important feature of mahjong is scoring a host of combinations. While a player should always try to mahjong, during the progress of the game it may become evident that this will be impossible. While the player who mahjongs collects chips from all the other players and pays none out, the other players pay each other the differences between their scores. A player who does not mahjong but holds good scoring combinations may collect more points than the player who mahjongs.

For example, suppose the number of points held in each hand is as follows:

- East Wind: 144 points
- South Wind: 22 points (including mahjong)
- West Wind: 4 points
- North Wind: 6 points

South Wind, who mahjonged, receives payment from all other players. Then, other players settle the differences between their scores. Sequence groups have no scoring value, but assist in mahjonging.

	Receives	Pays	Net Points Receives:	Pays

SOUTH WIND—has 22 points
    from WEST WIND
    from NORTH WIND
    from EAST WIND
	22
	22
	44
			88	

WEST WIND—has 4 points
    to SOUTH WIND
    to NORTH WIND
    to EAST WIND
		22
		2
		280
				304

NORTH WIND—has 6 points
    to SOUTH WIND
    to EAST WIND
    from WEST WIND
	2	22
		276
				296

EAST WIND—has 144 points
    to SOUTH WIND
    from WEST WIND
    from NORTH WIND
	280
	276
		44	512	

◀ The number of points paid and received by each player in the example

To determine the score, hands are divided into two groups:

A. *Exposed Hands*—Groups that have been obtained by punging or chowing and exposed to the other players.

B. *Unexposed Hands*—Groups that have been drawn and are unknown to the other players.

Tally the points as follows:

Exposed Groups

Three of a kind (except numbers 1, 9, Winds, and Honors): 2 points
Three of a kind (only numbers 1, 9, Winds, and Honors): 4 points

Unexposed Groups (Double the above points)

A player's own Wind or any Honor if paired: 2 points
Four of a kind: four times the amount of three of a kind

There are certain bonuses that apply only to the player winning the mahjong:

Mahjong: 20 points
No score in hand: 10 points
No sequences in hand: 10 points
Drawing winning tile: 2 points
Securing only possible tile to mahjong: 2 points
Drawing winning tile from loose tiles: 10 points

There are other bonuses that apply to all hands. After determining the number of actual points in the hand, these points are doubled the number of times indicated, if doubling combinations are held:

Three or four of Honors: 1 double
Three or four of own Wind: 1 double
All tiles of one suit with Winds and Honors: 1 double

All tiles of one suit (no Winds or Honors): 3 doubles
All Winds and Honors: 3 doubles

There are also several special hands, seldom held, which are valued more or less arbitrarily.

Should a hand contain more than one double, the total score is doubled for each doubling combination held. For example, a hand composed of all Honors and Winds would have three doubles, plus one double for each group of Honors or own Wind. If there were six doubles in the hand and the hand was valued at 36 points, the total value of the hand would be 2,304 points, as follows:

One double: 36 points doubled once = 72 points
Two doubles: 72 points doubled once = 144 points
Three doubles: 144 points doubled once = 288 points
Four doubles: 288 points doubled once = 576 points
Five doubles: 576 points doubled once = 1,152 points
Six doubles: 1,152 points doubled once = 2,304 points

Paying Scores

After a player has mahjonged and the number of points in his hand has been tallied, scores are settled with the chips distributed by the banker at the beginning of the game.

1. The player who mahjongs receives his full score from all the other players and pays no scores.
2. All other players pay each other the differences between their total scores. For example, if North Wind has 6 points and West Wind has 4 points, then West Wind pays North Wind 2 points.
3. East Wind receives and pays double. If East Wind mahjongs, North Wind, South Wind, and West Wind must pay East Wind double the total number of points in his hand. If some other player mahjongs beside East Wind, he is paid by East Wind double his total score. Among players not mahjonging, East Wind must pay or receive double the difference between his score and that of each other player.

The Flowers and Seasons

After the game has been mastered, the *flowers and seasons* may be added. The addition of these tiles adds an additional element of chance to the game.

There are generally four tiles of each, numbered from 1 to 4. If your set does not include these tiles, you can assign each wind to represent a flower and season, East Wind being number 1, South Wind number 2, West Wind number 3, and North Wind number 4.

Each flower or season counts for 4 points. Holding one's flower or season (for example, East Wind holding number 1) counts one double. Holding all flowers or seasons, from 1 to 4, with numerals all the same color, counts three doubles.

If your set includes the eight additional tiles of the flowers and seasons, the walls must be built eighteen tiles long instead of seventeen.

Flowers and seasons do not count in the fourteen tiles required to mahjong. They are additional tiles that are exposed to view and replaced by a loose tile when drawn. Generally, after drawing hands, all flowers and seasons in the hands are exposed and loose tiles are drawn first to replace these. East Wind has first draw, followed by the other Winds in turn. When a flower or season is drawn during the game it is exposed and replaced by a loose tile immediately.

Watch the discards of the other players, especially the player to your right. Your opponent will seldom discard a tile that is paired in his hand or one which, with some other tile in his hand, will form a sequence group in case he can chow. By watching the discarding, you can obtain a fair estimate of the opposing hands, which will assist in developing your own hand.

Cleared Hands

Many players prefer to play *all hands clear*; that is, each player must confine himself to one suit with Winds and Honors, or simply one suit, or all Winds and Honors. This makes the game somewhat more difficult but at the same time has the tendency to increase scores. There are two ways in which cleared hands are generally played:

1. The suits in which each player will undertake to mahjong are agreed upon *before* drawing hands. In this method East Wind has the choice of suits. West Wind then must choose the same suit. South Wind names his suit and then North Wind names the remaining suit.
2. Each player decides for himself the suit in which he will try to mahjong *after* drawing hands. The players concentrate on the suit in which they have the largest number of tiles, taking into consideration the suits decided upon by the other players.

If cleared hands are played it is especially important to watch the discards of the other players, particularly if suits are not named before drawing. To clear a hand, you should hold all Winds and Honors until you eliminate all but one of the three remaining suits—Circles, Bamboos, or Characters—from the hand. You should hold every tile drawn in the suit decided upon until the hand is cleared. After you have reduced the hand to one suit and Winds and Honors, you should discard the tile of least value, no matter if it is a Wind, Honor, or in the chosen suit.

ALERT!

Always try to arrange your hand so that you will have two or more places to mahjong. Don't let the thought that a chow is of no value in scoring make you save for too many pungs.

In choosing suits avoid, whenever possible, deciding upon the same suit as the opponent to your left. Unless you do this there is little likelihood of receiving either a chow or a pung from him, because he will hold all tiles in his chosen suit. As there are only three suits besides Winds and Honors and generally four players, two players can find themselves holding the same suit. If this case occurs, it is best for these two players to sit opposite each other rather than next to each other. They will have an equal opportunity to chow the discards of the opponents whose turns precede their own.

In playing cleared hands it is not difficult to determine, by a process of elimination, the suits that your opponents are holding. Each player will generally discard his shortest suit. If an opponent discards Circles you can be reasonably sure he will try to concentrate on either Characters or Bamboos. Of these suits, discard from the one in which you have the fewest tiles. His next discard may be a Bamboo so that you will know that his chosen suit is Characters. You can then decide on your own suit. If these discards have been made by an opponent to your left, you can choose either Circles or Bamboos yourself, depending on the number of tiles you hold in your hand.

If your opponents seem to be concentrating on the same suit, determine the suit your opponent opposite has decided upon and choose the remaining suit for yourself. You'll then have a better chance of winning in this suit. If, on the other hand, your opponents seem to be holding different suits, you should concentrate on the third remaining suit for yourself, which will in all probability be the suit chosen by the player opposite you.

Sometimes hands will be drawn in such a manner that three players will concentrate on the same suit. If you can determine that you are not one of the three, discard this suit immediately. If you should find that three players including yourself are concentrating on the same suit, do not hesitate to change to another suit even though you may have fewer tiles in that other suit than the one you had originally decided upon.

ALERT!

Do not be in too much of a hurry to claim four of a kind. Pung the fourth to three whenever possible, using only three of these and retaining the fourth in the hand for possible use in a sequence group. Nothing can be lost in so doing unless some other player mahjongs before you have a chance.

If you start out with a large number of tiles in one suit, say eight or nine, and no other player seems to be holding this suit, try to completely clear your hand. Discard all Winds and Honors each time you draw another tile in your long suit. A completely cleared hand counts three doubles, and Honors are slow to be discarded by your opponents. This is especially important in playing with the flowers and seasons because, should you draw your own flower or season, a completely cleared hand will give you four doubles. If you have only 32 points in your hand, doubling four times will count 512 points, more than the usual limit.

In playing cleared hands it is very difficult to hold a hand consisting of only Winds and Honors, though this occasionally can be done. Most players will hold their Winds and Honors until they have cleared their hands of all but one suit, so that unless you have completed groups of Winds and Honors, you will probably wait a long time for pungs. Remember, too, that there are only twenty-eight Winds and Honors tiles, though there are thirty-six tiles in each of the other suits, and also that Winds and Honors groups can only be punged.

If you draw a hand with an equal number of tiles in two or three suits and you must play first, it may be well to discard a Wind or Honor until you get some sort of an idea of your opponents' hands. Such a discard tells them nothing, and may prevent you from discarding from a suit that you might be able to build on later.

Yahtzee!

Rating: 8+

Yahtzee may be played by one or more people, in teams or alone. To determine who plays first, all players roll the dice. The player with the highest total score goes first, and play continues clockwise.

Players roll the dice three times in an attempt to get the best score possible. The score sheet has thirteen score boxes with different combinations of the dice to get the best score. The upper part of the scorecard contains types such as Aces (Ones), Twos, Threes, Fours, and so on. Players score adding the numbers on the dice rolled that correspond with the number in the box. For example, if you are scoring in the Five box and roll two fives, you get 10 points. If you earn 63 points or more in the upper section, you earn a bonus of 35 points. The bottom part has various combinations:

Three or four of a kind: sum of the dice
Full house (three of one kind, two of another): 25 points

Small straight (sequence of four numbers): 30 points

Large straight (sequence of five numbers): 40 points

Yahtzee (five of a kind): 50 points

In the bottom part, players either match the exact requirement and get all of the points or they get zero points. For extra Yahtzees players get 100 points, up to three Yahtzees.

Each player's first roll must be made with all five dice. After that the players choose whether or not to use their remaining rolls to try to get a better score. They may also choose the number of dice to roll. For example, if a player was going for the Twos box and rolls two twos, he or she may pick up the remaining three and try again with those dice. Score is taken on the last roll. Each player must score in each box before the game can end.

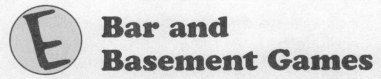

Chapter 10

Bar and Basement Games

The popularity of these games has become so great that many people are beginning to bring them into their homes. Whether you are looking to get in a little practice before showing off your skills in entertainment venues or simply just to have fun, the rules and strategies in this chapter will help you play.

Air Hockey

Rating: 8+

Air hockey requires two people and is played on a special air hockey table, which contains holes through which air is pumped. Each player has a round bottom mallet.

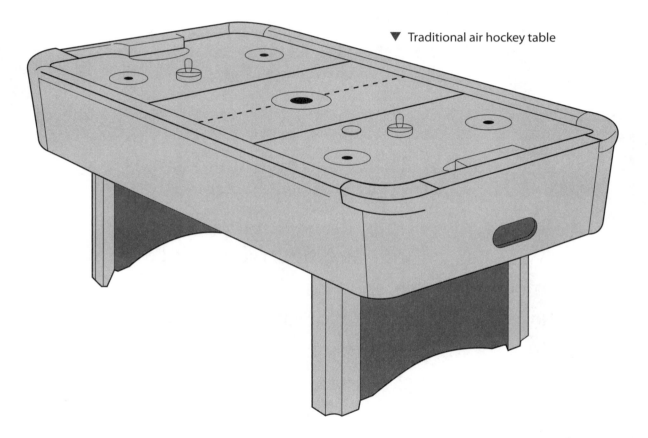

▼ Traditional air hockey table

The object is to get the puck past your opponent and into his goal. Each goal is 1 point. Games are usually played to seven goals. After a goal is scored, the scored-on player gets possession of the puck.

Additionally, violation of these rules counts as a foul:

1. Players may not place the mallet on top of the puck.

2. Players may only strike the puck on their respective sides of the center-line. However, if the puck is touching the centerline, either player may strike it.

3. Player's body or clothing may not touch the puck.

4. Players may not hit the puck off the table.

Fouls result in the player fouled against gaining possession of the puck.

Billiards Games

Rating: 8+

Billiards games are played on a pool table, but they may require slightly different equipment. You can alter your pool table to play these games by covering the pockets and assigning the balls different values.

FACT

Pool and billiards are two entirely different games, although their names are often used interchangeably. Most Americans are familiar with pool games and don't know how to play billiards. As you'll see, these games require different table setups, different balls, and totally different sets of rules.

The Four-Ball Game

Most billiards games require three balls. However, as its name implies, you use four for this game. In regulation play, two balls should be red and two white. One red ball is lighter in color than the other, and one of the white balls has a black center spot.

From the head to the lower end, the table is marked with three spots on its surface, placed on an imaginary line dividing the table lengthwise, with diamond sights on the end rails at the head and foot of the table. One spot is fixed at the head of the table and in line opposite the second diamond sight on each of the side cushion rails. This is the *light red spot,* and is known in the three-ball game as the *white ball spot.* The *dark red spot* is fixed in a similar measured position at the foot or lower end of the table. The white ball or *pool spot* is fixed five inches from the face of the lower end cushion and on a direct line with the other spots.

Playing the Game

Any number of players can participate in this game. As in standard pool, the players bank the ball for the choice of balls and lead. The player who wins the choice of balls and lead must either roll his ball down toward the lower cushion, as an object for his opponent to play at, or else compel his opponent to lead off.

In leading, you must play the ball from within the string-line and strike it with sufficient force to carry it beyond the deep-red ball on its appropriate spot at the foot of the table. But the ball must not pass again, after having come in contact with the lower cushion. The ball cannot touch either red ball, rest on the cushion, or jump off the table. In any of these cases, or if you did not strike the cue ball with sufficient force to make it pass beyond the deep red ball, your opponent may make you spot your ball on the pool spot nearest the lower cushion or lead again, or he may take the lead himself.

Should you fail to hit the white first, or fail to hit it at all, you forfeit 1 point, which is added to your opponent's score. You also forfeit 1 point if you fail to hit any of the other balls with your own. Again, the point is added to your opponent's score.

No count or forfeiture can be made or incurred until two strokes have been played. Once the lead is made, neither player can withdraw from the game. The game continues with each player playing on the white ball at the foot of the table.

Rules of the Game

1. The player forfeits 2 points when the ball rests on the cushion, or goes over the table, after having struck or been in fixed contact with the other white, no matter whether it has touched one or both of the reds.

2. The player forfeits 3 points when the ball that he plays with rests on the cushion, or goes over the table, after having come in contact with one or both of the reds, and not the white. The same applies if neither red nor white are struck.

3. If the player causes any ball to jump off the table, even if it is immediately returned to the table, it must still be treated as if it had fallen to the floor. If it is a red ball, it must be spotted; if a white, held in hand. Should it be the last player's ball, he forfeits 2 or 3 points.

4. If any player plays with his opponent's ball, the stroke is foul and doesn't count, unless the error is found out after a second stroke is made. Should two or more strokes have been made previous to the discovery, the progress of the game cannot be disturbed, and the player may continue his turn with the same ball, or he may have the balls changed. The same privilege is extended to the opposing player when his turn comes to play. If both players have used the wrong ball successively, whoever was first to play with the wrong ball cannot put in a claim of foul against his opponent.

5. When playing with the wrong ball, a player cannot count what points he may make, except in those cases mentioned above; he is bound to pay whatever forfeitures he may incur while playing with the wrong ball, as if he had been playing with his own.

6. Should, however, both the white balls be off the table together, and should either player, by mistake, pick up the wrong one and play with it, the stroke must stand, and he can count whatever he has made.

7. If the player attempts to strike a ball before it is fully at rest, or while any other ball is rolling on the table, the stroke is foul.

8. If the player, when playing with the butt or side of his cue, does not withdraw the butt or side before the cue ball touches the first object ball, the stroke is foul.

9. A stroke made while a red ball is off the table, provided its spot is unoccupied, is foul.

10. A red ball that has been forced off the table shall be spotted on another spot, provided its own is occupied, and provided, also, that the nonstriker's ball is off the table at the time. The light red ball is then to be placed on the dark red spot; and if that spot is occupied, the light red is to be placed on the pool spot at the foot of the table. The dark red ball is to

be placed on the light red spot. If both reds are off the table at the same time, and their spots are occupied by the two whites, one of the reds may be placed on the pool spot. The other must remain off the table until its proper spot is vacant.

11. If, after making a successful stroke, the player obstructs or otherwise affects the free course of any ball in motion, the stroke is foul, and he cannot score the points made.

12. A touch is a shot. And if, while the balls are at rest, a player touches or disturbs any ball on the table other than his own, it is foul. He has, however, the privilege of playing a stroke for safety, provided his own ball has not been touched, but he can make no count on the shot.

13. In playing a shot, if the cue leaves the ball and touches it again, the stroke is foul.

14. If the striker, through stretching forward or otherwise, has not at least one foot on the floor while striking, the shot is foul, and no points are earned.

15. If, when the player's ball is in hand, he does not cause it to pass outside the string before touching any of the other balls or cushion, the stroke is foul, and his opponent may choose whether he will play with the balls as they are, have them replaced in their original positions, or cause the stroke to be played over; or, should the player pocket his own ball under such circumstances, the penalty may be enforced.

16. Playing at a ball whose base or point of contact with the table is outside the string is considered playing out of the string, and the stroke is a fair one, even though the side that the cue ball strikes is hanging over, and therefore within the string.

17. Playing directly at a ball that is considered in the string is foul even though the cue ball should pass wholly beyond the string-line before coming in contact with the ball.

18. Giving a miss inside the string when the player is in hand is foul but he may, for safety, cause his ball to go out of the string and return.

19. If a player alters the stroke he is about to make, at the suggestion of any party in the room—even if it be at the suggestion of his partner—the altered stroke is foul.

20. Placing marks of any kind whatever, either upon the cushions or table, is foul; and a player, while engaged in a game, cannot practice a particular stroke on another table.

21. When the cue ball is in contact with any other ball, the striker may effect a count, either by playing first upon some ball other than that with which his own is in contact, or by playing first against the cushion. It doesn't matter which ball the returning cue ball strikes first.

22. Should the cue ball be in contact with all the other balls on the table or of the two balls only, while the remaining ball is on the table in such a way that the player cannot play on the free ball or the cushion first, it shall be optional with him to have all the balls taken up, and the reds spotted as in the beginning of the game.

Three-Ball Carom

Three-ball carom is played with two white balls and one red. The billiard table has three spots on an imaginary line, dividing the table lengthwise, running from the center of the head cushion to the center of the foot cushion. One of those spots, cutting the line in two equal parts, is called the *center spot,* and the other two are situated halfway between the center spot and the head and foot cushions.

A ball forced off the table is put back on its proper spot. Should the player's ball jump off the table after counting, the count is good, the ball is spotted, and the player plays from the spot.

The spot at the head of the table is called the *white spot,* and the one at the foot of the table the *red spot.* The center spot is only used when a ball forced off the table finds both white and red spots occupied. Therefore, should the white ball forced off the table have its spot occupied, it would be placed on the red spot and vice versa.

In beginning the game the red ball and one white are placed on their respective spots; the other white remains in hand, and the player who plays the opening stroke can take any position within a six-inch radius, of which the spot at the head of the table is the base, but he must strike the red ball first before a count can be effected.

Rules of the Game

1. The game is begun by banking for the lead; the player who brings his ball nearest to the cushion at the head of the table wins the choice of balls and the right to play first or compel his opponent to play. Should the striker fail to *carom,* his opponent then makes the next play, aiming at will at either ball on the table.

2. A *carom* consists of hitting both balls with the cue ball in a fair and unobjectionable way; each carom will count one for the player. A penalty of one shall also be counted against the player for every miss occurring during the game.

3. If the cue is not withdrawn from the cue ball before the cue ball comes in contact with the ball, the shot is foul, and the player loses his count and his turn.

4. If the balls are disturbed accidentally in any way other than by the player himself, they must be replaced and the player allowed to proceed.

5. If, in the act of playing, the player disturbs any ball other than his own, he cannot make a counting stroke, but he may play for safety. Should he disturb a ball after having played successfully, he loses his count on that stroke. His hand is out and the ball is placed back as near as possible in the position that it formerly occupied on the table, the other balls remaining where they stop.

6. Should a player touch his own ball prior to playing, it is foul. The player loses one ball and cannot play for safety. It sometimes happens that the player, after having touched his ball, gives a second stroke; then the balls remain where they stop, or are replaced as near as possible in their former position, at the option of his opponent.

7. When the cue ball is very near another, the player shall not play without warning his adversary that they do not touch.

8. When the cue ball is in contact with another, the balls are spotted and the player plays with this ball in hand.

9. Playing with the wrong ball is foul. However, should the player using the wrong ball play more than one shot with it, he shall be entitled to his score just the same as if he played with his own; as soon as his turn is up, the white balls must change places, and the game proceeds as usual.

10. No player is allowed to withdraw before the game is finished, otherwise he forfeits the game.

11. Should a ball that has once come to a standstill move without apparent cause while the player is preparing to strike, it shall be replaced. Should it move before he can check his stroke, it, and all other balls set in motion by that stroke, shall be replaced, and the player shall repeat his shot.

12. It is a foul if the player shoots directly at any ball with which his own is in fixed contact, and the striker must in this instance play from balls spotted, as in the opening stroke of the game.

13. It is a foul to place marks of any kind on the felt or cushions as a guide to play.

The rules of the four-ball game govern this game also, except when they conflict with the foregoing rules.

Dart Games

Rating: 8+

Originating in England, the many variations of darts are becoming increasingly popular in the United States, in family rooms, local bars, and in tournaments. Although the classic darts set includes a dart board with darts made of brass and feather flights, many sets are now produced for family enjoyment, with small Velcro balls, magnets, or suction cups used instead of darts. The illustration on page 192 shows a typical dart board. No matter what your dart set looks like, the following games will be popular pastimes for years to come.

ALERT!

Darts must remain in the dart board to count; bounce-outs can be reshot during this initial turn. At all other times, bounce-outs are considered to be *dead shots*, and they may not be reshot or scored for points.

In the following instructions it is understood that the reader has some knowledge of the necessary equipment, and its uses, for the games. The bull's-eye of the dart board must be 5 feet 8 inches from a level ground, and the players must stand 7 feet 9¼ inches from the board.

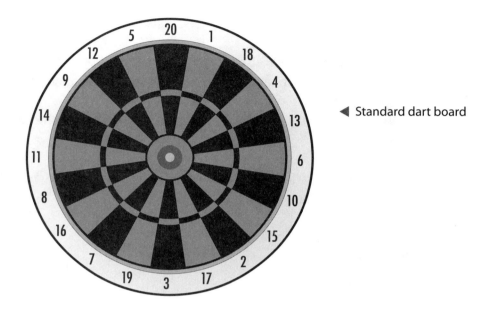

◀ Standard dart board

Cricket

The game of cricket is a game of skill and strategy. The object of the game is to be the first player to close all of the play numbers (15–20, and the bull's-eye) and to score the most points. Any number of people can play, as long as they are divided into two equal teams.

Play begins with a single dart shot aiming for the bull's-eye, with the player closest to the bull's-eye going first. Each player shoots three darts per turn, attempting to close his play numbers. A number is considered closed when it has been hit three times by the same player or team. All play-number wedge areas count as a single score with the exception of the outer ring, which counts as a double score, and the inner ring, which counts as a triple score. The bull's-eye is divided into two sections: the inner ring (double), and the outer ring (single).

Points are scored in cricket when the shooter has closed a play number and the opponent's play number has not yet been closed. For example, suppose you hit the #16 wedge three times, closing that number for your team.

As long as the opposition's #16 is not yet closed, any additional hits landing on #16 will score 16 points each for you.

Points can be scored on any *open* play number and are worth their own face value. The bull's-eye is worth 25 points for each single and 50 points per double. The score is tallied on a scoreboard. Record the hits alongside the numbers in two columns, one for each team. Record the three hits as an X within a circle: one slash of the X for the first hit, the second slash for the second hit, and the circle around the X on the third hit.

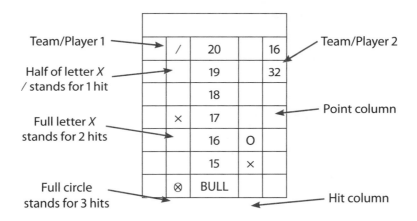

▲ Keeping score in Cricket: In this example, Player 2 has #16 closed and has pointed Player 1 for two additional 16s, giving the team 32 points. Player 1 has hit one #20, two #17s, and three bull's-eyes so far in this game.

Killer

Killer is a competitive game for which you need two or more players. The object of the game is to be the only player left with points at the end of the game. You first must earn enough points to become a *killer* and then you must knock all other opponents out of the game by taking their points away.

Killer begins with a one-dart shot at the bull's-eye, but each player must use his alternate shooting hand. The player closest to the bull's-eye will shoot first. Remember each shooter's play number, which corresponds to the wedge in which his first dart landed. This will be marked on the score-board as a point of departure.

Using his regular shooting hand, each player will try to become the killer. To become a killer you must hit your play number five times. All double and triple areas do count, but you can never have more than five hits on one number at one time. For example, if Player 1 hits four 16s and he later hits a triple 16, then he would only have a total of five 16s.

Reaching killer status allows you to go after your opponents' play numbers. For every play number of your opponents' that you hit, they will lose one hit previously scored. Suppose Player 2s number is 2, and he has 5 points. On his turn, Player 1 hits two of Player 2s play numbers. Player 2 is no longer a killer. Player 2 then has to regain killer status in order to score more points. Once a player loses all of his points, he is out of the game. The killer left is the winner.

To improve the challenge level of this game, you can make the qualifications to become a killer more difficult. For example, you can require each player to hit five triples, instead of singles, or any other combination that you can think of.

The score is tallied on a scoreboard. Each player or team records their play number, and records their points under it.

Foosball

Rating: 8+

Foosball is played on a special table with rods holding the men. The object of the game is to get the ball into your opponent's goal by maneuvering the men by means of the rods, and also to protect your own goal. Games are usually played to nine goals or best of nine. The first player to reach nine or five wins. Players are not allowed to spin the rods. The ball can only remain in one place for fifteen seconds or less.

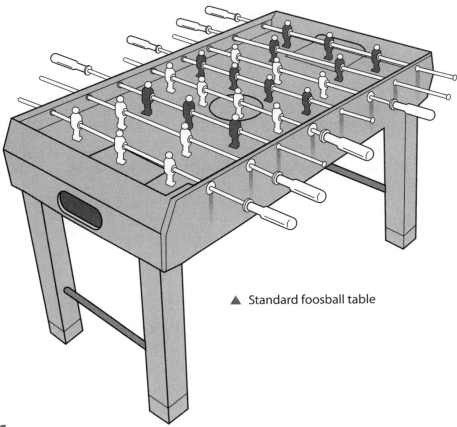

▲ Standard foosball table

Pool

Rating: 8+

The most popular version of this game, known as solids and stripes, is played with fifteen numbered balls and one white ball, not numbered. The white ball is known as the *cue ball*. The cue ball is used to hit the other balls into the pockets. The object of this game is to pocket as many balls, of all varieties, as you can.

The fifteen balls are numbered from one to fifteen: numbers 1 through 8 are solid; numbers 9 through 15 are striped. In this game the numbers on the balls are simply used for convenience in calling the balls that the player intends to pocket, and do not in any way affect the score of the player.

Before beginning the game the fifteen balls are placed within a triangular frame (the rack) on the table, and rolled so that the first ball covers one of the two spots on the felt. The highest-numbered balls must be placed nearest the apex of the triangle, pointing toward the head of the table.

The pool game is begun by *banking*. Each player rolls one ball across the table, directly from where he stands. The player whose ball returns closest to the starting point is the winner. The winner of the lead has the option of playing first, or passing to his opponent to play first. When you play a series of games, the players must alternate who shoots first.

Each and every ball pocketed counts 1 point for the striker, and the player who first scores eight balls wins the game. Any number of players can participate in this game.

The rules of the game are as follows:

1. The player who makes the opening stroke must strike the pyramid of balls with sufficient force to cause two or more balls to strike a cushion, or cause at least one ball to go into a pocket. Should the player fail to do either, he must forfeit one ball to the table from his score, and the next player plays. Should a player have no balls to his credit, the next ball he scores is replaced on the table. All balls pocketed on the opening stroke count for the player, and it is not necessary for him to call the number of the ball he intends to pocket before making the opening stroke.

2. Before making a stroke, except for the opening stroke, the player must distinctly call the number of the ball he intends to pocket (but he need not name the particular pocket into which he intends to put it). If he fails to do so, the ball pocketed does not count for him and must be placed on the spot where the pyramid of balls was first placed (called the *foot spot*), or, if that is occupied, as near below it as possible. The player loses his turn, but does not pay a forfeit, and the next player plays. Should he call more than one ball, he must pocket all the balls he calls, otherwise none of them can be counted for him. A player does not receive a scratch for failure to remove or hit a called ball, provided he hits any other ball or balls on the table.

3. After the opening stroke, each player must either pocket a ball or make contact with a ball, or strike a cushion with the cue ball, under penalty of forfeiture of one ball.

4. Should the player pocket, by the same stroke, more balls than he calls, he is entitled to all the balls he calls, and all the other balls pocketed by the stroke.

5. All strokes must be made with the point of the cue, otherwise they are foul.

6. When two players are engaged in a game, he who pockets or scores eight balls first is the winner of the game. But when more than two players are engaged, the game is ended only when the number of balls remaining on the table does not amount to enough to tie or beat the next lowest score.

7. A ball going into a pocket and rebounding onto the table must be regarded in the same light as if it had struck a cushion, and is not counted as a pocketed ball. It remains in place where it came to rest on the table. Any ball forced off the table must be replaced on the foot spot, or, if that is occupied, as near below it as possible. If it is the cue ball, it is to be regarded as being off the table and *in hand.*

8. A ball resting on the cushion must be regarded as off the table and in hand.

9. When the cue ball is in *hand,* the player may play from any place behind the spot from which he started. He may shoot for any ball outside of (or across) this string. Should none of the balls be outside the string, the ball that is nearest outside is moved to the foot spot, and the player may play at it.

10. Should the striker touch the cue ball with the point of his cue, or with any other part of the cue, or with his clothing or anything else, it shall be counted a stroke.

11. If the player, before his stroke has been delivered, touch a ball with the point or any part of the cue, or with his clothing or anything else, so that the ball moves, it must be returned to its original position. The striker loses his turn for that round only.

12. A stroke is complete when all balls set in motion have come to rest.

13. A stroke made when any of the balls are in motion is foul. Should such a stroke be made, the balls are either replaced or left as they come to rest,

at the option of the next player. The striker loses his turn and forfeits one ball.

14. Should a player play out of turn, his stroke is foul. The balls must be replaced in the position they occupied before the stroke, and whoever's turn it was plays. But should a player, playing out of turn, make more than one stroke before being checked, the strokes made are fair, and he is entitled to any points he may have made by such strokes, and he may continue his play until his turn is out. After his turn is out (and the player whose turn it was plays), the offending player, having had his inning, is not to play again when his regular turn comes, but must wait for his regular turn to come around the second time.

15. Should the balls on the table be accidentally disturbed by any person or cause other than the player, they are to be replaced as nearly as possible in their original position, and the player may continue.

16. Push shots are allowed; that is, it is not necessary to withdraw the point of the cue from the cue ball before the latter touches the ball. When the cue ball is in contact with another ball, the player may play directly at the ball with which it is in contact, or directly from it, and the latter play shall not be recorded as a miss, provided a cushion is struck.

17. When the striker is in hand, should he play at any ball that is within the string-line, or if, when in hand, he plays from any position not within the string-line, without being checked previous to the stroke being made, any score he may make from such stroke he is entitled to; but if he is checked before making the stroke, and then makes it, it does not count for him, his hand is out, and the next player plays. All balls disturbed by the stroke must be replaced or left as they are, at the option of the next player.

18. It is a foul, and the striker forfeits one ball, if, while in the act of striking, he does not have at least one foot on the floor.

19. Should the striker, by a clear, fair stroke of the cue, pocket a ball and, after the stroke, move, touch, or foul one or more of the balls, he is entitled to the pocketed ball, and loses his hand only because of the foul, and the next player plays.

20. Should a ball that has come to a standstill move without apparent cause while the player is preparing to strike, it must be replaced. Should it move before he can stop his stroke, it and all the other balls set in motion by the stroke must be replaced, but the player shall repeat his stroke.

21. When two persons are playing, should a player incur three penalties, scratches, or forfeitures in succession, he shall forfeit every ball remaining on the table to his opponent. Should more than two persons be playing, then the offending player is automatically declared the loser of the game.

22. No player is allowed to withdraw before the game is played out; by so doing he forfeits the game.

Shuffleboard

Rating: 8+

In shuffleboard, players shove weights across a shuffleboard playing field. Players can either play one-on-one or in teams. Players attempt to outscore each other by getting their weights further into the scoring field. The weights may either pass the opponent's weights (out-drawing) or dislodge them. There are eight weights, four red and four blue.

Players stand at the same end of the board. They take turns sliding their weights by hand on the shuffleboard. After all eight weights have been slid, the score is tallied and the round is over. The next round begins from the other end of the board. In singles matches, the first player to receive 15 points wins; in other matches the first to receive 21 points wins.

When keeping score, players count only the weights of the lead color that are ahead of the furthest of the other color. Only one side gets points in a round. Points are weighted as follows:

1. Weights on or in front of the deuce line equal 1 point.
2. Weights between the deuce line and the trey line (or on the trey line) equal 2 points.
3. Weights between the trey line and the end of the board equal 3 points.
4. Weights hanging over the end of the board (hangers) equal 4 points.

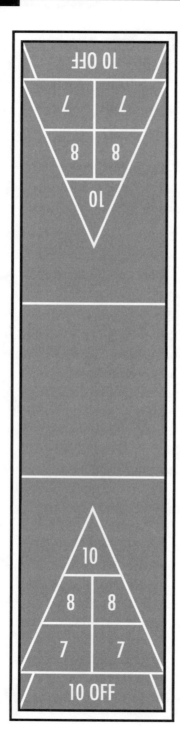

◀ The shuffleboard playing field

Table Tennis
Rating: **8+**

Table tennis, also known as Ping-Pong, can be played by either two (singles) or four players (doubles). It is played on a special table with a small plastic ball and paddles. The first side to get 21 points wins the game; however, the side must win by at least a 2-point margin. Matches are usually decided by the best of three or five.

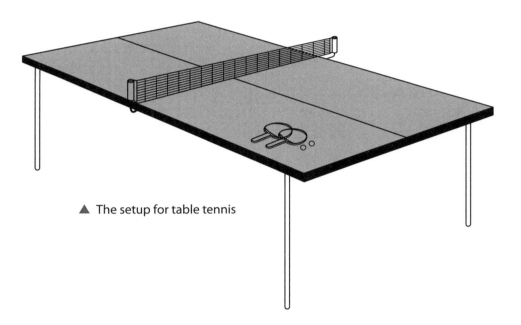

▲ The setup for table tennis

Players choose which side will serve first. To serve, a player tosses the ball up and hits it so that it bounces once on his side of the table and then onto the other side of the table. The ball may not touch the net. If it does and goes onto the other side of the table, it is called a let and must be re-served. If it hits the net and stops or hits the net and then the floor, the server loses the point to the other player. One player serves until 5 points (total of both sides) are scored, and then the other side serves for 5 points, and so on. If the players reach a score of 20-20, serve is alternated between the two.

The rules of the game are as follows:

1. The ball must bounce before the receiver may hit it. No volleying.
2. The ball may bounce only once.
3. The ball may touch the net on a return shot.
4. If the ball hits the net and misses the table on a return shot, the hitting player loses the point.

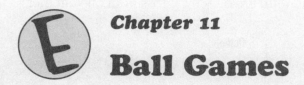

Chapter 11

Ball Games

Ball games are favorites among children and adults alike. Who needs high-tech computerized games when you have a ball? This chapter offers a variety of games, from the classics to newcomers. But don't stop with the suggestions in this chapter. If you're feeling creative, you can make up your own games or change the rules any way you like.

Baseball
Rating: 8+

Baseball is played on a diamond with four bases: home, first, second, and third. Home base is at the base of the diamond with second base directly across from it. First and third are directly across from one another.

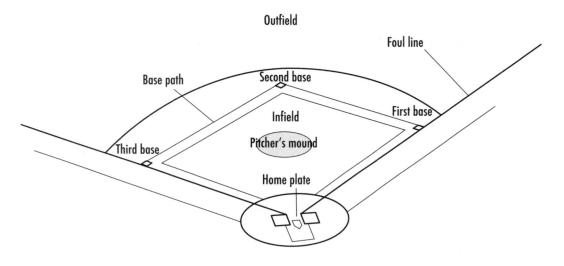

▲ Baseball playing field

The game is played by two teams. To start the game, players decide which team will begin at bat (the offensive team); the other will be in the field (defensive team). A team remains at bat until it incurs three outs. The object is to score as many runs as possible. The game is played in nine innings. An inning is constituted by a period in which both teams have turns at bat.

The offensive team sends one player at a time to bat. Players waiting to bat remain off the field. The defensive team takes up positions in the field. The infield players are the pitcher who delivers the ball; the first, second, and third basemen and the shortstop (standing between second and third bases), who try to catch the ball and tag runners on their respective bases; and the catcher, who is behind home plate and catches the ball if the batter does not hit it. The outfielders are outside the diamond. Their duty is to catch the ball if it leaves the infield.

The batter becomes a runner if he hits the ball (as long as it's not a foul ball); if the pitcher throws four "balls" (pitches that are out of the strike zone); or if the pitch hits the batter.

FACT

Though baseball as described here isn't suitable for young kids, there is now a form of baseball called T-ball, in which children as young as three can participate. The youngsters hit a ball off of a batting tee, thus eliminating the need for pitching.

Unless the batter hits the ball, he may take first base without being taggable. If the batter does hit the ball, it must be a "fair" ball. A ball is "foul" if it goes outside the line from home to first or home to third when a batter hits it. That is, the ball does not go over the playing field. The runner's objective is to get to home base without getting an out. Each time a runner touches all three bases and home, a run is scored, which is worth 1 point. A home run occurs when the batter strikes a ball, rounds all the bases, and makes it home without being tagged in one run.

You get an out if:

1. At bat, you get three strikes. A strike is called when a batter either misses a fair pitch or does not swing at a fair pitch.
2. You are tagged when the ball is live. In order to tag, the infielder must be touching the base and tag the runner while holding the ball.
3. A member of the defensive team catches the ball you hit before it touches the ground.

Players are safe on bases until the next batter makes a hit and a runner runs to that base. The previous runner is then forced to the next base.

After three outs the teams switch places. The team with the most runs at the end of nine innings wins.

Stickball
Rating: 8+

Stickball is an urban version of baseball. It is played with a stick of some sort, usually a broom handle, and a rubber ball. Bases are arranged in a baseball diamond and most often are made from whatever is available. Play follows baseball rules except that players are usually only allowed one or two strikes, and teams are often quite small.

Basketball Games

In addition to the game of basketball, there are several other games you can play with the same kind of ball. Here are a few games you can play in big groups or with just a few people.

Boundary Ball
Rating: 8+

Any number of players can participate, but it's best to form a group of ten to sixty players. Mark out the ground or floor in a rectangle about fifteen by thirty feet, and divide the rectangle in half with a line drawn across the center of it. After sides are chosen, they take their places in their respective fields. Players stand facing one another in two rows about ten feet from the center line and parallel to it. Any player may start the game by throwing the ball into his opponents' field. His opponents catch the ball, or, if it is rolling, stop it. The opponents' line then advances or retreats, so as to cross the spot on which the ball was caught or stopped. The catcher of the ball next throws it back to the first side, which in its turn must catch or stop it. This continues until one side succeeds in passing the ball across the outer boundary of its opponents' side, and scores a point. The winner is the team that first scores 10 points.

Corner Ball
Rating: 8+

Any even number of players can participate, but the best groups are between ten and thirty. To set up the game, draw a line across the center of the floor and mark four goals, one in each corner. The players divide into two teams, which take their positions on opposite sides of the center line. Each team appoints two goal men, who stand in the goals on their opponents' territory, opposite their own side.

The object of the players on each team is to throw the ball to either of their own goal men. Whenever a goal man, without stepping outside his own goal, succeeds in catching a ball that has not been touched by an opponent, he scores one for his side. The opposing team tries to intercept the ball as it is thrown; if, before it is caught, they can in any way touch it without entering a goal, they score one. The players are numbered, and throw in turn, the sides alternating. A thrower must not advance beyond the middle line. A game is ended when all the players on each side have thrown. The side having the higher score wins.

Kickover Ball
Rating: 8+

Any number of players can participate, but the best groups are between ten and thirty players. You also can use a volleyball for this game.

If you plan to play kickover ball, it is a good idea to have an adult act as umpire. The umpire is not only responsible for beginning play, but also for deciding whether the players are keeping their hands on the floor.

The players choose sides. Each side sits on the floor in a straight row, with the two rows facing one another. The players place their hands on the floor behind them and stretch their feet out in front of them, leaving space so the ball can be rolled between them. Mark a goal at one end of the room, equally distant from both rows. The player who is the farthest from the goal in each row is the scout for his side.

The umpire rolls the ball down the center from whichever end of the line he chooses. Each player tries, as the ball passes, to kick it so as to send it over the heads of his opponents. If a player on team A succeeds in doing this without removing his hands from the floor, the A scout runs to the goal while his team's line moves down one space away from the goal. The scout then sits down at the goal end of his line, in the place left vacant when his line moved away from the goal. At the same time that the A team is making these moves, the B scout picks up the ball and runs to seat himself at the goal end of his line, which also has moved one space away from the goal. In other words, the object for the B scout is to sit opposite the place left for the A scout. If the A scout is the first to get seated, his side scores 2 points, one for the kickover and one for the goal run; if the B scout is the first seated, the A side scores only the 1 point for the kickover.

Box Ball

Rating: 8+

Any number of players can participate, but the best groups number between six and twenty. You will need a box for each player (the boxes should all be about the same size), a red rubber ball, and some small stones.

Because one of the objects of the box ball game is to strike other players with the ball, be sure to play with a light rubber ball that won't hurt the players when they are struck. Avoid using heavier balls such as a basketball.

Place the boxes in a row on the floor, with the open side up. The players stand in a line at some distance from them, each player opposite his own box and facing it. The player at the right of the line tosses the ball into any one of the boxes. All the players scatter except the one whose box the ball has fallen into. He runs, picks up the ball, and tries to throw it so as to strike one of the other players.

If the player fails to hit another player, put a stone in his box. The other players then form in line as at first, and he starts the game again by tossing the ball into one of the boxes. If, however, he succeeds in hitting the player he aims at, the player who is struck is the one who receives a stone and starts the game again. If anyone fails in his attempt to toss the ball into a box, he also receives a stone, and the player next to him in line makes the attempt. When a player has five stones in his box, he goes out of the game. The last player left is the winner.

Double Pass

Rating: 8+

Any number of players can participate, but the best groups have between ten and sixty players. You will need two balls or two beanbags for this game.

The players stand in a circle, with one taking his place in the center with the balls in his hands. Each player in the circle counts the players around him, to find out which is the fifth player at his right and which is the fifth at his left. Then the player in the center throws one ball to any player, saying at the same time, "Right!" or "Left!" The player at whom the ball has been thrown catches it, and immediately throws it to the fifth player on the correct side. This player catches the ball and returns it to the player in the center, who meanwhile has started the second ball in the same way as the first, by throwing it to any other player.

The first ball is returned to the center at about the same time the second ball is leaving, so that there is constant passing. A player who misses the ball leaves the circle. Whoever is left with the player in the center wins.

Drop Ball
Rating: 8+

Any number of players can participate, but the best groups are between ten and sixty players. You will need a tennis ball for this game.

One player stands in the center, and the rest form a ring round him. The player in the center tosses up the ball, and calls the name of any one of the players in the ring. The player whose name has been called tries to catch the ball before its second bounce. If he succeeds, he changes places with the player in the center. If he fails, the player in the center continues until someone does catch the ball. When a player has failed to catch the ball three times, he is out.

FACT

To make this game more difficult, first draw a chalk circle. No player may step inside the circle until his name is called. Breaking this rule counts the same as a failure to catch the ball.

Another variation is catch ball, in which the players can run freely about the room instead of standing in a ring. The player who tosses the ball may call the name of someone who is at a considerable distance, so that great speed and alertness are required to enable the player whose name has been called to catch the ball before its second bounce.

Lawn Ball
Rating: 8+

Any number of players can participate, but the best groups number between four and twenty. You will need a colored ball for each player. Choose one color for half of the balls and another color for the other half. You also will need a single ball of a third color.

Choose sides, and distribute the balls so that all the players on a side have the same color. The leader of one side takes the *jack*, which is the ball of the third color, and throws it a considerable distance. The other players, alternating from the two sides, stand in turn at the place from which the leader threw and throw their balls, trying to make them land as near to the jack as possible. When all have thrown, the side that has a ball lying nearest the jack scores.

The score is 1 point for each ball that lies nearer the jack than the best ball of the opposing side. Whichever team reaches 50 points first wins.

Medicine Ball

Rating: 8+

Any even number of players can participate, but the best groups are between six and sixty. You will need as many basketballs, medicine balls, or other large balls of uniform size and weight as there are pairs of players (one for every two players).

Divide the players into two or more rows, according to the number of players. The players in each row stand at equal distances from one another, and the leader of each row holds a ball. The positions of the leaders and of those at the rear of the rows are marked on the floor.

A variation of medicine ball is called arch ball. Instead of passing the ball between the feet, throw it backward over the head from one player to another. You also can combine these two relays in the game called under and over, in which the players in each row alternate passing the ball through their legs and over their heads.

At a signal, each leader passes the ball between his feet to the player behind, who, in turn, passes it along between his feet to the next player, and so on to the end player. After making sure that the ball has touched the mark that he's standing on, the end player runs with it as quickly as possible to the leader's position in the front of the row, and immediately starts it down the line again as before.

Every time a player runs forward with the ball, the others of that row all move backward somewhat, in order to give the runner room in front and keep the spaces equal. The ball must always pass between the feet of every player in the row. If a crooked pass sends it out to one side, it should, as soon as possible, be brought back to the line, and started along by the player next in turn. The row that is the first to get back to its original position wins.

Preliminary Ball

Rating: 8+

This game is an organized version of an old-fashioned egg toss. Any even number of players can participate, but the best groups are between ten and sixty. You will need balls (don't try to use raw eggs!) for half the number of players.

The players stand in two lines facing one another. The players of one line hold the balls. At the signal, each throws his ball to the player opposite him, who catches the ball and throws it back. The winning team is the first to complete the entire drill without dropping the ball once.

The method of throwing and catching can be anything that you determine, but the following options will add variety to the game:

- Throw three times with the *right* hand, and catch with *both*
- Throw three times with the *left* hand, and catch with *both*
- Throw three times with the *right* hand, and catch with the *right*
- Throw three times with the *left* hand, and catch with the *left*
- Throw three times with the *right* hand, and catch with the *left*
- Throw three times with the *left* hand, and catch with the *right*

Soccer

Rating: 8+

Soccer is one of the most popular sports in the world. It is played at all levels from the backyard to the professional leagues. The object of the game is for each team to get the soccer ball into the goal of the opposing team (each

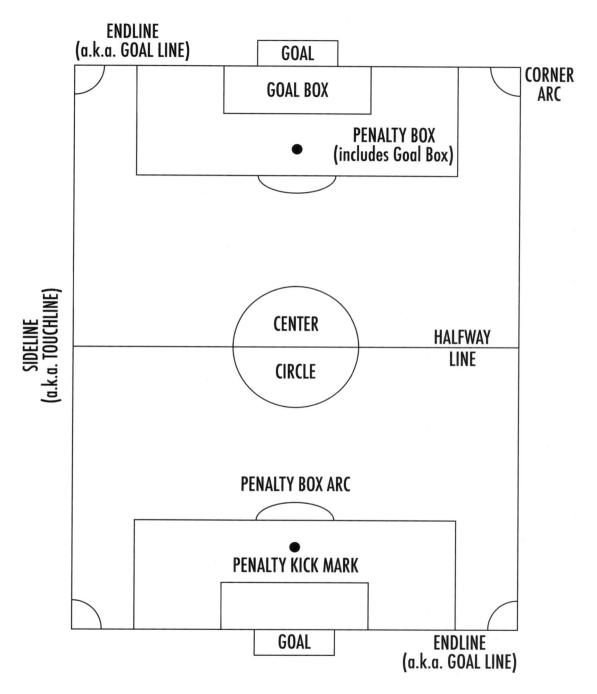

ENDLINE
(a.k.a. GOAL LINE)

GOAL

GOAL BOX

CORNER
ARC

PENALTY BOX
(includes Goal Box)

SIDELINE
(a.k.a. TOUCHLINE)

CENTER

CIRCLE

HALFWAY
LINE

PENALTY BOX ARC

PENALTY KICK MARK

GOAL

ENDLINE
(a.k.a. GOAL LINE)

▲ Traditional soccer field

goal is equivalent to a point). The team with the higher score at the end wins the game.

The game begins with a coin toss that determines which team will kick off and allows the winning team to decide which goal they want to defend. After kickoff, players are free to run up and down the field. However, offensive players must have at least two defensive players between them and the goal line when the ball is played forward (if they do not, they are offsides, which is an infraction).

FACT

A soccer field comes in various sizes. Regulation fields are 100 to 130 yards by 50 to 100 yards. However, you can adjust the field size to your needs. In general the width should be two-thirds the length of the field.

Returning the Ball to Play

The ball cannot leave the field at any time. If it does, there are three ways to return it to play:

1. If the ball is kicked out by the offensive team, a goal kick is used. The ball is placed on the side of the goal to which it went out. A player from the defensive team then kicks it out of the penalty area.
2. If a team kicks the ball across its own goal line, a corner kick is used. The ball is placed at a corner arc and the offensive team will then kick the ball.
3. If the ball crosses the touchline, the team that was not the last to touch the ball receives possession.

The Positions

Forwards: The purpose of forwards is basically to score goals. They play near the other team's goal.

Midfielders: Midfielders, as the name suggests, play near the center of the field. They are charged with trying to steal the ball from the other teams and get it to their team's forwards.

Defenders: Defenders play near their own team's goal to defend it from the other team's forwards. The goalie will direct returns toward them. They in turn try to get the ball to their team's midfielders.

Goalies: Goalies defend their team's goal. They are the only players in the game who may touch the ball with their hands.

Fouls

There are basically three types of fouls with two types of penalties.

Handballs: Players other than the goalie are not allowed to intentionally touch the ball with their hands or arms. When they do, the other team gets a direct free kick.

Offside: As explained above, a player is offsides when, after having touched the ball, she does not have two defensive players between her and the goal line (not including kicks to return the ball into play). This infraction incurs an indirect free kick.

Contact fouls: This category basically includes any sort of deliberate contact with another player (such as hitting, kicking, pulling clothes, pushing, tripping, and so on). These usually incur a direct free kick for the other team as well as a yellow card (warning) for the offender. If the player commits more than one of these offenses or a particularly vicious one, she may get a red card and be ejected from the game.

Penalties

Direct free kick: The fouled team gets a free kick from the offense point at the goal without the ball having to touch another player.

Indirect free kick: The fouled team gets a free kick from the point of the offense. However, the ball must touch another player before the goal is scored.

Penalty kick: If a direct kick offense occurs within the penalty area, the fouled player gets a chance to score with just him and the goalie in the penalty area.

Stool Ball

Rating: 8+

Any number of players can participate, but the best groups are between ten and thirty players. You will need a tennis ball and stools. There should be one less stool than the number of players participating in this game.

The stools are placed in a circle several feet from one another. A player stands in back of each stool, in any position previously agreed upon (for example, "heels together and hands on the hips"). The bowler, who stands in the center of the circle, tosses the ball at any one of the players. If the player at whom the ball is tossed succeeds in batting it with his hand, all the players behind the stools change places.

The bowler catches the ball or picks it up, and then throws it so as to hit any player who is out of the required position. The one who has been hit changes places with the bowler. (In a variation of stool ball, you can try having the player who has been hit fall out of the game instead of having him change places with the bowler.) If no one has been hit, repeat the game with the same bowler. If at any time the ball is not batted back, the bowler repeats the throw until it is.

Stoopball

Rating: 8+

Stoopball has several variations. In one, the batter stands 10 to 15 feet from the stoop of a building and throws the ball at it. When the ball returns, the player must catch it at one or zero bounces in order to get points. One bounce equals 5 points; zero bounces equals 10 points. If the ball bounces off the corner of the stoop and the player catches it, the ball is called a pointer and is worth 100 points. Players usually play to 1,000 points, though they may choose any number to play to. If the player fails to catch the ball, his or her turn is over.

Another version of stoopball is more like baseball. The batter throws the ball at the stoop, and "ghost runners" round a number of bases equal to the number of times the ball bounces before the defense catches it. For example, if the ball bounces two times, the runner is on second base. Players must keep track of their ghost runners and scores. The batter bats until he gets three outs. Outs occur when the defensive player catches the ball before it bounces.

Tetherball
Rating: 8+

Each player stands on one side of the pole. The object of the game is for each player to wrap the ball around the pole by keeping the ball moving one way. The opponent tries simultaneously to block the ball and move it the other way. It does not matter whether you prefer to hit the ball in a clockwise or counterclockwise motion.

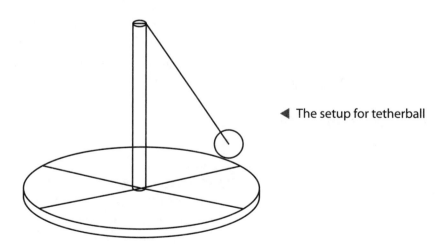

◀ The setup for tetherball

Players move the ball by hitting it with their hands. The players decide before the beginning of the game whether the ball can be hit with two hands or one. The winner of the game is the one who wraps the ball around the pole the most times during an agreed-upon period.

Rubber Ball Games

Lots of games require nothing more than a rubber ball to get you started. Here are some games to keep you playing for hours.

Bound Ball
Rating: 8+

Any number of players can participate, but the best groups number between ten and thirty. To start, mark a line on the floor. The players divide into two equal teams, taking their positions five feet from the opposite sides of the line. The players of each team spread out, so that each individual has space to move. One player begins by throwing the ball into the midst of the players so that it will rebound from the floor as near as possible to the line.

After the ball has bounced, the player who is then nearest to it strikes it from above, and either he or some of the players of his side continue to strike it after each rebound until there is an opportunity to bounce it across the line. A player commits a foul if he strikes the ball when it has not rebounded from the floor, fails to strike it after the first rebound, fails to strike it from above, or permits it to roll on the ground. The side that first has twelve fouls scored against it loses the game.

Center Stride Ball
Rating: 8+

Any number of players can participate, but the best groups are between ten and sixty players. One player stands in the center, and the other players form a ring around him by standing with their feet apart, each foot touching a neighbor's foot. The player in the center tries to send the ball out between the players' feet by batting it with his hand so that it will roll along the floor.

The players protect themselves by batting the ball back. If any player fails to do this, and so allows the ball to pass out between his feet, he must change places with the player in the center. If the circle is large, there should be two players in the center and two balls in play.

Center stride ball may also be played with variations. The players may kick the ball instead of batting it; or they may keep the ball moving around the circle, either to the right or the left, so that the player in the center has difficulty in getting an opportunity to bat the ball out.

Dodge Ball
Rating: 8+

Any number of players can participate, but the best groups are between twenty and sixty. After choosing sides, the players of side A stand in a circle around those of side B. The A's try to throw the ball so as to hit the B's, while the B's attempt to save themselves by running and dodging inside the circle. The A's may pass the ball among themselves as much as they choose, and leave the circle when it is necessary to regain possession of the ball. However, while they are out of the circle, they may not throw at their opponents. They must either return to the circle or throw to one of their own side. When a B has been hit, he is "killed," and must stand in the circle with the A's and help them "kill" the remaining B's. The last B left in the circle is the winner.

Dodgeball should be played with adult supervision. Because the players throw balls to intentionally hit someone, adults need to make sure that the balls aren't thrown too forcefully.

Guess Ball
Rating: 8+

Any number of players can participate, but the best groups are between ten and twenty-five players. First, all the players except one form a line, standing side by side. The remaining player stands several feet in front of the others, with his back toward them, and counts aloud to a number previously agreed upon. Meanwhile the ball is passed back and forth along the line.

When the given number is called, the person who then holds the ball throws it so as to strike the back of the player who stands in front. If the player is hit, he turns quickly, and tries to guess by the attitudes of the players which of them threw the ball. If he guesses correctly, the player who threw the ball changes places with him. If he does not guess correctly, he remains in front, and the game is repeated. If the player in the line fails to hit the one in front with the ball, they change places.

Numbers
Rating: 8+

Any number of players can participate, but the best groups are between six and sixty. The players are all assigned numbers and stand together. The player who is first chosen as "It" throws the ball high into the air, at the same time calling one of the numbers given to the players. Thereupon all the players except the one whose number has been called run as far away from the ball as they can.

The player whose number was called tries to catch the ball as quickly as possible. As soon as he has it, he stands still, and calls out "I got it." The rest of the players must stop running and, without turning their heads, stand with their backs to the one who has the ball. The latter, after taking time to aim, throws the ball to hit someone on the back. The thrower can take up to the number of steps that equal his player number. If he is successful at hitting someone, the one who has been struck calls out "I was hit." The player hit then gets to throw the ball into the air and call out another number. This game continues through an allotted period of time. There are no winners or losers.

One-Legged Football
Rating: 8+

Any number of players can participate, but the best groups are between ten and sixty. In addition to a rubber ball, you'll also need a stopwatch.

Mark goal lines at the two ends of an area. The distance between them varies according to the number of players, being always large enough to allow the players to run about freely. Players choose sides and appoint captains. Then the ball is put into play between the two captains. Each player stands with his right foot held behind him in his left hand or his left foot in his right hand. With his free hand or with the foot on which he is standing, he tries to hit the ball.

FACT

A variation of one-legged football is having the players assume the same position as before, but hit the ball only with their free hands. Or the players may stand on both feet and run about freely, and hit the ball with either hand. Players may not throw the ball in any case.

The object of the game is to force the ball over the opponents' goal line. Each goal scores 1 point. After the goal has been made, put the ball into play again at the center. Whoever scores the most points in the allotted time wins.

Any Ball Will Do

For any of the following games, just about any ball will do. As long as it can bounce, you can start playing.

Roll Ball
Rating: 8+

Any number of players can participate, from two to twenty. Draw a line to divide the floor into two courts. On each side of this line, parallel to it, and seven or eight yards from it, draw a boundary line. There are two teams, A and B. Each team takes a court, and stands behind the boundary line.

The first player from A comes forward, and takes his place on his boundary line with the ball on the line beside him. The first player from B stands opposite on his boundary line. The A player then tries to send his ball across B's boundary line by batting it with his hand or his fist. The B player tries to prevent the ball from crossing his line by running to meet it and batting it back without first catching it. If the A player fails to send the ball across the middle line, B scores a point. But if the ball crosses the middle line and B fails to bat it back before it crosses his boundary line, A scores a point. The game continues between these two players until one of them scores a point or makes a foul. Then two other players take their places.

A player commits a foul if he stops the ball before batting it back; bats the ball so that it flies up above the knee; or sends the ball so that it lodges in a piece of apparatus before it crosses the middle line. If the ball lodges in the apparatus after it has crossed that line, no foul has been made, and the player on whose side the ball is may roll it out a short distance in a direction parallel to the middle line, and from there bat it. If the ball hits the wall, it is still in play, and no foul has been made. Each foul scores 1 point for the opponents' side. The side that first scores 30 points wins the game.

Target Ball
Rating: 8+

Any number of players can participate, but the best groups are between ten and twenty-five. The players choose one person to be thrower. The other players are runners, and stand in a row. The thrower stands several paces distant from them toward the center of the row. At a given signal the first runner starts, runs around two sides of the room, and stops on the farther side, opposite the last player in the line of runners. During the run the thrower tries to throw the ball so as to hit the runner. If he succeeds, the one he hits remains opposite the line of runners, and a second runner is called out.

The game continues until the thrower fails to hit the runner. The runner who has escaped becomes thrower, and the thrower takes his place as the last runner in line. The game goes on as before. When all the runners have been hit, the game ends. The thrower who has hit the most runners wins.

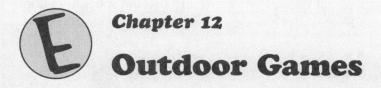

Chapter 12

Outdoor Games

Who doesn't love to be out in the sunshine, enjoying the fresh air? The games offered in this chapter provide the perfect incentive to turn off the television and go outside. With games like badminton and the ultimate Frisbee, you can get some exercise and have a blast at the same time.

Badminton

Rating: 8+

This lawn game is played with one or two players to a team. To play, you'll need a badminton net, rackets, and shuttlecocks (birdies). Most people set up a badminton net in their backyard and use the space on either side as the court. Each team gets one side of the court as their territory.

▲ Badminton rackets and shuttlecocks

In badminton, there are three ways to score a point:

1. When the birdie lands inside the court of the nonserving team (having gone over the net).
2. When the nonserving team hits the birdie outside of the serving team's court area (or under the net).
3. If the nonserving team commits a rules violation.

To begin playing, the serving team must serve from behind their end line. The serve must be underhand. The serving team serves the birdie over the net into the court of the nonserving team. The nonserving team returns, and the volley continues until one team loses the point by hitting the birdie out of the other team's area or under the net, by allowing the birdie to touch the ground inside their court area, or by hitting the birdie twice consecutively.

If teams are playing, the serve goes to the other side when both parties on the team have served. The players on each team rotate positions after every point.

Badminton is generally played to 15 or 20 points. Only the team serving can score a point. The nonserving team gains the serve, should it win the point played, and then has the opportunity to score.

Beanbag Target
Rating: 5+

The minimum number of players for this game is nine. You will need five beanbags for each group of nine or more players.

For every group of nine or more players, draw three concentric circles on the floor. They should be about one, two, and three feet in diameter. About twenty feet from the circles, draw a straight line to serve as the baseline. In each group a referee is appointed, and sides are chosen. The players alternate from the two sides. Each in turn stands with his toe on the baseline, and tosses the five beanbags, one after another, toward the circles. Each beanbag that falls within the inner circle counts fifteen, each within the second circle counts ten, and each within the outside circle counts five.

You also can substitute a board for the circles on the floor. The board should be about 2½ by 2 feet, with a large hole cut near the upper left-hand corner and a small one near the lower right-hand corner. It should stand at an angle of forty-five degrees. When a board is used, the point count is fifteen for every bag thrown through the small hole, ten for every one through the large hole, and five for every bag remaining on the board at the end of the player's turn. Whichever group totals 100 points first wins.

Bocce

Rating: 8+

Bocce is an Italian lawn game that is becoming very popular in the United States. Four or more people can play. If four play, they play individually. Otherwise, the players are divided into teams of four. Create a playing field with clearly marked lines. Each team uses four bocce balls. The balls have distinctive colors and patterns so that each player can identify his ball.

The rules of the game are as follows:

1. Toss a coin to decide which team will go first. The winner tosses the *pallino* (the smallest ball) to put it into play. The pallino must pass the midfield line and stay in bounds. If the pallino is not tossed properly by the first team, the second team tosses the pallino to put it into play.
2. The team that tosses the pallino properly then tosses their first bocce ball as close to the pallino ball as possible. The first team then steps aside and lets the second team toss their first bocce ball. Whenever a team gets their bocce ball closer to the pallino ball than the other team did, they step aside and let the other team toss their bocce ball. If a team does not toss their bocce ball closer to the pallino, then the other team continues to toss their remaining bocce balls until they get a ball closer or they have tossed all of the balls. This continues until both teams have tossed all their bocce balls.

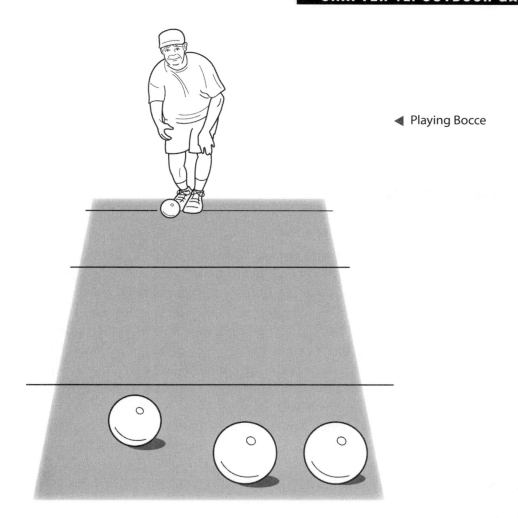

◀ Playing Bocce

3. A player can use his bocce ball to knock his opponent's bocce ball away from the pallino. All balls must stay in bounds at all times. If a bocce ball goes out of bounds it is removed from the game. Play will resume from the opposite end of the court, with the team that originally tossed the pallino tossing it again.

4. Only one team scores in a frame. One point is given for each bocce ball that is closer to the pallino than is the closest ball from the opposing team.

5. All balls must be tossed from behind the foul line. Balls may be tossed, rolled, or bounced underhanded.

6. If a player rolls the wrong color ball, simply replace it with the correct color ball when it comes to rest. If a player rolls out of turn, the other team has the option to replace any moved balls to their original position or leave all balls as they are.

7. The team that reaches the agreed-upon number of points for that game wins.

Crisscross

Rating: 8+

Any number of players can participate, but the best groups number between four and sixty. You will need half as many beanbags as there are players for this game. Decide on a time limit for the game before play begins.

Divide the players into groups of not more than ten. Each of these groups plays a separate game. Each group chooses sides, which stand facing one another at a distance of eight or ten feet; give the beanbags to the players of one side. The player at the right end of the beanbag row is number 1 of that line. He begins the game by throwing his bag to the player opposite him in line, who catches it and throws it back. Number 1 of the beanbag row then throws his bag to Number 2 of the opposite line, and so on until he has come to the last player, after which he begins again with Number 1.

FACT

Another fun beanbag game is catch it, drop it. Players create a circle around a player who is holding a beanbag. The player throws the bean-bag to any player in the circle and calls out "Catch it" or "Drop it." The player must do the opposite of what is called; if he doesn't, he must sit down. The last player left standing in the circle wins.

Meanwhile, as soon as Number 1 of the beanbag line has received his bag after his first throw, Number 2 of the same line begins throwing to Number 1 of the opposite line, and so on. In like manner, when Number 2 has received his bag after his first throw, Number 3 begins. This continues until all the players in the beanbag line are throwing, each beginning as soon as his right-hand neighbor has made his first play. Keep score of the number of times each side drops a bag. When the time limit has expired, the side that has dropped the fewer bags wins.

Croquet

Rating: 8+

Croquet is a lawn game the entire family can enjoy. The game requires an official croquet set, which includes eight balls, eight mallets, nine arches, and two stakes. You also can play a *half set,* consisting of four balls, four mallets, nine arches, and two stakes.

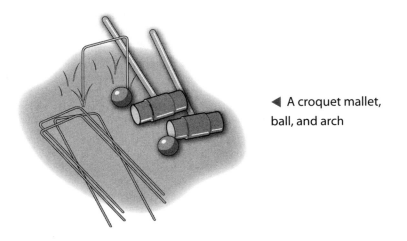

◀ A croquet mallet, ball, and arch

While the game can be adapted to any size lawn, the official dimensions are as follows: length, 72 feet; width, 36 feet; corner pieces, 8 feet long; inside measurements, with a line denoting boundary of the field, 30 inches from the inside of the border. Place the stakes 72 feet apart; the first arch 7 feet in front of the starting stake; the second, 7 feet from the first; the third, 14 feet to the right of, and one foot in advance of the second; the fourth, in line with the first and second, and 22 feet in advance of the second; the remaining five at the same relative distance. In the end, there will be five arches in line between the stakes, and four wing arches.

You can play croquet with up to eight people, four on each side. Six or four, however, make a better game, and if there are only two players, each can use two croquet balls. Regardless of the number of participants, each takes a mallet and ball of the same color.

Playing the Game

The game begins with the leader of one side placing his ball about a mallet's length in front of the starting stake, and striking it with the head of his mallet, driving it through the first arch. If he succeeds, he then tries to drive it through the next arch, and so on. As soon as he misses going through an arch his turn is over. If at his first turn he does not send his ball through the first arch, he gives his place to the next player. The leader of the other side then plays, and then the others in the order of the colors on the starting stake.

▲ Hitting the croquet ball

The aim of each player is to drive the ball from the starting stake throughout the seven arches to the turning stake, which must be struck. This is called *pegging* or *staking*. The player then drives the ball back to the starting stake.

When a player strikes his own ball so as to hit another, however lightly, he is said to *roquet* it. Having hit a ball, he can *take the croquet*, meaning that he places his own ball against the roqueted ball so that it touches it; he then strikes his ball, driving one or both balls in any direction he wishes. The player can do this before proceeding further in the game, or not, at his option.

As soon as the ball has gone through the first arch, the player may use the ball to *croquet* (meaning to strike one's own ball when in contact with a roqueted ball) any ball that has also passed through the same arch. A player may use this opportunity to help out a fellow teammate, or derail an opponent. It is done as follows: When a ball has hit another at a distance, the player lays his own ball against the other ball so that it touches it. At this point two different methods of playing come in. One is called *tight croquet*, and the other *loose croquet*. In the former the player places his foot on his own ball, and strikes the ball with the mallet. The effect of this will be to drive the other ball in any direction the player may choose, which will be governed by whether the ball belongs to a player on his own side or not.

If the player adopts the loose croquet method, he does not place his foot on the ball, but merely places the two balls in contact and drives them both together by striking his ball. The result of this is that they fly off at different angles.

When a player has returned to the starting stake, he may either strike the peg and retire, or not strike it and be a *rover* with the privilege of traveling over the ground to assist players on his own side or damage the prospects of the opponents. Therefore, the player who reaches the turning stake first has great advantage. As soon as he begins his return journey he is able to croquet the other players, considerably impeding their progress. The side whose balls are first driven around, and then peg the starting stake, wins the game.

ALERT!

Do not play a selfish game; that is, do not be in too great a hurry to make your own arches. You may often help your side more by going back and roqueting than by running your own ball through half a dozen arches. Remember, if you are playing on a team you cannot win the game by your own ball alone.

Rules of the Game

1. The players on each side are to play alternately according to the colors on the starting stake.
2. On the first play, each player may place his ball at a distance from the starting stake not exceeding the mallet handle.
3. The first stroke must be to pass the ball through the first arch.
4. The ball is struck with one of the faces of the mallet head, never with its side.
5. The ball must never be pushed. A ball is considered to be well struck when the sound of the stroke is heard. A ball is pushed when the face of the mallet is allowed to rest against it, and the ball is propelled without the mallet being drawn back.
6. If a ball is struck with other than the face of the mallet, if it is pushed, or if in striking at his own ball a player hits another, it is a found stroke, and the player loses his turn; any balls disturbed shall be replaced or remain, at the option of the opposite side.
7. If, in making a stroke, a ball is driven beyond the limits of the croquet ground, it may be taken up and placed at the point where it crossed the boundary line.
8. When a ball is accidentally driven from its resting place, it is to be returned to the spot from which it was started.
9. A player can rest the head of his mallet on the ground at a distance from the ball and strike it by sharply advancing the mallet from its resting place.
10. Instead of aiming at his arch or at another ball, a player may strike his ball toward any part of the ground he pleases.

11. The balls are to pass through the course in the regular order of the arches. If a ball passes through an arch other than the arch next in its turn, or from the wrong side, it doesn't count.

12. If a ball is struck through its right arch by another ball, or is roqueted through, it is considered to have gone through its arch.

13. Any player missing the first arch takes his ball up, and when his turn comes, plays from the starting place as at the beginning of the game.

14. A ball is considered to have passed through an arch when it passes within and beyond it to any extent, or when, if the handle of the mallet is laid across the two sides of the arch whence the ball came, the ball does not touch the handle.

15. Hitting the turning stake is equivalent in its privileges to the passing of an arch.

16. When the ball of a player hits the starting stake after he has been through all the arches, whether by his own play or by being roqueted or croqueted, he is out of the game.

17. A ball is a *rover* after going through all the arches, without hitting the starting stake.

18. A rover has liberty to croquet consecutively all the balls during anyone of his turns, but cannot croquet the same ball twice in a single turn.

19. If a person plays out of turn, and the error is discovered before the turn is completed, the ball must be placed where it stood before, as well as any balls it may have moved. If, however, the turn is completed, the player loses his next turn.

20. When a player roquets two or more balls by one stroke of the mallet, he is said to *ricochet,* and may croquet one or all, at his option.

21. As soon as a player has gone through the first arch, he is at liberty to croquet any ball that has also gone through the arch.

22. A player cannot croquet a ball that he has not roqueted.

23. A *booby* (a ball that has failed to pass through the first arch) cannot croquet another ball, or be croqueted.

24. A player is forced to move the croqueted ball at least six inches, and cannot croquet the same ball a second time until he has passed through an arch.

25. If a player ricochets, and wishes to croquet, he must do so in the order in which the balls were roqueted, but the striker has only one additional stroke when he has croqueted.

26. If a player hits another ball that is a rover and drives it against the winning stake, he is allowed another turn, but cannot croquet the ball, as it is dead the moment it touches the stake.

27. If in tight croqueting the ball slips from the foot and goes through the arch, or strikes the stake, the stroke does not count.

28. If, in an attempt to croquet a ball, the player's ball *flinches* (slips from beneath the player's foot), the ball on which the croquet was to be executed is free, and can be struck in its turn by its owner.

29. A player, after striking a ball, is not necessarily compelled to croquet it, but is allowed to play in any direction he pleases. He must, however, play from the place where his ball is, and not move it to another position in order to touch the ball he struck.

30. If a player croquets a ball illegally, he loses his next turn.

31. If a ball, when croqueted through its arch in a wrong direction, rolls back through the arch, it does not have to pass through the same arch in the same direction again.

32. Should the course of a ball be interrupted by any person, the player can allow it to remain at the point where interrupted, or it can be moved to where he supposes it would have reached.

33. If a player plays with a wrong ball, he has to replace the ball and lose his turn. This is not enforced unless the error is discovered before the player's second turn.

34. If a ball is moved by a player when it should not have been touched, it must be restored to its former position.

35. The first side to have all its players pass through the arches and strike both stakes wins the game.

36. All the games shall be opened by scoring from an imaginary line through the middle wicket, and playing two balls each (not partner balls) together toward the home stake. The player whose ball rests nearest the stake shall have the choice of play, using that ball.

37. A player, in each turn of play, is at liberty to roquet any ball on the ground once only before making a point.

38. A player makes a point in the game when his ball passes through an arch or hits a stake in proper play.
39. If a player makes a point, and immediately afterward roquets a ball, he must take the point and use the ball.
40. If a ball roquets another and immediately afterward makes a point, it must take the ball and reject the point.
41. A player continues to play as long as he makes a point in the game, or roquets another ball to which he is in play. A ball making 2 or more points at the same stroke has no additional privileges.
42. Should a player find his ball in contact with another, he may hit his own as he likes, approaching it as though the balls were separated by an inch or more.
43. A rover has the right of the roquet and consequent croquet on every ball once during each turn of play, and is subject to roquet and croquet by any ball in play.
44. Rovers must be continued in the game until partners become rovers and go out successively. A rover that has been driven against the stake cannot be removed to make way for the next rover.

Hide-and-Seek

Rating: 5+

Hide-and-seek can be played either outdoors or indoors, depending on the number of players and the amount of space you have. Any number of participants can play this game.

Appoint one player as "It." This player stands at a *home base,* turns around or closes his eyes, and counts out loud to twenty, while the other players hide. He then opens his eyes and begins to search for the other players. If he finds a player, he chases her, and tries to tag her. She has to run back to home base before It catches her. If It does catch her, she then becomes It and everyone else hides. If she is not caught and makes it safely back to home base, the first player is still It and must find and tag another player, and so on.

Pickleball

Rating: 8+

Pickleball is played on a badminton-sized court with a 36-inch-high net. There are two teams of one or two players each. Players hit a large, plastic, perforated ball with a large wooden paddle. The ball is served underhand diagonally into the opponent's court.

Points are awarded only to the serving side. Points are scored when the opponent fails to return the ball or hits it out of bounds. The serve switches to the other side when a server faults. A fault occurs when the server hits the ball into the net or out of bounds. If the ball hits the net and goes into the correct court the server reserves the ball. The first side to reach 11 points wins. However, they must win by a 2-point margin.

Rules of the game are fairly simple:

1. The server can have one foot in the baseline if the other is out.
2. After the serve, the ball must bounce once before volleying.
3. When the serving team wins the point, the teams switch serving areas of the court. If they lose the point, they turn the ball over to the other side.
4. In doubles, the first serving team can fault only once before the serve changes to the other side. After the first fault, both members of the team serve and fault before the other side serves.
5. Faults include: ball out of bounds, ball hits the net, stepping into a non-volley zone while volleying, and volleying the ball before it bounces once.
6. The ball may land on the line and be counted.

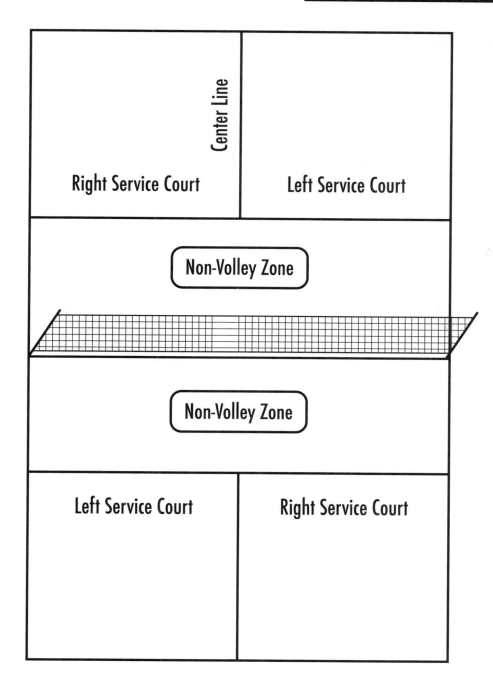

▲ Standard court for pickleball

Tennis

Rating: 8+

Tennis is either played one-on-one (singles) or two-on-two (doubles). The object is to gain enough points to win a game. When you win six games, you win a set. When you win the best of either three or five sets, you win the match. The first player to win 4 points wins the game unless the two players tie at the third point (40-40). This is called deuce. If there is a deuce, the winner is the first player to score 2 points in a row.

Playing

The game starts with the server serving behind the baseline in the right-hand court. The server then hits the ball into the court diagonally opposite. Each server has two chances to get the ball into the appropriate court. If the ball hits the net or post or goes out of bounds, it is a fault. A ball that hits the line is in. After two faults, the opponent gets the point. When a player fails to return the ball, hits it out of bounds, or hits it after more than one bounce, the other player gets the point. After each point is scored, players switch service areas of the court. Serve switches after games.

Scoring

Scoring in tennis is as follows:

0 points = Love
1 point = 15
2 points = 30
3 points = 40
4 points = Game

The server's score is called first. For example, if the server has gained 2 points and the receiver one, the score is 30-15.

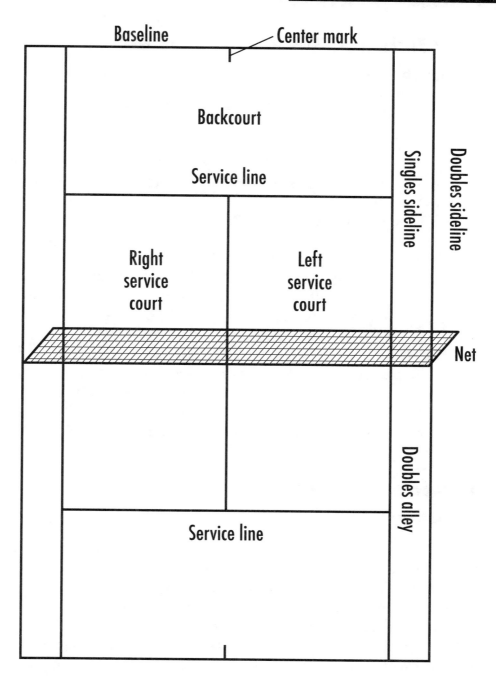

▲ Traditional tennis court

Time Ball
Rating: 8+

Any number of players can participate, but the best groups number between ten and sixty. You will need as many balls or beanbags as there are rows of players.

Seat the players so that there is the same number of players in each row. Draw a line about four yards from the rows of players, and another at about two yards from them.

The leader of each row takes his ball, and stands opposite his row on the far line. Then, at a given signal, the first player in each row runs toward the leader to the halfway mark. When the player has reached it, the leader throws him the ball, which he catches and returns. Immediately he runs back to his seat. As soon as he is seated, the next player in the row runs to the mark and catches the ball. So the game goes on, with the players running in turn, and each starting as soon as the previous player has seated himself.

A player commits a foul if he throws when he is not on the mark, or misses the toss from the leader, and he must repeat the play. When all have run, the leader returns to his row and seats himself with the ball in front of him. The first row that succeeds in doing this wins the game.

Ultimate Frisbee
Rating: 12+

Ultimate Frisbee is played on a field with end zones. A field is usually 70 by 40 yards. End zones are 25 yards into the field. Teams are composed of seven players. The game is started with players lined up at their respective end zones. The defense throws the Frisbee to the offensive team. Offensive players score points by completing passes in the end zone of the other team.

Players must not run with the disk and must throw it within ten seconds of gaining possession. If the pass is not completed, the other team gains possession. Defensive players attempt to block or intercept passes. Players are not allowed to touch one another. Intentional physical contact between players results in a foul. Games are usually played to 9 points or for forty-five minutes. A team must win by 2 points.

Are there any other games that people play with a Frisbee?
Another fun game is Frisbee golf. It is played on a course of nine or eighteen "holes." Players divide into groups of up to four. Groups start at different holes—for example, group 1 starts at hole 1, group 2 at hole 2, and so on. Players attempt to throw the Frisbee into the "hole," which is a basket. The basket and "tee" are usually about 200 feet apart. The number of throws it takes to get the Frisbee in the basket is counted. The player with the fewest accumulated throws at the end of the round wins.

Volleyball

Rating: 12+

Volleyball is a popular outdoor game that can be adapted to either the beach or the backyard. Any even number of people can play, from two to eighteen. You'll need a volleyball net, a stopwatch, and a volleyball.

The object of the game is to score points by making the opposing team miss the ball and have it land on the ground. The ball must be kept in motion, back and forth above the net, by striking it with the open hand or with the forearms. At no time can the ball go outside the court or touch the floor.

While the volleyball serve described here applies to adult players, the game can also be enjoyed by kids by allowing the children to serve the ball underhand, thus improving their chances of getting it over the net.

A member of one team starts the game by standing with one foot on the back line of the court and with the other foot behind the line, usually standing in the right corner of the court. From there the player serves the ball by tossing it lightly from one hand and batting it with the palm of the other hand. Two trials are allowed to send it into the opponents' court. If a ball in service strikes the net or fails to enter the opponents' court after two tries, the opposing side gets to serve. A player continues serving until he makes two faults in succession during service or until his side does not return the ball.

◀ Player striking ball with open hand

In returning, as well as in serving the ball, any number of players on the same side may strike the ball to send it across the net; but no player may strike it more than twice in succession. Volleying continues until one side fails to return it or it touches the floor.

A ball that hits the net, if not a service ball, counts as a failure in returning. If the ball hits the net during service, it is dead, and counts as a trial serve. If any player touches the net while playing, the ball is out of play, and the opposite side scores a point. If any player catches or holds the ball for even an instant, that also scores a point for the opposite side.

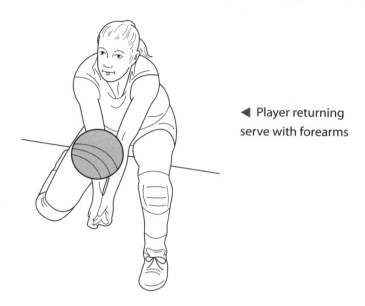

◀ Player returning
serve with forearms

If the ball strikes any object except the floor and bounces back into the court, it is still in play. Each good service that is unreturned scores a point for the serving side, and the serving side also scores whenever the opponents fail to return a ball that is in play. A side only scores when serving. An inning is finished when each player has served in turn, and a game consists of any number of innings previously agreed upon.

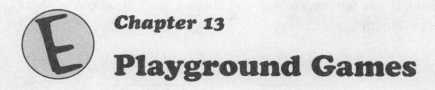

Chapter 13

Playground Games

While school may be boring at times, the playground needn't be! Within this chapter you will find several popular playground games that can accommodate any number of players. When you introduce these games on the playground, you can have fun and make new friends at the same time.

Hopscotch

Rating: 8+

Hopscotch is a popular children's game that requires only a few stones, a piece of chalk, and a concrete surface. While the hopscotch grid can be drawn to suit the players' size and abilities, the official one is about twelve feet in length.

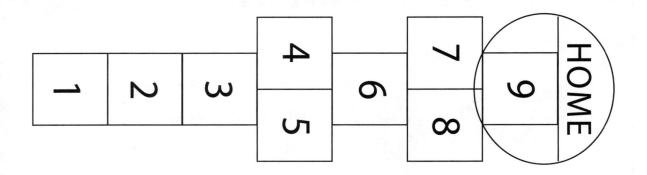

▲ Hopscotch grid

The first player stands at a starting line drawn a foot or two from the beginning of the court. She tosses a stone into box number 1, hops into the box on one foot, and then kicks out the stone, which she throws into box number 2. Then she jumps backward to the starting line. Next, the player again hops into number 1 on one foot, and then jumps and lands both feet so that one foot is in box 1 and the other foot is in box 2. The player kicks the stone into box number 3, and then out, and so on, until she fails to throw the stone into the right place, or to kick it into the right division, or lands on a line, or touches her raised foot, or steps on a line. Any of these would cause the player to lose her turn, allowing the next player to go. The player who can complete the grid first without faltering is the winner.

The player must straddle boxes 4 and 5, landing one foot in each; in the others a hop only must be taken.

In another popular variation of hopscotch, no straddling step is taken, but the player, in certain boxes, is allowed to place the stone on her foot, and so expel it from the grid at a single kick. The grid also can vary in the number of boxes and their arrangement.

Kickball

Rating: 8+

This game is an outdoor game played by two teams of at least nine players each (there can be fewer players, if necessary). Kickball is played in a manner similar to baseball, but is much easier, especially for younger players.

The players are arranged as in baseball: three in the outfield, three in the infield, one pitcher, and one catcher. The first team up "bats," or kicks, the ball. The pitcher rolls the ball toward the first player, who kicks it as hard and as far as he can. He then tries to run to first base, and if he can go farther he may. If not, he stays at first. At the same time the team in the field tries to catch the ball and get it to the base the player is trying to get to, and tries to tag him out. If the team succeeds in tagging him out, he has gotten an out for his team and returns to the bench. Each team gets three outs before they switch positions in the field. The team that was in the field will then kick, and the other team will field.

The game usually has nine innings. The team with the highest score wins.

Mother May I

Rating: 8+

This popular game is best played with ten or more players. One player is selected to be the "mother." The object of this game is to tag the mother; once you've done this you become the mother and everyone else tries to tag you.

The mother stands in front of a line of players about fifty yards away. The mother calls out one of the players' names, and he answers, "Yes, Mother." The mother then asks them to do a specific task; for example, "Take three giant steps forward." At this time the player has to ask the mother if he can do it by responding, "Mother, may I?" The Mother then either answers, "Yes, you may," and the task is carried out, or, "No, you may not," and the player stays where he is.

The mother then has to keep track of all the players. Once she forgets where they are, she will surely lose her position.

FACT

This game can either be played with the mother facing the players or with her back turned to them. Obviously, it is more difficult if the mother isn't facing the players, because she will have to rely on the sound of the players' voices to determine how close they are.

Red Light, Green Light

Rating: 8+

This is an outdoor game that is best suited for ten or more players. One player is selected to be the *traffic light*. This person stands at the front of a line about fifty yards away from the other players. The object of the game is to tag the traffic light. The person who makes the tag then becomes the traffic light for the next round.

The players line up and the traffic light turns his back to the players. The traffic light begins counting out loud, at any speed that he wants, "Red light, green light, one, two, three." After that he quickly turns around. While the traffic light is counting, the rest of the players try to run up and tag him. But as soon as he turns around, everyone has to freeze. If the traffic light catches another player moving, that player must return to the starting line.

Red Rover

Rating: 8+

This game is best suited for large groups, with no fewer than twenty players. First, divide the players equally into two teams. Each team stands at opposite ends of a field, holding hands to form a wall. One team begins the game by shouting, "Red Rover, Red Rover, send [insert name] right over," using the name of someone on the other team.

A good strategy for this game is to seek out the weak links in the chain. Especially if the runner is a smaller player, he or she should run toward the link between the two smallest players on the opposing team.

That person must run toward the opposing team and try to break through the wall. If he succeeds in breaking through, he goes back to his team, and it is their turn to call someone over. If he does not succeed, he changes sides and is added to the team that he tried to break through, becoming a part of the wall. That team then gets another turn. In the end, the team that captures all the players wins.

Relay Races

Rating: 8+

Relay races are popular outdoor games, and can easily be organized by children or adults. The games listed here are the classic relays of all time.

Tag the Wall Relay Race

Divide the players into equal rows. One player gives a signal (for example, shouts out a certain word). The first player in each row then runs forward to touch the wall, immediately returns to the end of the row, and sits down. The next player on his team does the same thing. The first row to complete the race wins.

Relay Flag Races

Any number of players can participate, but the best groups are between ten and sixty participants. You will need chalk and a variety of flags for this game. If you can find lots of different-colored flags, or U.S. state flags, that would be best.

Draw two long chalk lines to create a starting point and an ending point, with five to ten yards between them. Divide the participants into rows that each have the same number of players. Give a flag to the first in each row. The rows then line up behind the starting line.

At the signal, the player holding the flag turns around, runs to the farther chalk line, turns around, and runs back to his starting point. Then the second player in his row takes the flag as quickly as possible, and runs with it, and so on. The row that finishes first wins.

The race may be varied by having the players jump or hop down the course, or by having them stop halfway and perform definite tasks, such as picking up and replacing beans or stones or performing some gymnastic exercise.

Simon Says
Rating: 8+

This classic party game is perfect for any number of players, but between ten and sixty make for the best game. All the players stand in long lines, except for one player, or parent, who is chosen to be Simon. Simon will instruct the rest of the players to perform certain physical movements, and the players will follow him with that movement, until he suggests another. However, Simon must say "Simon says" before naming the movement in order for the rest of the players to follow along. If Simon omits saying "Simon says" in the command, the rest of the players do not perform the movement, even if Simon is demonstrating it.

Any player who fails to obey Simon's commands promptly, or who obeys commands that are not accompanied by the words "Simon says," must leave the game. The last player left in the group is the winner.

FACT

A variation on Simon says: The leader of the game calls out "Ducks fly," and raises his arms to represent flying. The players imitate him. He continues, naming any animals he chooses instead of ducks. As long as he names an animal that can fly, the players continue to imitate him; but if he names one that cannot fly—for example, if he calls out "Cats fly"— the players remain motionless.

Tag
Rating: 5+

There are hundreds of versions of tag, a universally enjoyed children's game. Some are more complicated than others. Any number can participate in any game of tag, but the best games have six to sixty players.

Classic Tag—One player is chosen to be "It." He chases the other players and tries to tag one of them. If he succeeds, the one who has been tagged becomes It.

Secret Tag—This game is played without telling who is It. All the players pretend to tag; but any player who is not It whispers to the one whom he tags, "I am not It," while the one who is It must say, "I am It."

Stoop Tag—In this game no player may be tagged while he is in a stooping position. You can create a rule and limit the number of times that a player may be allowed to stoop. After a player has stooped the allotted number of times, he can escape only by running. A further variation may be created by substituting any gymnastic position for stooping.

Goss Tag—If any player runs between the one who is It and the one who is pursued, the latter cannot be tagged; the one who has crossed between must be chased instead. This brings cooperation into the game.

Iron Tag—A player may not be tagged when he is touching iron with his hand. The game may be varied by substituting wood or stone for iron, or by requiring that the object be touched in some special way (with the elbow, or the foot, or with four fingers at once, and so on).

Japanese Tag—The one who has been tagged must place his right hand on the spot where he has been touched, whether it is on his arm, his chest, his back, or his ankle. With his hand in that position he must chase the other players until he has tagged one of them.

Clasp Tag—The one who is It clasps his hands behind his back and keeps them there until he has tagged one of the other players with them.

Pickadill—This is a kind of tag played during the winter. Make a large circle in the snow, with paths; if there are many players, make two circles. One person is selected to be It for each circle, and the center of the circles is the place of safety.

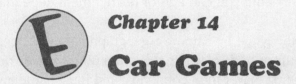

Chapter 14

Car Games

Let's face it; road trips can be rather boring. Within the confines of a vehicle, people tend to get a bit antsy. This chapter offers the solution car games. Choose any or all of these games to play, and you won't hear the dreaded "Are we there yet?" again.

Geography
Rating: 8+

Geography is the perfect family game for long drives or quiet summer nights. Any number of people can participate in the game. The rules given here are for the most general game, but you can add or restrict them depending on the level of play.

One player begins the game by naming a geographical reference, such as a town, city, state, country, body of water, mountain range, and so on. The player to the left of the first player then continues, and must name another geographical reference that begins with the last letter from the first reference. For example, if the first player says "Oklahoma," the next player must name a state that begins with A, such as "Alabama."

Continue the game with each player adding on to the last player's reference. You may not repeat any references; each player must keep a mental list of what has been said. If a player cannot think of a reference, or repeats one that has already been mentioned, he is out of the game. The last player to remain in the game is the winner.

I Spy
Rating: 8+

One player picks an object in the view of the other players and describes its color: "I spy something with my little eye and the color is blue." Players then try to guess which object she has in mind. The first player to guess correctly wins and gets to pick the next object.

License Plate Bingo
Rating: 8+

Each player writes the letters of the alphabet on a piece of paper in bingo-card style, five squares by five, for a total of twenty-five (skip one letter, for example "z"). You may cross off each letter only when you see it on a license plate. The first player to get five squares across, up, down, or diagonally calls out "Bingo."

For a more challenging variation, cross off letters in alphabetical order. That is, you may only cross off C after you have crossed off B, and so on.

For longer road trips, someone may make up bingo-style cards with the states' names in the squares. Players may mark off squares when they see a license plate from that state. The first player to get five squares across, up, down, or diagonally calls out "Bingo."

Road Sign Bingo

Rating: 8+

Players make up bingo-style cards, five squares by five, marked with the various road signs. As you spot the road signs, mark them off on your card. The first player to get five squares in a row, up, down, across, or diagonally wins and calls out "Bingo."

Twenty Questions

Rating: 8+

One player thinks of a famous noun, person, or thing. Players then ask yes-or-no questions to try to get information about the object. For example, the other players ask questions such as "Is it an animal?" Players get twenty questions. The first player to guess the thing that the first player is thinking of wins and becomes the thinker for the next round. If players fail to guess within the twenty questions, the thinker tells them and goes again.

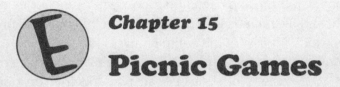

Chapter 15

Picnic Games

This chapter is a must-read for anyone planning a picnic or a family reunion. In these pages you will find a variety of classic picnic games for all ages that will be sure to bring family and friends closer together—sometimes even in a heap, as often happens with the three-legged race!

Horseshoes
Rating: 8+

Horseshoes, or horseshoe pitching, was a very popular pastime back in the days before cars. Today, real horseshoes are pretty hard to find (originally, the stakes were made of iron, and each horseshoe was 7½ inches in length, 7 inches in width, and 2½ pounds in weight). You can buy a plastic or light-weight metal set, which is easy for the entire family to play with.

Any number of participants can play this game, although only two people play against each other. More players can play together on different courts, or alternate turns. Each player must have two horseshoes in order to play.

The Horseshoe Court

While the court can be created to suit the players' individual needs (and sizes), the official court should cover an area of level ground at least ten feet wide and fifty feet long. The court consists of two pitcher's boxes, with a stake in the center of each. The pitcher's box is three feet square, and does not extend more than one inch above the ground level. For indoor play, the pitcher's box must not exceed six inches in height above the floor.

The pitcher's box should be filled with potter's clay or any similar substitute. The clay should be at least six inches deep at the beginning of each game, and the surface of the clay should never be more than one inch below the top of the box.

FACT

If, in a three-handed game, two of the players each have a ringer and the third player no ringer, the two players having ringers score their closest shoe; the third player is out of this play. If each of the three players has a ringer, the one who throws his next shoe closest to the stake scores.

Set one stake in the center of each pitcher's box. The stakes must incline two inches toward each other and project ten inches above the top of the box. Where several courts are constructed, place the adjacent stakes on a straight line not less than ten feet apart.

Rules of the Game

1. No player shall make any remarks or utter any sounds within the hearing of his opponent, nor make any movement that might interfere with the opponent's playing.
2. No player shall walk across to the opposite stake and examine the position of his opponent's shoe before making his first or final pitch.
3. All players shall pitch both shoes from the pitcher's box into the opposite pitcher's box or forfeit a point to his opponent.
4. The outer edges of the pitcher's box are known as the *foul lines*.
5. In delivering the shoe into the opposite pitcher's box a player may stand anywhere inside of the foul lines. A player's toes are allowed to extend slightly over the foul line.
6. Each player, when not pitching, must remain outside and behind the pitcher's box until his opponent has finished pitching.
7. At the beginning of a game the players shall decide who has the first pitch by the toss of a shoe or a coin. The winner chooses whether or not he should go first. After the first game, the loser of the preceding game pitches first.
8. The shoe is considered pitched as soon as it leaves the player's hand.
9. A shoe pitched while the player is standing outside the foul lines is foul.
10. If a shoe first strikes outside of the foul lines or any part of the pitcher's box before entering the pitcher's box, it is considered a foul.
11. Foul shoes are removed from the pitcher's box at the request of the opponent, and are not scored or credited.
12. No player shall touch his own or his opponent's shoes after they have been pitched, until the final decision has been rendered as to their scoring value. Failure to comply with this rule shall result in both shoes of the offender being declared foul, and his opponent shall be entitled to as many points as the position of his shoes at the stake should warrant.
13. A *ringer* shall be a shoe that encircles the stake far enough to permit a straight edge to touch both heels simultaneously.

14. Whenever a player knocks off his own or opponent's ringer, such knocked-off ringers lose their scoring value and the player making the ringer is credited with a ringer.

15. If a player knocks on one of his own or his opponent's shoes from a non-ringer position to a ringer position, the changed shoe has scoring value.

16. When a thrown shoe moves a shoe already at the stake, all shoes are counted in their new positions.

17. A regulation game consists of 50 points. Each game is divided into innings and each player pitching two shoes constitutes an inning.

18. All shoes shall be within six inches of the stake to score. The closest shoe scores 1 point. Two shoes closer than an opponent's score 2 points. One ringer scores 3 points; two score 6. One ringer and the closest shoe of same player scores 4 points. If a player has two ringers and his opponent one, the player with two scores 3 points. No points are scored for ties.

19. If each player has a ringer, the next closest shoe, if within six inches of the stake, shall score. If each player has a double ringer, both double ringers are canceled and no points scored. In case there is a tie of all four shoes, no score shall be recorded, and the player who pitched last is entitled to pitch first on the next throw.

20. Any shoe leaning against the stake in a tilted position shall have no advantage over a shoe lying flat on the ground against the stake. All such tosses are considered ties. If a player has a shoe leaning against the stake it shall count only as the closest shoe.

21. All shoes shall be scored and announced only in their final position after all scores have been pitched.

Leap Frog
Rating: 8+

This game requires at least two players. All players but one kneel on the ground in a line and cover their heads with their hands. The remaining player goes to the end of the line, puts her hands on the last frog's back, and jumps over. She continues down the line until the end, at which point the jumper kneels down. The last person in the line then becomes the jumper. Repeat until everyone has a chance to be the jumper.

Sack Race

Rating: 5+

Give each person a large burlap sack. Step into your sack with both feet and pull it up, holding it up with your hands. Everyone lines up at the starting line. One nonplayer starts the race. Players must hop inside the sack to the finish line. The first player across wins.

Three-Legged Race

Rating: 8+

Players form teams of two. Standing next to each other and facing the same direction, players tie their inside legs together. Each team lines up at a designated starting line, and a nonplayer calls "Ready, set, go!" Each team tries to make it to the designated finish line before the other teams do. The first team across wins.

While it is a good strategy to find players of approximately the same size, it can be a lot more fun for you and for the audience to pair up with someone smaller or bigger than you are.

Tug of War

Rating: 8+

Divide the players into two teams (roughly matching in weight). Designate a center mark with a line marked on the ground or with a string stretched through a mud pit or wading pool. Each team takes one end of the rope and tries to pull the other team across the line or into the mud or water. The first team to cross the center mark loses.

Water Balloon Toss

Rating: 8+

Players form teams of two. Then each pair stands across from the other, so that there are two rows of players facing each other, at about one foot apart. One player in each pair takes a balloon filled with water. When a designated person calls "Go!" each player holding the balloon tosses it to their partner. If their partner catches it without the balloon breaking, both players take a step backward (away from each other). Then, the balloon is tossed back to the other player. After each successful toss, both team members continue to take a step back. The team that is farthest apart when their balloon breaks wins.

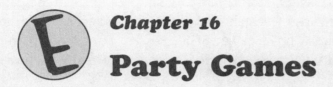

Chapter 16

Party Games

Whatʼs a party without games? For children, game-playing is a time to cut loose and have a blast. For parents, games provide organization and control. This chapter provides a variety of games for any number of participants. Whether you are having a large or small party, you will find great suggestions here.

Blind Man's Bluff
Rating: 5+

Any number of people can participate, but the best games have ten to sixty players. You will need a handkerchief for this game.

Blindfold one player and turn him around three times in the center of the room. He then tries to catch one of the other players. When he succeeds, he must guess who he caught. If he guesses correctly, the player who has been caught is blindfolded. If he does not guess correctly, he must catch another player.

Bobbing for Apples
Rating: 8+

This game can be played with any kind of apples, but candied or caramel apples make for more of a mess, which is always more fun!

FACT

For a variation of this game, partly fill a tub with water and throw the apples in. The object is for the players to dive in and try to retrieve the apples with their mouths. No hands allowed! Each player keeps the apple he rescues from the water.

Tie strings to the stems of the apples, and hang the apples just high enough that the players must jump to catch them with their mouths. Tie the players' hands behind their backs before the first jump. The first player to eat his entire apple wins.

Cat and Rat

Rating: 8+

This party game can be played by any number of players, but between ten and thirty players make for the best game.

Choose one player to be the cat and another to be the rat. The rest of the players join hands and form a ring, with the cat on the outside and the rat in the center. The cat then tries to catch the rat. The players favor the rat, and allow him to run in and out of the circle under their clasped hands. They try to prevent the cat from catching the rat by lowering or raising their hands, whichever is necessary. When the rat is caught, he joins the circle; the cat becomes rat, and chooses a new cat from the players.

Cushion Dance

Rating: 8+

Cushion dance requires six to thirty players. You will need half as many cushions (or pillows) as there are participants for this game.

A variation to this game is called slow poison. The players form a ring, hands joined, as in cushion dance. Instead of dancing, though, each player tries to pull or push his neighbors into the center of the ring, so as to make them knock down the cushions, while not knocking down any himself. The penalty for knocking down a cushion, or for letting go of hands to avoid knocking one down, is to go out of the game.

Set the cushions upright in a circle on the floor. The players join hands and form a ring around them. The circle formed by the cushions should be nearly as large as the ring formed by the players, and the cushions may be placed at a considerable distance apart. The players in the ring dance around the cushions, and each player, as he dances, tries to make his neighbors knock over the cushions while he avoids knocking over any himself.

The penalty for knocking over a cushion or for letting go of hands is to go out of the game. If you prefer, substitute upright bowling pins for the cushions.

Duck, Duck, Goose
Rating: 5+

This party game can be played by any number of players, but more than ten make for the best game.

All players sit in a circle. Choose one player to be "It." The player who is It walks around the circle and taps every person on the head, calling out "Duck" as he taps. He then picks one random person, taps that player's head, and says "Goose." That person then has to get up and chase the tapper around the circle. The person who is It has to run around the circle, and get back into the spot where he tapped the "goose." If he is successful he sits in that spot and the goose is now It. The new It then goes around the circle, just as before, and the game continues.

If anyone is unsuccessful in making it back to the open spot in the circle and is caught by the goose, he is sent into the middle of the circle, called the *pickle jar.* He has to sit there until someone else doesn't make it around the circle in time, at which point they trade places.

Musical Chairs
Rating: 5+

This party game can be played by any number of players, but more than ten make for the best game. You will need chairs or stools (one less than the number of players), and a tape recorder or radio that can easily be turned on and off.

For a small group, place the chairs in a line, facing alternately right and left. For a larger group, place the chairs in a giant circle, facing out, or facing right and left. Appoint one player or supervisor to control the music.

The game begins when the music is turned on. The players march around the line of chairs. Suddenly the music stops, and the players all try to seat themselves. The one who fails to get a seat takes one chair away, and goes out of the game. The game continues until only one player is left—the winner.

Observation
Rating: 8+

This party game is perfect for large groups, especially from ten to sixty players. You will need twenty different small- to medium-sized objects, and enough paper and pencils for each player.

Place the objects on the table. Each player in turn looks at them for half a minute, and then goes to a seat facing away from the table, where she writes down the names of all the objects she can remember in the allotted time. The players can sit together to write down their answers, but they cannot compare notes or talk until time has run out. The one who remembers the greatest number correctly wins the game.

Pin the Tail on the Donkey
Rating: 8+

This party game can be played by any number of players. For this game you will need Scotch tape or thumbtacks, one picture of a donkey, and several cutout tails that are either numbered or colored, one for each player.

Hang the picture of the donkey on the wall. Give each player one paper tail with a tack or tape attached to the top. Blindfold the first player and spin him around several times. Then face him in the direction of the donkey. The player tries to walk toward it and pin the tail to the donkey's behind. Repeat for all of the players. The player who gets his tail closest to where it belongs on the donkey's behind is the winner.

Piñata

Rating: 8+

Part of the traditional Mexican birthday celebration, the piñata is a game for the birthday boy or girl to play, and all of the guests to enjoy. A piñata is always made out of papier-mâché, but the style can vary greatly. Sometimes it is made to look like an animal, or a hat, or a birthday cake. Piñatas are always beautifully decorated and stuffed with candy. Any number of players can play.

You can find piñatas in all sorts of varieties—cartoon characters, holiday themes, and more. Ask at your local craft store.

Hang the piñata from the ceiling, about a foot out of the player's reach. Give the player a stick, blindfold him, and spin him around. The player then has to figure out where the piñata is, and aim his stick in that direction. The player swings at the piñata while the rest of the crowd cheers him on, giving him directions. If he breaks the piñata, the candy comes out, and all of the guests rush to get their share. If not, the next player takes a turn.

Scavenger Hunt

Rating: 8+

This game can be played by any number of participants. If there are more than ten players, you can divide them into teams of equal number. This party game needs to be prepared for in advance; you will need several small objects that can easily be hidden, and paper and pens.

Each player or team is given a list of items. The object of the game is to find the items in the time allotted. The first team to make it back to the start with either the items or a list of their locations wins.

You can develop this game to varying degrees of difficulty. For younger players, you can make the lists of the exact names of the objects to find. For older players, you can give clues instead, so that each player or team has to first figure out the clue, and then find the object. The lists can be thematic or random, depending on the party and your own creativity.

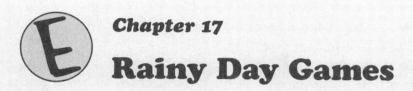

Chapter 17

Rainy Day Games

Rainy days needn't be gloomy. Make the indoors more fun and have more than a few laughs with charades; test your hand-eye coordination with games such as jacks and Jenga; and get the blood flowing with Twister. Any of the games in this chapter will provide great family fun on not-so-sunny days.

Charades

Rating: 8+

Charades is a classic game for adults and children. Charades can be altered to be difficult or simple, depending on the participants. To play, you will need some paper, a pen, and a stopwatch. Any number of people can participate, either playing alone or in teams. The object of the game is to guess specific actions that are being presented to you.

Before playing, appoint one individual to be the referee. This person does not participate in the game, but is responsible for writing down a number of topics on small pieces of paper, resolving disputes, and watching the clock. The topics can be either a noun or a verb. They could be thematic—for example, a group of songs, movies, celebrities, or actions—or a random mix of all of the above.

Before play begins, teams can decide among themselves specific pantomimes that can be used as clues to help the team guess the idea. These actions can represent a book, a movie, a song, an action word, and so on. However, once the game begins, the team cannot converse at all, especially about what the previously agreed-upon actions mean.

If participants are playing as individuals, the referee gives each player a piece of paper with one topic written on it. The game begins with the referee choosing one player to go first. That player must convey to the other players the idea that was on his paper, within the time allotted. The player acts out either the entire idea, or parts of it. At no time is he allowed to utter a word, sign specific letters, or use any physical props to get his idea across. The player who guesses what the first player is trying to convey takes the next turn. If time runs out and no one has guessed correctly, the player to the left of the first player takes a turn, and so on. In individual play, there are no winners or losers.

If teams are playing, the referee gives one topic to each member of each team. The referee then chooses which team shall go first. One player on each team takes a turn, and acts out his idea for the rest of his team only. If his team guesses correctly, another player on the same team takes the next turn, and so on. If the team does not guess correctly within the allotted time, the team to the left of the first team takes the next turn. In team play, the first team in which all of the players have taken a turn is the winner.

Hot Potato

Rating: 5+

Players form a circle. One player starts out holding a beanbag, which is the hot potato. A nonplayer starts the music. The players must pass the bag from one to another as quickly as possible while the music plays. The person controlling the music stops the music at random. The person holding the hot potato when the music stops is out. The last player standing wins.

Jacks

Rating: 8+

Jacks is a popular game of skill and coordination. It can be played alone or with any number of players. You will need a set of twelve jacks, which are small six-legged objects, usually made of either metal or plastic, and a very small rubber ball. Jacks is usually played on a smooth surface or floor.

ALERT!

While these are the most general rules for playing jacks, players can vary the game by making up their own rules and creating new games. There are also several established variations of jacks—you can find the rules for the variations online.

To play, gather all of the jacks into the palm of your hand and toss them across the floor. A good toss separates all the jacks so that they can easily be picked up one at a time. Once the jacks are on the floor, begin collecting them. Do this by throwing the ball up, and with the same hand scooping up one jack while the ball bounces. The ball is only allowed to bounce once, and may be caught before it bounces at all. You must throw the ball, catch the jack, and catch the ball all with the same hand. Place the captured jack in your opposite hand. Repeat until all of the jacks are picked up, one at a time.

When you have picked up all of the jacks, toss them again. This time, pick up two jacks at a time. The game continues in order, each player completing a round by picking up the appropriate number of jacks. For odd numbers, the leftover jack is picked up last. A player continues from one round to the next until he loses his turn.

While you are in the process of picking up jacks, you cannot disturb any of the other jacks. You lose your turn if you fail to catch the ball, or if you disturb the other jacks. Once you lose your turn, the next player tosses the jacks, and so on. The winner of the game is the first to pick up all twelve jacks in one swoop.

Jenga

Rating: 8+

Jenga is a game of coordination. To start, build a tower by stacking Jenga wood blocks, three adjacent horizontally and three more on top vertically. Repeat this pattern until all of the blocks are used up. Players then take turns removing one block from the tower and stacking it on the top of the tower in the appropriate pattern (horizontal or vertical). The last person to stack a block without toppling the tower wins.

Marbles

Rating: 8+

The various marbles games have been played for centuries. There are two principal styles of play. In the first, you strike marbles out of a ring by shooting from a line; in the second, you play by making the tour of a series of holes, or goals, made specifically for the game. Any number of participants can play these games, unless otherwise specified.

FACT

The best method of shooting a marble is to bend the thumb at the first joint and grasp it firmly with the middle finger. Place the marble above the thumb and hold it in position with the first finger; then suddenly, having taken good aim, let go of the thumb and the marble will be shot forward.

Bounce Eye

Draw a circle, about a foot in diameter, on the ground. Each player adds a marble into the center of the circle, creating a pool.

The first player takes a marble and aims it at the center of the pool. He tries to scatter as many marbles as he can outside the ring; those that land outside are picked up and kept by the shooter. If he does not succeed in moving any marbles outside the ring, the one he shot with must remain in the pool.

When all the marbles are removed from the pool, the game is over. Whoever holds the most marbles at that time wins.

Bridge Board

You can create a bridge from a narrow piece of board in which you cut out nine arches. The arches should be about an inch in height and width. Place numbers over the arches, but not in consecutive order.

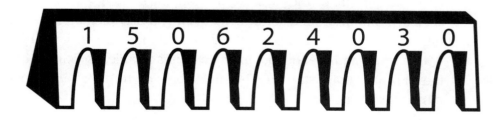

▲ Bridge board

One player is appointed the bridge keeper, and the others take turns aiming at the bridge. If a marble passes under one of the arches, the bridge keeper gives the player a number of marbles corresponding to the number marked over the arch. If a player fails to shoot through an arch, he must pay one marble to the bridge keeper.

A different player should be the bridge keeper for each round. Whoever holds the most marbles after an allotted period of time wins.

Pickup Sticks

Rating: 8+

Pickup Sticks is another classic family game. Any number of people can play this game, or it can be played alone. You will need a set of Pickup Sticks to play, or you can create your own set by finding a large number of identical long objects, such as pencils or pens. This game is usually played on a smooth surface or floor. While these are the most general rules, players can vary the game by making up their own rules.

The object of the game is to pick up all of the sticks, one at a time, without disturbing the rest. In this way, the game is very similar to jacks. However, in Pickup Sticks you are allowed a tool to separate the sticks. The tool is one stick that is slightly different from the rest, either in color or weight.

Gather the sticks in one hand so that they are perpendicular to the playing surface. Then release your hand, causing the sticks to spread out into a larger circle (they will be overlapping). Then, try to pick up one stick at a time without disturbing the rest. You may pick up the sticks with one hand, or use the tool to lift the stick, and then retrieve it with your other hand. You can use the tool in any way imaginable, as long as the rest of the sticks are not disturbed. The sticks that you retrieve can be put aside during the turn.

A player loses his turn if he fails to pick up a stick, or disturbs the other ones. The players rotate turns, each time laying out the sticks for a new round. The winner of the game is the first to pick up all the sticks on one turn.

Pictionary

Rating: 8+

Players divide into two teams. If the teams are small, players may elect one person to draw all the clues for the team. However, players may rotate this duty. Teams roll the dice to determine which goes first. Each team selects a playing piece and puts it on the start space on the board. The first team's drawer takes a card. She gets five seconds to think about how to draw the picture, and sixty seconds to draw clues for her teammates.

ALERT!

The rules of Pictionary state that the drawer may not speak or use body gestures in order to give hints. Additionally, she may not draw words or numbers.

Teammates must guess the picture in sixty seconds. If they succeed, they roll again and repeat the process. If they fail, the play passes to the next team. The first team to reach the finish space and successfully guess the final picture wins.

Tiddlywinks

Rating: 8+

Tiddlywinks is played by two people, or by four people who are playing against each other or in pairs. The chips come in four colors, and each color is controlled by one player. There are six disks, called winks, per color. Red and blue are partners, as are green and yellow. In singles, one player controls red and blue, while the other controls green and yellow. There is also a squidger, which is a disk that is used to play the winks.

The *squidge-off* determines the order of play. Put the pot in the middle of the mat with the winks arranged in the corners (one color to each corner) in the following order clockwise: blue, green, red, yellow. Each player then plays his wink. The color closest to the pot is deemed the winner of the squidge-off. After the squidge-off, return the winks to their position behind the baseline.

The winner of the squidge-off starts the play. Play continues in the sequence of the other colors as above. Winks that land in the pot are referred to as *potted*, while those outside the pot are *free* or *squopped*. A wink is squopped when another wink (the squoppering wink) hits it. To make a shot, press down on a free wink of the color you want to play. Then use the squidger to hit the other winks that have been squopped by the first wink. If you pot a wink of the color being played, you get another shot. When a wink leaves the mat, it is replaced in the position it was in before it left the mat. If your shot causes one or more winks of the color being played to leave the mat, the color being played loses its turn in the next round.

The game ends when all the winks of one color are potted. This color is then potted out. As an alternative, players may agree on a prearranged time limit, which is when the game will end regardless of how many winks are potted. The game also may end if there are no winks remaining to be played (they are all squopped). The score is counted by awarding tiddlies. Each wink in the pot gets three tiddlies; free winks played from behind the baseline get one tiddly. The team with the most tiddlies wins.

Twister

Rating: 8+

Lay out the Twister mat, which is a large rectangle with four columns with six rows of colored circles: green, yellow, blue, and red. There can be up to four players on the mat. One person sits out the game to be the spinner. That person spins the game spinner, which matches a color with a body part (for example, left hand; blue). You must put that body part on that color. If you get a new color for the body part, you move that part. Players who fall or have an elbow or knee touch the mat are out. The last player remaining wins.

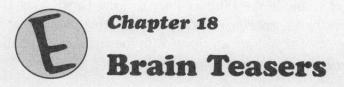

Chapter 18

Brain Teasers

This chapter is for those of you who like to stimulate your mind. Here you will find a variety of challenging games that will test your brain power against that of your opponent. A word of warning: Some of these brain teasers can become addictive!

Anagrams

Rating: 12+

To make an anagram, you rearrange all of the letters in one word or phrase to form another word or phrase. People have enjoyed playing anagrams for thousands of years. In the third century B.C., the Greek poet Lycophron scored points by transposing the king's name into a phrase that meant "made of honey." See if you are as clever with these anagram challenges. The clue for the following three is "presidents":

1. HUG GORES WEB
2. MARRY JIM ETC
3. VETOED HORSE LOOTER

The answers are: George W. Bush, Jimmy Carter, and Theodore Roosevelt.

Dots

Rating: 8+

Dots is a thinking game for two to four people. However, it is best played with just two. For this game you will need blank paper, and as many pens as there are players. The object of the game is to connect the lines drawn to create squares. The player who creates the greatest number of squares wins the game.

To begin, create a board on the blank paper. Draw horizontal and vertical lines of small dots, evenly spaced. A very quick game would consist of ten dots across and ten dots down. You can make the board as large or small as you would like, depending on the level of play and the number of players.

Once the board is created, each player takes a turn drawing one line at a time, connecting two dots. The dots can be connected horizontally or vertically, never diagonally. As soon as a player finishes a square, he places his initial inside the square, and gets another turn, and so on, until he can no longer create a square with the addition of one line.

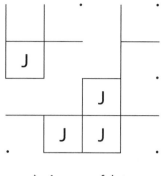

▲ A game of dots

There are two strategies for dots. The first is to block the opponents from creating a square. The second is to connect the dots on the board so that many squares can be created from the addition of one line.

Hangman

Rating: 8+

Hangman is another popular brain teaser created especially for two players. You will need blank paper and a pen to play this game.

Think of any word imaginable. It must be a real word, and you must know that the other player is familiar with the word and its spelling. Draw out the number of blank spaces necessary to spell out the word. Next, draw a diagram that represents a gallows and a noose.

The game begins when your opponent guesses a letter that might be in the word. If it is, write it on the correct blank space. If the letter is not in the word, write the letter off to the side, and begin to draw in the *hangman*, by adding a circle to the noose to represent the head. Your opponent continues to guess letters until he can guess the entire word. For every wrong answer, you add one body part to the hangman: body, arms, legs, eyes (draw one at a time for the last three), and mouth.

If the body is complete before your opponent can guess the word, you are the winner. If your opponent guesses the word correctly before the body is complete, he is the winner and it is then his turn to think of a word.

Inky Pinkys
Rating: 12+

This word game can be played with any number of people. In this game, the leader comes up with the clue—a sentence that should lead the others to a pair of single-syllable words that rhyme. The other people must guess the correct rhyming pair. The player who guesses correctly wins the round.

For example, if you want people to guess "ump jump," you can use "baseball referee hop" as your clue. If the clue is "an informal conversation with a rodent," the right answer is "rat chat."

Tick-Tac-Toe
Rating: 8+

This classic brain teaser is for only two players. You will need a pen and paper to play this game. On the paper, draw a grid of nine squares using two vertical and two horizontal lines. Then, choose which one of you will be represented by X's and which by O's.

The player who has chosen to be X goes first. He places an X in any of the squares within the board. The next player then places an O in another square. Continue until one player has lined up three of his symbols in a row, horizontally, diagonally, or vertically. The first player to do this wins the game.

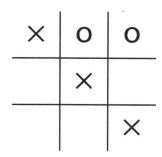

▲ In this game, the winner is X.

Tick-tac-toe often ends in a draw, as neither player is able to get three symbols in a row. The best games are played when the two players are of equal skill level.

Chapter 19

Swimming Pool Games

Children love to play in the water and some adults do, too! This chapter provides a variety of popular swimming pool games that may be just the right refreshment on those sultry summer days. However, remember that children must always be supervised by an adult when playing in or near water.

Marco Polo
Rating: 8+

This game requires three or more players. After one person is chosen to be "It," he closes his eyes and walks around the inside of the pool. When he calls out "Marco," the people he is in pursuit of call out "Polo." The object is for the person who is It to tag the other players as he tries to find them only by the closeness of each voice answering "Polo." The player who is first tagged becomes the next It.

Poison Ball
Rating: 8+

Poison ball is played by about five to ten people in the pool. The players form a circle holding hands around a beach ball (or other floating ball), which is "poison." Using only their linked hands, the players try to push and pull other players to make them touch the ball. Players who touch the ball are out. As the circle gets smaller, it becomes more and more difficult for players to keep from touching the ball. The last person to touch the ball wins.

Sharks and Minnows
Rating: 8+

This swimming pool game requires at least three players. One person volunteers to be the shark. All of the other players are minnows. Players pick a category, such as colors or numbers one through five. Each minnow then picks a member of this category. For example, if the category is colors, each minnow chooses one color. The minnows line up on one side of the pool, while the shark stands outside the pool, with her back to the minnows. The shark starts the game by calling out colors. When a minnow's color is called, he must quietly swim to the other side of the pool (if other minnows chose the same color, they too must swim). The shark listens for minnows to swim across after she calls each color. When the shark hears a minnow, she must jump into the pool and attempt to tag the minnows as they swim across.

Water Polo
Rating: 8+

Water polo is a highly competitive water sport when played at the collegiate or professional level. However, it is also a fun and exciting game that you can play at home. Each game is divided into four quarters, which are seven minutes each, with two minutes between quarters. Teams are made up of seven players: one goalie and six field players.

FACT

Water polo first began in England and was played a little differently from what we know today. Because many water sports tried to copy land sports, those playing water polo rode around in the water on barrels painted to look like horses, and they hit the ball with a stick.

The object of the game is for each team to try to get the ball (a floating ball about the size of a volleyball) into their opponent's net. Each goal is awarded 1 point. The team with the most points at the end of the final quarter wins. Players must adhere to the following rules; violation of any of the rules constitutes a foul. Rules may be modified in an agreed-on fashion for backyard games.

1. Players may only touch the ball with one hand at a time.
2. Players may not push off the bottom or sides of the pool.
3. Players may not touch or rest on the bottom or sides of the pool but must tread water.
4. Players may not hold the ball under water.
5. Players may not hit or dunk or push off another player.
6. Players may not hit the ball with their fists.
7. Players may not be within two meters of the opponent's goal if the ball is

behind them. This is called offsides.

8. The ball may not be thrown out of bounds.
9. A team may keep the ball for only thirty-five seconds without taking a shot.

Water Tag
Rating: 8+

Water tag, a variation on the classic game of tag, has several variations. Three of the most popular are squirt-gun tag, freeze tag, and white whale.

In squirt-gun tag, one player is selected as "It." She uses a squirt gun to tag other players with water. The first person tagged is It for the next round.

In freeze tag, the person who is It must swim around and tag other players. Once a player has been tagged, he is frozen (he cannot move) until another player swims over and unfreezes the player by tagging him. The game continues until everyone is frozen. The last person to be frozen becomes It for the next round.

Underwater tag is the same as the other forms of tag except that players are safe as long as they are completely submerged. One person is "It." He tries to tag other players, but can only tag body parts that are above the water. The first person tagged is It for the next round.

In white whale, one player volunteers to be the whale. All the other players are fish. The whale swims around in the pool with the fish swimming around her. While the whale is swimming around like this, she is called a "black whale," which is safe for the fish. The whale suddenly yells "Thar she blows!" At this point, the whale becomes a "white whale" who swims around and tries to tag the fish. If all the fish successfully evade the white whale, the whale yells "Black whale," and begins swimming around again. The first fish to be tagged becomes the whale for the next round.

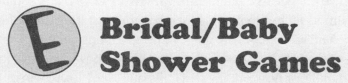

Chapter 20

Bridal/Baby Shower Games

Games at baby showers and bridal showers are a good opportunity to liven things up a bit and keep your guests amused and entertained. Alas, even with the most engaging party games you may encounter some initial resistance from a party pooper or two. If you offer prizes for the winners of these games, though, even the biggest wet blankets may be encouraged to play.

Bridal/Baby Bingo
Rating: 12+

This is a great game to play while the bride or mother-to-be is opening gifts, because it keeps the guests busy during what could otherwise be a somewhat boring event. Give the guests a bingo card with twenty-five blank squares and ask each of them to fill in the blank squares with items they think the bride or mother-to-be will receive. As the guest of honor opens her gifts, the guests mark off those squares that correspond to the gift. Whoever gets five in a row diagonally, vertically, or horizontally first calls out "Baby!" and wins.

Famous Couple Trivia
Rating: 12+

Try developing some trivia questions with a love theme for your shower. Chances are that your guests will do better answering these questions than inquiries about the first space launch, which always seem to be the stumpers in the board-version trivia games (unless, of course, your girlfriends happen to be rocket scientists—in which case, they may actually prefer some more challenging mathematical trivia questions, like figuring out how many different boyfriends a certain starlet has had).

ALERT!

A word to the wise: Keep it clean, especially if you're in mixed company. It's one thing to play rowdy games when you're sitting around with your girlfriends, but it's quite another to include Grandma and Great-Aunt Ruth. You'll send them packing, and they won't look back—ever.

Here are some sample questions:

- Who was Tom Cruise's first wife? (Mimi Rogers)
- Who did Prince Rainier marry? (Grace Kelly)
- Who dies first in *Romeo and Juliet*? (Romeo)

Make up your own questions—it's a fun game and most of the guests will have an equal chance of winning if you include questions about couples from every generation represented at your shower. Set a time limit for answers, and give a prize to the winner. The person with the most correct answers wins.

Finish the Phrase
Rating: 12+

This game can be adapted to fit either a bridal shower or a baby shower. Each guest should receive a piece of paper with twenty sayings that need to be completed. The sentences should be well known and suited for the event at hand. For a bridal shower, for example, some sayings may include:

Start	Finish
A woman's work . . .	is never done.
A penny saved . . .	is a penny earned.
Home is . . .	where the heart is.

For a baby shower, it's fun to have the guests finish lines from nursery rhymes. For example, some lines may include:

Start	Finish
Little Miss Muffet . . .	sat on a tuffet.
Mary, Mary, quite contrary . . .	how does your garden grow?
Peter, Peter, pumpkin eater . . .	had a wife and couldn't keep her.

Give the guests five minutes to finish the sentences. Whoever correctly finishes the most sentences in the least amount of time wins the prize.

Guess the Goodies
Rating: 12+

Fill a large decorative jar with white or colored candied almonds. Ask the guests to guess how many almonds are in the jar. They can take as long as they want to hazard a guess; at the end of the shower, they hand in their answers on a slip of paper. The person who comes closest to the number without going over wins the jar and the almonds. (You can substitute chocolate kisses, M&M's, jelly beans, or anything else you can think of.)

FACT

All these games require some of your time and creativity. If you do not have the time or inclination to make these games yourself, you can find premade versions online or in party supply stores.

Make sure that whoever filled the jar knows how many what-have-yous are inside and has written the number down somewhere for safekeeping (and also for the ultimate last word on who has won). Otherwise, this contest could start to resemble the 2000 presidential election, with countless recounts and various contestants claiming victory.

Memory Game
Rating: 8+

Place twenty items on a large tray and allow the guests to look over the tray for fifteen seconds. Take the tray into another room and ask the guests to write down as many items as they can remember. The guest with the most correct answers wins. The items should be appropriate for the event. For instance, at a baby shower, the tray could include items such as a pacifier, baby bottle, diaper pin, rattle, and jar of baby food. At a bridal shower, the tray could include items such as a ring, garter, a scrap of lace, an apron, and a flower.

Word Scramble

Rating: 12+

Word scramble for a bridal or baby shower can be played in a couple of different ways. Give each guest a pencil and a piece of paper with the names of the bride and groom or the mother- and father-to-be at the top. Give the guests five to ten minutes to create a list of words using the letters from the two names. The guest who creates the most words within the time limit wins. To make this game more difficult, specify that the words created must relate to the event at hand (marriage or birth).

Another word scramble game requires the guests to unscramble words. Make a list of twenty words that are appropriate to the event and scramble the letters of each word. Give the guests five minutes to complete the game. Whoever unscrambles the most words in the least amount of time wins.

Here's a bridal shower spin on a game of pin the tail on the donkey: pin it on the groom. Draw the silhouette of a man on a large piece of paper. Attach a photo of the groom's face to the top. Blindfold the guests, spin them, and have them try to pin a flower on his lapel, or a bow tie on his neck.

 **Index**

THE EVERYTHING SERIES!

BUSINESS & PERSONAL FINANCE

Everything® Budgeting Book
Everything® Business Planning Book
Everything® Coaching and Mentoring Book
Everything® Fundraising Book
Everything® Get Out of Debt Book
Everything® Grant Writing Book
Everything® Homebuying Book, 2nd Ed.
Everything® Homeselling Book
Everything® Home-Based Business Book
Everything® Investing Book
Everything® Landlording Book
Everything® Leadership Book
Everything® Managing People Book
Everything® Negotiating Book
Everything® Online Business Book
Everything® Personal Finance Book
Everything® Personal Finance in Your 20s and 30s Book
Everything® Project Management Book
Everything® Real Estate Investing Book
Everything® Robert's Rules Book, $7.95
Everything® Selling Book
Everything® Start Your Own Business Book
Everything® Wills & Estate Planning Book

COOKING

Everything® Barbecue Cookbook
Everything® Bartender's Book, $9.95
Everything® Chinese Cookbook
Everything® College Cookbook
Everything® Cookbook
Everything® Diabetes Cookbook
Everything® Easy Gourmet Cookbook
Everything® Fondue Cookbook
Everything® Grilling Cookbook
Everything® Healthy Meals in Minutes Cookbook
Everything® Holiday Cookbook

Everything® Indian Cookbook
Everything® Low-Carb Cookbook
Everything® Low-Fat High-Flavor Cookbook
Everything® Low-Salt Cookbook
Everything® Meals for a Month Cookbook
Everything® Mediterranean Cookbook
Everything® Mexican Cookbook
Everything® One-Pot Cookbook
Everything® Pasta Cookbook
Everything® Quick Meals Cookbook
Everything® Slow Cooker Cookbook
Everything® Soup Cookbook
Everything® Thai Cookbook
Everything® Vegetarian Cookbook
Everything® Wine Book

HEALTH

Everything® Alzheimer's Book
Everything® Diabetes Book
Everything® Hypnosis Book
Everything® Low Cholesterol Book
Everything® Massage Book
Everything® Menopause Book
Everything® Nutrition Book
Everything® Reflexology Book
Everything® Stress Management Book

HISTORY

Everything® American Government Book
Everything® American History Book
Everything® Civil War Book
Everything® Irish History & Heritage Book
Everything® Middle East Book

HOBBIES & GAMES

Everything® Blackjack Strategy Book
Everything® Brain Strain Book, $9.95
Everything® Bridge Book
Everything® Candlemaking Book

Everything® Card Games Book
Everything® Cartooning Book
Everything® Casino Gambling Book, 2nd Ed.
Everything® Chess Basics Book
Everything® Crossword and Puzzle Book
Everything® Crossword Challenge Book
Everything® Cryptograms Book, $9.95
Everything® Digital Photography Book
Everything® Drawing Book
Everything® Easy Crosswords Book
Everything® Family Tree Book
Everything® Games Book, 2nd Ed.
Everything® Knitting Book
Everything® Knots Book
Everything® Motorcycle Book
Everything® Online Genealogy Book
Everything® Photography Book
Everything® Poker Strategy Book
Everything® Pool & Billiards Book
Everything® Quilting Book
Everything® Scrapbooking Book
Everything® Sewing Book
Everything® Woodworking Book
Everything® Word Games Challenge Book

HOME IMPROVEMENT

Everything® Feng Shui Book
Everything® Feng Shui Decluttering Book, $9.95
Everything® Fix-It Book
Everything® Homebuilding Book
Everything® Lawn Care Book
Everything® Organize Your Home Book

EVERYTHING® KIDS' BOOKS

All titles are $6.95
Everything® Kids' Animal Puzzle & Activity Book
Everything® Kids' Baseball Book, 3rd Ed.

All Everything® books are priced at $12.95 or $14.95, unless otherwise stated. Prices subject to change without notice.

Everything® Kids' Bible Trivia Book
Everything® Kids' Bugs Book
Everything® Kids' Christmas Puzzle
    & Activity Book
Everything® Kids' Cookbook
Everything® Kids' Halloween Puzzle
    & Activity Book
Everything® Kids' Hidden Pictures Book
Everything® Kids' Joke Book
Everything® Kids' Knock Knock Book
Everything® Kids' Math Puzzles Book
Everything® Kids' Mazes Book
Everything® Kids' Money Book
Everything® Kids' Monsters Book
Everything® Kids' Nature Book
Everything® Kids' Puzzle Book
Everything® Kids' Riddles & Brain Teasers Book
Everything® Kids' Science Experiments Book
Everything® Kids' Sharks Book
Everything® Kids' Soccer Book
Everything® Kids' Travel Activity Book

KIDS' STORY BOOKS

Everything® Bedtime Story Book
Everything® Fairy Tales Book

LANGUAGE

Everything® Conversational Japanese Book
    (with CD), $19.95
Everything® French Phrase Book, $9.95
Everything® French Verb Book, $9.95
Everything® Inglés Book
Everything® Learning French Book
Everything® Learning German Book
Everything® Learning Italian Book
Everything® Learning Latin Book
Everything® Learning Spanish Book
Everything® Sign Language Book
Everything® Spanish Grammar Book
Everything® Spanish Phrase Book, $9.95
Everything® Spanish Verb Book, $9.95

MUSIC

Everything® Drums Book (with CD), $19.95
Everything® Guitar Book
Everything® Home Recording Book
Everything® Playing Piano and Keyboards
    Book

Everything® Reading Music Book (with CD),
    $19.95
Everything® Rock & Blues Guitar Book
    (with CD), $19.95
Everything® Songwriting Book

NEW AGE

Everything® Astrology Book
Everything® Dreams Book, 2nd Ed.
Everything® Ghost Book
Everything® Love Signs Book, $9.95
Everything® Numerology Book
Everything® Paganism Book
Everything® Palmistry Book
Everything® Psychic Book
Everything® Reiki Book
Everything® Spells & Charms Book
Everything® Tarot Book
Everything® Wicca and Witchcraft Book

PARENTING

Everything® Baby Names Book
Everything® Baby Shower Book
Everything® Baby's First Food Book
Everything® Baby's First Year Book
Everything® Birthing Book
Everything® Breastfeeding Book
Everything® Father-to-Be Book
Everything® Father's First Year Book
Everything® Get Ready for Baby Book
Everything® Getting Pregnant Book
Everything® Homeschooling Book
Everything® Parent's Guide to Children
    with ADD/ADHD
Everything® Parent's Guide to Children
    with Asperger's Syndrome
Everything® Parent's Guide to Children
    with Autism
Everything® Parent's Guide to Children
    with Dyslexia
Everything® Parent's Guide to Positive
    Discipline
Everything® Parent's Guide to Raising a
    Successful Child
Everything® Parent's Guide to Tantrums
Everything® Parent's Guide to the Overweight
    Child
Everything® Parenting a Teenager Book
Everything® Potty Training Book, $9.95

Everything® Pregnancy Book, 2nd Ed.
Everything® Pregnancy Fitness Book
Everything® Pregnancy Nutrition Book
Everything® Pregnancy Organizer, $15.00
Everything® Toddler Book
Everything® Tween Book
Everything® Twins, Triplets, and More Book

PETS

Everything® Cat Book
Everything® Dachshund Book, $12.95
Everything® Dog Book
Everything® Dog Health Book
Everything® Dog Training and Tricks Book
Everything® Golden Retriever Book, $12.95
Everything® Horse Book
Everything® Labrador Retriever Book, $12.95
Everything® Poodle Book, $12.95
Everything® Pug Book, $12.95
Everything® Puppy Book
Everything® Rottweiler Book, $12.95
Everything® Tropical Fish Book

REFERENCE

Everything® Car Care Book
Everything® Classical Mythology Book
Everything® Computer Book
Everything® Divorce Book
Everything® Einstein Book
Everything® Etiquette Book
Everything® Mafia Book
Everything® Philosophy Book
Everything® Psychology Book
Everything® Shakespeare Book

RELIGION

Everything® Angels Book
Everything® Bible Book
Everything® Buddhism Book
Everything® Catholicism Book
Everything® Christianity Book
Everything® Jewish History & Heritage Book
Everything® Judaism Book
Everything® Koran Book
Everything® Prayer Book
Everything® Saints Book
Everything® Torah Book
Everything® Understanding Islam Book

All Everything® books are priced at $12.95 or $14.95, unless otherwise stated. Prices subject to change without notice.

Everything® World's Religions Book
Everything® Zen Book

SCHOOL & CAREERS

Everything® Alternative Careers Book
Everything® College Survival Book, 2nd Ed.
Everything® Cover Letter Book, 2nd Ed.
Everything® Get-a-Job Book
Everything® Job Interview Book
Everything® New Teacher Book
Everything® Online Job Search Book
Everything® Paying for College Book
Everything® Practice Interview Book
Everything® Resume Book, 2nd Ed.
Everything® Study Book

SELF-HELP

Everything® Great Sex Book
Everything® Kama Sutra Book
Everything® Self-Esteem Book

SPORTS & FITNESS

Everything® Fishing Book
Everything® Fly-Fishing Book
Everything® Golf Instruction Book

Everything® Pilates Book
Everything® Running Book
Everything® Total Fitness Book
Everything® Weight Training Book
Everything® Yoga Book

TRAVEL

Everything® Family Guide to Hawaii
Everything® Family Guide to New York City, 2nd Ed.
Everything® Family Guide to RV Travel & Campgrounds
Everything® Family Guide to the Walt Disney World Resort®, Universal Studios®, and Greater Orlando, 4th Ed.
Everything® Family Guide to Washington D.C., 2nd Ed.
Everything® Guide to Las Vegas
Everything® Guide to New England
Everything® Travel Guide to the Disneyland Resort®, California Adventure®, Universal Studios®, and the Anaheim Area

WEDDINGS

Everything® Bachelorette Party Book, $9.95
Everything® Bridesmaid Book, $9.95

Everything® Elopement Book, $9.95
Everything® Father of the Bride Book, $9.95
Everything® Groom Book, $9.95
Everything® Mother of the Bride Book, $9.95
Everything® Wedding Book, 3rd Ed.
Everything® Wedding Checklist, $9.95
Everything® Wedding Etiquette Book, $7.95
Everything® Wedding Organizer, $15.00
Everything® Wedding Shower Book, $7.95
Everything® Wedding Vows Book, $7.95
Everything® Weddings on a Budget Book, $9.95

WRITING

Everything® Creative Writing Book
Everything® Get Published Book
Everything® Grammar and Style Book
Everything® Guide to Writing a Book Proposal
Everything® Guide to Writing a Novel
Everything® Guide to Writing Children's Books
Everything® Screenwriting Book
Everything® Writing Poetry Book
Everything® Writing Well Book

- -

We have Everything® for the beginner crafter!
All titles are $14.95

Everything® Crafts—Baby Scrapbooking
1-59337-225-6

Everything® Crafts—Bead Your Own Jewelry
1-59337-142-X

Everything® Crafts—Create Your Own Greeting Cards
1-59337-226-4

Everything® Crafts—Easy Projects
1-59337-298-1

Everything® Crafts—Polymer Clay for Beginners
1-59337-230-2

Everything® Crafts—Rubber Stamping Made Easy
1-59337-229-9

Everything® Crafts—Wedding Decorations and Keepsakes
1-59337-227-2

Available wherever books are sold!
To order, call 800-872-5627, or visit us at *www.everything.com*
Everything® and everything.com® are registered trademarks of F+W Publications, Inc.